CHIEF

Edited by
Inéz Cardozo-Freeman

Chief

The Life History
of Eugene Delorme,
Imprisoned
Santee Sioux

University of Nebraska Press
Lincoln and London

Portions of chapter 2 are reprinted
from Inez Cardozo-Freeman (in collaboration
with Eugene P. Delorme),
*The Joint: Language and Culture in a
Maximum Security Prison*, 1984.
Courtesy of Charles C Thomas, Publisher,
Springfield, Illinois.

The paper in this book meets
the minimum requirements of
American National
Standard for Information
Sciences—Permanence of
Paper for Printed Library
Materials, ANSI z39.48-1984.

Library of Congress Cataloging in Publication Data
Delorme, Eugene P.
Chief: the life history of Eugene Delorme,
imprisoned Santee Sioux
/ edited by Inéz Cardozo-Freeman.
p.   cm. – (American Indian lives)
Includes bibliographical references.
ISBN 0-8032-1469-3 (cl : alk. paper)
1. Delorme, Eugene P.
2. Santee Indians – Biography.
3. Criminals – Washington (State) – Biography.
4. Prisoners – Washington (State) – Biography.
I. Cardozo-Freeman, Inez.
II. Title. III. Series.
E99.S22D453   1994
364.3′4975–dc20   *Bt 26.00/NET 4/96*
[B]
94–7336
CIP

For Gina Marie Delorme

I looked and saw that the leaves were falling from the holy tree. And the Voice said: "Behold your nation, and remember what your Six Grandfathers gave you, for henceforth your people walk in difficulties."

Black Elk, a holy man of the Oglala Sioux

Contents

ACKNOWLEDGMENTS

I owe thanks to many who helped to make this book a realization. First, Robert A. Freeman, who opened the doors for me to the Washington State Penitentiary in Walla Walla, where I met Eugene Delorme in 1978. I thank the officials at the Washington State Penitentiary for their cooperation in allowing me to work and communicate freely with Eugene Delorme. My thanks, also, to the Ohio State University College of Humanities and the OSU Newark Campus Research Fund for their generous travel grants.

Thanks to my folklorist colleague at the Ohio State University, Patrick B. Mullen, who discussed aspects of the manuscript with me and gave me much helpful advice, particularly on the Introduction, and thanks to my godson, Michael Olivas, for his loving support, advice, and encouragement.

My deep appreciation goes to James Welch, who read the book manuscript for the University of Nebraska Press and made useful, insightful, and constructive commentary. And I especially thank LaVonne Brown Ruoff, General Editor of the American Indian Lives series of the University of Nebraska Press, for her excellent guidance and wise advice through all the stages of the book's development.

I thank my gentle and beloved son, John Freeman, for teaching me that sometimes the humblest and most rejected of us are precious jewels. Last of all, I thank my friend Eugene Delorme, who so trustingly and generously gave me his life history and permission to seek its publication. Both he and I have the impression that throughout all that has surrounded the creation and publication of *Chief,* the presence of the Great Spirit has been with us.

Inéz Cardozo-Freeman

An autobiography . . . is but an extended
reply to one of the simplest and profound-
est of questions: who are you and how did
you come to be that way?

Albert E. Stone

Eugene Delorme began telling me the story of his life in 1978. I met him
in June of that year when I first came to the Washington State Penitentiary
to begin a study of prison slang and culture. Delorme, one of eight men
whom I interviewed, agreed to help me conduct the ethnolinguistic fieldwork. Over a period of two and one-half years we compiled nearly two
hundred hours of taped conversations and interviews—some two thousand pages of transcribed data, about one-fourth of which was used to
produce our book, *The Joint: Language and Culture in a Maximum Security Prison* (1984). After explaining my goals to him, which were to learn
as much as possible about prisoner culture and to elicit the prison slang in
its natural or near-natural context, Delorme, an expert on the language
and culture of the prison, determined how to gather the information and
whom to interview. It was he who decided early on in our collaboration
that I needed to look carefully at the life of one imprisoned man in order
to understand how he came to be there. Delorme chose himself for that
life story.

Delorme was thirty-eight years old when I first met him. He had been
in and out of prison since 1962, mainly for property crimes (theft) and pa-

role violations. He was highly respected and trusted by the prison population, identified as "good people," a term used to describe a small number
of men in the prison who are leaders exercising a positive influence on the
population. His close friends and Indian brothers called him "Chief."

It is important to emphasize that Delorme, although born on a reservation in South Dakota, is not a reservation Indian. He spent his childhood
in a small town in western Washington, and his adolescence and adult-
hood, when not incarcerated, in Tacoma, Washington. His worldview, for
this reason, is not particularly Native American. Arnold Krupat points
out the difference in worldview between Western and Native American
autobiography: the centrality of the self is uppermost in Western perspective, whereas the self subordinated to the whole group is paramount in
Native American tradition (1991:176). In considering this statement in
the light of Delorme's autobiography, it is obvious that his worldview is
highly individual, highly subjective in the Western sense. The strongest
cultural impressions in his life have been made by the American criminal
justice system, the white society at large, and, in his infancy and early
childhood, the Catholic Church. The cultural and traditional worldview
of his people was not a part of his upbringing: he grew up with a Western
(Christian) perspective.

Much of what Delorme knows and understands today about his heritage has been gleaned in prisons from other Indian prisoners; from the oc-
casional medicine man allowed to enter the prison to teach the mostly urban Native Americans about the rituals of the sacred pipe and sweat lodge
and to hold ceremonies that strengthen their spirit and help them to survive; and from his informal association with the Puyallup Tribe in Tacoma, Washington.

Although Delorme's autobiography reveals a propensity for what
Krupat identifies as the "centrality of the self," it would be incorrect to say
he is not thinking at all of his people in this ethnography of the self. Indeed, part of his reason for wanting to tell his story in the first place was to
demonstrate "what happens to Indians in the criminal justice system."
While many white–Native American collaborative autobiographies in
the nineteenth and early twentieth centuries recorded the confrontations

that took place between these cultures, Delorme joins forces with me to record this confrontation in another dimension: Native Americans who are caught up in the criminal justice system.

With respect to those Native Americans who live their lives breaking the law, Delorme's story is not atypical. In *The Joint* (1984: 142–43), Delorme describes the situation of reservation and urban Indians in the prison at Walla Walla:

Reservation Indians, in particular, suffer greatly from prison confinement and often retreat into alcohol or sniffing glue [carbon tetrachloride] to escape their condition in prison. Officials have recognized the need to allow Native Americans to practice their religion, and a sweat lodge is maintained; however, prejudice and misunderstanding of the function of the sweat lodge by some guards causes much bad feeling. Native Americans are greatly feared by the prison population, particularly when they go on the "warpath."

Reservation Indians are very quiet and don't mix with the population. They are slow to make friends and are drawn toward each other. These guys are defensive and generally uneducated, seldom reaching the eighth grade. Their beliefs clash with urban values. One of the things they have in common is booze. Reservations are very isolated places. Some places have electricity, although some don't; but they do see TV. Their view of the world comes from TV, or the advice and stories from the old people. So it must be very confusing. Reservation Indians come in for violent crimes like murder. Seldom sophisticated crimes like paper hanging [forged checks] or armed robbery. Murder, committed either in a tavern or at a party while blind drunk, is the usual story.

Their religious beliefs run from none to very traditional. Indian religion is kept quiet and is practiced almost at the drop of a hat. The ceremonies are not elaborate—a pipe, a drum, and eagle feathers are the tools. The Medicine Man is for special occasions.

Indians pray together more than just Sundays. Indians pray alone in their *houses* [cells] while holding the eagle feathers. They speak to the Grandfathers, the ancestors. They praise the Mother

Earth. They honor the four spirits of the earth—wind, earth, sun, north for the land of the Snow People; the eagle, the four-leggeds, the winged people, the fish people, all the animal brothers and sisters.

These beliefs are somewhat removed by the forced attempt at assimilation into the white culture that the urban Indian goes through. We [urban Indians] relearn our truths from the traditionals, but we do not live the way our religion teaches. The Indian path is one of beauty; not one of death and destruction.

The urban Indians are on that fast track and move too fast for our reservation brothers in the prison. The reservation Indian suffers more from the closeness of the prison; he does not accept the prison and resists the rules just as all Indians have fought control and genocide by the white man in power. We learn from each other, but more often than not we lead each other into the jaws of the monster.

The reservation Indian is so far removed from education that his learning ability is affected. It is a very hard chore for him to enter the completely white-oriented school in this prison and make any progress. When he tries to work in the industries or the vocational school, he will get into trouble because he will discover that there are chemicals that when put on a rag and inhaled will eliminate the pressures of the insitution and the world. He will discover that he can see visions if he continues. The Indian believes that these visions are not only of the gods, but very often since they are a product of the self-conscious, they will carry a man back to the plains, the buffalo, a war party, buckskins, and blue sky. So he is hooked.

The urban Indian also searches for visions, so both groups are constantly in trouble with "sniffing glue," as it is called. It is seldom glue, but that's what is always written on the tag [infraction slip]. Both groups are very proud, or at least they try to be. Very sensitive and defensive as hell. The Indian is not very far removed from the violence of the old days, in my observation. It takes very little booze or chemical to eliminate what small bit of control there is.

Some poor urban Indians in Washington survive, in part, by stealing.

They are often so good at it that non-Indians who are also thieves identify their skill as "professional." For example, Indians in the state of Washington are expert at "boosting" (shoplifting). A brief explanation about a very complex subject, the underworld, in particular that of professional thieves, is needed at this point to set Delorme's criminal activities into proper perspective.

There are several kinds of theft recognized in the underworld. Each possesses its own slang (argot), each is placed within a hierarchy by professional thieves according to the degree of skill and intelligence needed for successful performance of the "craft," and all share adherence to the "thieves' code." (This code is identified in prisons as the "convicts' code.") Confidence men are considered the most skilled thieves, whereas boosters are among those at the bottom. David W. Maurer (1964: 9–11) points out the difference between the professional and amateur thief. The amateur identifies with the dominant culture; in fact, he is a member of that culture and therefore "feels shame, guilt, and severe loss of status for having become involved in crime. . . . The professional [on the other hand] works at crime as a business; he makes his living by it; he is recognized and accepted by other professionals in his class as a professional; he knows and uses the argot or semi-secret language of the profession; he subscribes to the code of behavior long established for professionals in his group; he has status and is known within a considerable circle of other professionls; he adopts certain attitudes toward other criminals, the law, the *sucker,* society in general; he feels no shame or guilt for his acts against the dominant culture, and seldom if ever 'reforms.' *He is, in short, a member of the parasitic subculture.*" In addition, all underworld subcultures possess "well-defined behavior patterns, with mores which are often enforced more rigorously than those of the dominant culture, [and] technology which enables the subculture to live parasitically at the expense of the dominant culture." Furthermore, the argot of these subcultures reflects not only their behavioral patterns but their attitudes toward the dominant culture.

Native Americans in the state of Washington who are boosters not only steal clothing, TVs, cigarettes, food, drugs (from pharmacies), and so on, but some even specialize, for example, those boosters who steal only meat from grocery stores. They take great pride in their "craft," making their living in this way by selling what they don't need for themselves. Delorme is a professional thief who happens to be a Native American. He has spent his entire life—since age six when he began stealing food—living outside the law. Certainly, most Native Americans are not thieves, but Delorme is not the only Indian caught up in defying the American criminal justice system and his identity as a thief places him in direct opposition to the value structure of the majority culture.

What has been described above emphasizes that Delorme is not middle-class. Most people don't realize that criminals possess subcultures of their own, and consequently can't understand why "those people are not like us." We of mainstream society, like most people, view groups outside our own from an ethnocentric perspective and this can cause problems with expectations about others who are different from ourselves. Although people of the underworld don't understand what it means to be middle-class, they understand far more about the culture and values of "square johns" than square johns understand about underworld culture and values.

When we speak of the underworld, we are looking at a group of people who live their lives antithetically to that of the majority culture. They actually pride themselves in refusing to live within the value system of the mainstream. In fact, this is how they define themselves—by being or doing the opposite of what is expected by society. To espouse the values of the middle class—be law-abiding, hard-working, responsible—is to be disloyal to their own culture and its values. Because the identity of underworld people is tied to being antithetical, this nonconforming attitude shows up in their language. For example, "to cop a slave" means to get a job; "gaming and capering" means stealing.

Since the majority culture does not realize that the underworld has its own system of values to which it strictly adheres, it does not understand why it is so difficult, perhaps impossible, to "rehabilitate" underworld people when they end up in jails or prisons. Persons with middle-class values who break the law and are imprisoned can be turned around, but, in general, people like Delorme cannot. Breaking the law is part of his value system, his way of life. Much of what he values revolves around this antithetical worldview. For example, people like Delorme refuse to get proper driver's licenses or pay parking fees. Delorme has been sent back to prison more than once for refusing to abide by these simple rules. To this day, he refuses to get a driver's license, and it is certain at this very moment that he has hundreds of dollars of outstanding fines owed the city of Tacoma for refusing to pay parking tickets. Although it sounds ridiculous to us, to him and those like him it is a matter of principle: beat the system; refuse to conform, refuse to live by the rules of the square world.

Charles Dickens wrote about the thieves' underworld of nineteenth-century London in *Oliver Twist,* and the anonymous autobiography of the trickster rogue, *Lazarillo de Tormes,* describes the Spanish underworld during the sixteenth century. All countries in the world possess criminal subcultures: all are parasitic; all possess worldviews that are antithetical to their mainstream cultures; all possess distinct argots. These criminal subcultures, along with their values, are passed from parent to child, from generation to generation, decade after decade, century after century.

Delorme's system of values began forming when he was very young. He tells us that as a child his mother stole food and clothing for her younger brother, her blind sister, and herself in order to survive. When at age six Delorme began to steal food to help feed the family, his mother praised him. He tells us that he felt like a hero when he came home with sacks of stolen food. People like Delorme who begin their lives in this manner almost never join the law-abiding world. Once the cycle of arrests and imprisonments begins, their experiences with the criminal justice system reinforce their value system and their determination not to conform, and they sharpen their underworld skills by learning from other, more experienced criminals how to perfect their trade.

Often I have pleaded with Delorme not to steal, to live, rather, by *my* values, but that was before I finally understood how strongly his value system was opposed to mine. No matter how often he may have told prison officials, parole boards, judges, or parole officers, that he would "straighten his hand," he probably never will: his cultural values demand, insist that he live a life outside the law. Although there are times when he has suggested to me that he might change, to do so would be for him an act of disloyalty to his own people (those of the underworld) and their values, and loyalty is one of the cornerstones of the thieves' code. It is not that Delorme is lacking in intelligence; indeed, he is a very intelligent man, but his way of thinking does not incorporate a middle-class perspective. His values are too deeply ingrained to change. This fact serves to illustrate how little is understood about the value system of a large group of people in our society who live their entire lives outside the law. Applying a middle-class perspective to a person like Delorme will only produce misunderstanding. One must look at Delorme through his eyes in order to better understand who he is; one must become for the moment an "outsider" in order to see him clearly.

My approach to the presentation of Delorme's life history is through the lens of what anthropologists and folklorists call "reflexive ethnography." Such an approach legitimizes and explains the very personal and revealing passages in this introduction which tell why Delorme and I became "like family" and why he trusted me despite the fact that I am a square john and not a part of his underworld culture. Within the scholarship of reflexive ethnography, talking about my reasons for caring for Delorme and others like him who are often regarded as pariahs in our society is extremely important. As a reflexive ethnographer I must tell the truth about myself, show how my life experience affected my methodology, which in turn influenced Delorme and caused him to connect to me, a square john whom ordinarily he would never trust or confide in. Life histories, which are always oral, hence folk genres, always bear the stamp of the influence of the researcher (the "Other") on the narrator.

The question arises whether to call Delorme's story an autobiography or a life history. Vincent Crapanzano (1980: 8–10) writes that life history and autobiography are literary genres which "shape a particular preselected range of data into a meaningful totality. . . . The life history, like the autobiography, presents the subject from his own perspective. It differs from autobiography in that it is an immediate response to a demand posed by an Other and carries within it the expectation of that Other. . . .

The life history is a product of its author's desire for recognition by this essentially complex Other. It is not simply information; it is evocative as well. Its evaluation requires an understanding of the relationship between the author and the Other, the inevitable interlocutor whom he is addressing." Crapanzano's definition of life history prompts me to identify Delorme's story as life history rather than an autobiography per se because it was elicited in response to a "demand posed by an Other" carrying "within it the expectation of that Other." Although the demand was unstated, his life history was produced because of his "desire for recognition" from me.

Crapanzano correctly states that an evaluation of a life history requires an understanding of the relationship between the author and the Other. Why did Delorme share his life story with me? People in the underworld do not generally trust people in the law-abiding world, whom they refer to as "square johns." When I first met Delorme it was obvious that he regarded me with some suspicion. After all, I came from that other world; I was a square john. He was willing to work with me, however, for two reasons: he would be earning money and he had a genuine interest in talking to someone about prison life, something about which he knew a great deal. The relationship that developed between us, however, soon went beyond friendship. Delorme and I recognized early on that we were "family," not just "friends." How could two such disparate people—a university professor of Latino heritage and a prison inmate of Native American heritage—come to recognize that they were family to one another?

While gathering data for the book on prison culture that Delorme and I collaborated on in 1978–80, I disregarded Gresham Sykes's warning in *The Society of Captives* about the problems a researcher confronts when attempting to study a prison culture. He admonishes first against "the peril of being 'conned' by highly articulate, glib prisoners who seek some personal advantage," and, second, against the danger of becoming "partisan," consciously or unconsciously, adding that "only by remaining firmly neutral in one's sympathies can a valid picture of prison life be uncovered" (1958:135–36). I disregarded both these warnings because I firmly believed that being partisan was not only the key to not being conned but also the reason I was able to uncover a valid picture of prison life. But it was more than that: I had a genuine concern for imprisoned men and my concern went beyond the bleeding-heart syndrome. My perspective of sympathetic interest included all the imprisoned men that I met and spoke with, including Delorme—when conducting research in a prison one never refers to the men as informants—and this had an important influence on the book he and I produced.

I was also strongly influenced in the structuring of this life history by James M. Freeman's comment in *Untouchable: An Indian Life History:* "No comparison of life histories is possible without knowledge of the editor's perspectives and values that influenced the final form of the history. Failure to assess or at least recognize the observer's or editor's role leads to an image of a life history that is distorted and incomplete, since each editor, though not consciously, is necessarily influenced by his own perspectives" (1979:393). I realize, therefore, that my attitude toward imprisoned men has profoundly influenced my relationship with Delorme and that my perspective needs to be revealed for a more complete understanding and interpretation of the results of my collaboration with him in the production of his life history.

Many ask if conducting fieldwork among prisoners is intimidating and I answer no. I feel comfortable from the moment I walk through the barred gates and locked doors of maximum-security prisons—I have gathered data in nine such facilities—down the long breezeways, up to the education areas or wherever I am taken to sit and talk with prisoners. Why? Because although I am one who has led a sheltered and comfortable middle-class life, I have a deep sympathy for the rejected and disinherited of our society. While it is true that many of the middle class share my point of view, few share my reasons. I am well acquainted with society's contempt for the lowly; I know about asylums and their often cruel, inhumane methods from a deeply personal perspective and, therefore, identify strongly with anyone who lives that demeaning experience. My only child suffers from schizophrenia. He has been beaten on the street by the police; thrown into jail (in a small college town in a nearby state) for "acting crazy and breaking a window" and left there, fortunately in a one-man cell, for one month before I was informed of his whereabouts by a court-appointed attorney and rescued him; beaten and robbed in mental institutions and on the street; overdrugged by psychiatrists; and trussed hand and foot like a turkey and thrown into the "quiet room" of a psychiatric hospital in a major research university because he was a "problem." So, yes, I feel comfortable with imprisoned men. In fact, I like them very much: they are my sons.

In getting to know Delorme, I shared, on one of the first tapes I sent to him, the deep sadness I felt about my son's suffering and told him that although imprisoned men did not share the exact same experience as my son, it was similar enough for me to feel empathy for them. On the very day he learned about my son, September 21, 1978, Delorme began to tell me about himself. Previous to this—he had already sent me sixteen tapes—he had revealed nothing of himself; he had only spoken impersonally, irreverently, humorously, and even impudently about the language and culture and current happenings in the prison, and it was very obvious on these tapes that he regarded me as an outsider. But because he and my son shared experiences in common—asylums, rejection, revilement, brutalization—I became the person with whom he could share his life experiences, including the sadness and pain he had shared with no one before: I was a square john who understood. Something very special happened in that first moment of trust and recognition between us:

> Hello Chiquita. [From the beginning Delorme identified me as "Chiquita." When I was first introduced to him his response was "Hello, Chiquita." Delorme is about six feet tall and I am barely five feet.] Hey, babe, this is Gene. This is not Gene Burnett. My name is Gene Delorme, but that's all right. I noticed you got the names backward on this tape. I enjoyed your tape. I thought it was beautiful and I really . . . you're my favorite singer now, you know that? You should play a song like that [on guitar] every time [you send a tape]. I really enjoy it. You've got a beautiful voice. Kind of sad. Or maybe just thoughtful; I don't know. I sure liked it, though. You're a good singer. I'm glad you sent this tape. I'll listen to it again. I'll take it over to the library with me tomorrow night. I've got it to my-

self now. John gave it to me when I headed for chow, so I brought it in with me and I'll get all settled back here [in his cell] and put you on the big speaker and see what you have to say. Thank you for sending it, because I took a lot of notes while I was listening to the tape, so that gave me—that gives me—a lot of material, suggestions that you have, questions you asked. That's what I wanted, too, you know. I know that we tend to go along on our sessions over there [Delorme and an Indian friend, Duane Burnett, working in the prison library, were updating the prison's slang collection from the 1950s for me] and we get to talking pretty free on our sessions. I can't put any constraints on it, you know, like you said.

I get a mental picture of you: you're a little toughy. You're not so naive. You couldn't be; you've got too much inside. You got a love and compassion for your fellow man. So you're one of the very few that try to understand. Of course you're frustrated because you can't do anything, and, like you say, too, a book could do so much good, and you never know until we try. I didn't know what sort of writing you planned to do. It really didn't sound like there would be a great demand for a book on slang, so that's why I asked to try to get an idea on what you might be planning, and really hoped that we were going to do a book in depth. I know it's hard for you to hang around in here. You can't run around and get a feel of the place, being a woman, a pretty woman; you could never walk around here, you could never do that. There's two writers in here now. They will be here for the next two, three months. They're *Walla Walla Bulletin* [newspaper] employees.

I'll tell you a little about myself, Chiquita. [Here begins his self-initiated life history.]

While at the penitentiary Delorme chose what to tell me about his life. He had plenty of time to think and talk about all that had happened to him, and he seemed genuinely to enjoy the reliving of his life experiences. When he was transferred in 1980 from the Washington State Penitentiary to the University of Washington—he was still a prisoner—to complete the college program he had begun at Walla Walla, the taping of his life story came to an end. Chapter four of this book, "The Old Rebel in the Free World," was gathered through a series of interviews that I conducted when I visited him in Tacoma, Washington, for seven days in June 1992. "The Old Rebel in the Free World," therefore, differs from the rest of Delorme's story: he was not locked up in a prison freely selecting what he chose to tell me about his life; rather, he was in the free world specifically responding to my questions about his life since leaving the prison in 1980.

The material Delorme collected for our book, *The Joint,* consisted, in addition to his interviews and conversations with other prisoners, of countless hours in which he spoke on the tape recorder about prison life to me, far away in Ohio, while he sat in his house (cell) or in the prison library. On these tapes he also told me about himself and his life experiences, his dreams, his fears. And I responded by sending tapes to him on which I either sought to encourage him to continue his studies in the prison college program or sang lullabies and Mexican folk songs to cheer him up.

Delorme's story was told to me orally. He did not sit down and write his life history for me. The structure and character of an oral narrative are different from those of a written narrative, which is revised and rewritten and reorganized over and over until it satisfies the rules of formal written prose. Because Delorme's story was spoken, it rambles, it repeats, switching from one topic to another, then back again; it moves like the mind. In many ways it is a stream of consciousness pouring forth, lively, rapidly changing, spontaneous. One aspect of this naturalness is the appearance of incremental repetition that is formulaic in oral narrative. There are instances in which Delorme returns to a subject again and again. In each instance he adds something to it. In each instance he reveals more about himself. These incremental repetitions allow us to see more deeply into his persona. He keeps coming back, for example, to his experiences in the "hole" (solitary confinement) and to his outrage at the way he was treated as a child by other children because he was Indian. These repetitions are signals of revelation for us; indeed, an awareness of these incremental repetitions and the way they unfold present us with a greater understanding of this very complex and contradictory man. The narrative flow, the way he tells his tale, is a fascinating study in itself.

For reasons explained above, I have transcribed what he told me as accurately as possible, editing out only what I deemed extraneous to his life story. To protect the privacy of persons mentioned in the narratives, with the exception of his daughter, Gina; his sister, Mary Jan; and his brother, Donny, I have changed all names. In some instances I have eliminated repeated words or phrases, sacrificing them for aesthetic reasons. I have not, however, censored his language in any way. The "you know's," "anyway's," "as I was telling you's," "like I said's," "you know what I mean's," "in the meantime's," and so on all serve as links or bridges between narratives, or as communication markers to let me know he is aware of my presence: he knows that he is talking to me even though I am almost three thousand miles away.

Anyone who has been imprisoned for any length of time knows how to create this imaginative "you are here with me" world, knows how to make real what is a dream or desire. This distance between us, of course, produced an unusual performance situation. There is no face-to-face interaction here. That is impossible. This man is in a maximum-security prison in Washington and the person he is speaking to is in Columbus, Ohio. But in his (and, later, my) imagination, we are together and he is sharing his innermost thoughts with me face to face. How does he overcome this barrier? With a tape recorder. It becomes the communication link closing the distance between us. There is no personal interaction, yet he speaks to me as if there were. I cannot see his facial expressions, his gestures, but his voice eloquently brings his performance to life. In Delorme's imagination, Inéz (Chiquita) is sitting right next to him as he tells his stories to her, and in Inéz's imagination, when she listens to him talking to her on the tape, she is there with him.

Actually, using a tape recorder is common in many prisons. It is one of the most important ways prisoners have of communicating with people in the free world. Indeed, it has evolved into a tradition that incorporates technological change and development and has come into being since the widespread availability of inexpensive tape recorders. Prisoners have incorporated into their communication patterns this tradition of speaking on tapes to their families and friends in the free world, overcoming in the process some of the communication barriers that are produced by imprisonment. Both prisoners and their families and friends use this method of communication in those prisons where such communication is allowed. So the context in which Delorme told me about his life was not artificial: it was a way of communication that he was very familiar and comfortable with, one that he had used many times before.

Delorme's life history is presented chronologically exactly as he ordered it, although part of it was told to me in scattered places throughout the many recordings he made in which he spoke of prison life or interviewed other prisoners. Several tapes were devoted completely to his life story, but as he progressed through his collection of field data, something he was talking about might trigger a personal memory and he would launch into a story about himself, then return to his original intent of describing life in prison. I have searched these narratives out and included them here. I want to emphasize, however, that I did not rearrange the sequence of his story. Not only was it unnecessary, but rearranging might well have spoiled the artistry of his style. Whenever he needed to back up in time, he provided markers that set the event in its proper context.

Embedded within Delorme's autobiography are adventure tales such as the harrowing cliff-hanging and rescue when a child, the haunted-house episode, the Greenhill escape, the Red Mill riot, the wilderness camp experience, and the airplane caper. All these tales are masterfully told: taut, well crafted, dynamic, highly entertaining. These adventure episodes are announced by certain formulaic signals or markers. When Delorme suddenly says, for example, "I started to tell you about . . . ," "This is really true," "Well, one time when I was in the hole . . . ," "One night we had a helluva fight . . ." "I was telling you about how . . . ," "The first armed robbery I ever pulled . . . ," or in a transition in which he backs up in time by many years, "I'm just going to go back a step in time here before I met Linda," or "When I was thirteen years old . . . ," he is signaling that he is prepared to take me on another interesting or exciting adventure. These annunciatory signals or formulas have the effect of drawing me, through his performance, into his world. I, as the appreciative audience of one, regard him and his tale with a "special intensity" (Bauman 1984:11).

"The last time I was in the hole" is a formulaic cultural marker signaling that something from his past is about to be revealed which I should listen to. This marker serves as a frame announcing that I must give what is about to transpire the utmost attention (Mullen 1991:20). Delorme often shifts into quoted speech in his storytelling, the effect of which is to highlight the frame aspect of his performance. He also employs codes, the lingo of the prison, to frame his performance, codes which I understand, since I have been included as one who understands and accepts his cultural worldview.

Through his verbal artistry he recreates his adventures in such a manner that we are both transported back in time and place to the actual happening. There is also the illusion that I am sitting right beside him, either in his cell or in the prison library, listening avidly to his adventures. Delorme constructs a frame within a frame within a frame. Like Boccaccio's *Decameron,* his creation is built on a complicated structure: Delorme sits in prison alone speaking into a tape recorder; his storytelling is for an appreciative audience of one, who in his imagination is sitting right beside him but who, in reality, is nearly three thousand miles away. As he narrates adventure after adventure it has the effect of pulling me, the appreciative listener, into the exciting episodes with him. This, of course, takes place within a different time frame which excludes his actual presence; his re-creation is, for him, a reliving: *he is there.* This, the re-creation, is very seductive for me, the audience; consequently, I, too, am drawn into the tale. So we have an audience immediately present in the imagination, as well as present in reality, though far away and in a later time frame. The audience is drawn into the actual tale itself through its lively and imaginative re-creation. It is as if the audience of one is an invisible spectator standing by, watching the adventure unfold when it is happening. Past, present, and future seem inextricably mixed into an instantaneous now.

Some of Delorme's narrative endings also take on formulaic patterns: "Hell, I never played that game again"; "Boy, that cop slid up on me and almost got my ass that time"; "Believe me, I stayed away after that"; "So I went wild after that"; "That was the last time I ever went to the hole." These leave-taking phrases seem to signal that a lesson has been learned and serve, in a manner of speaking, almost as statements meant to be didactic.

Each separate episode or adventure, juxtaposed against the totality of his story, seems to be a building block that firmly places him within a context out of which he seems unable to escape. These episodic experiences in his past, together with happenings which he is living immediately in the present of the actual tape-recorded performance, have the effect of revealing a portrait of a particular and unique man, trapped both physically and psychically in a past/present, with his future obscured by two walls: the actual wall surrounding the prison, and the invisible wall trapping his spirit. Here he sits in a now, reviewing his past life, past actions, past feelings and thoughts. Rarely, however, does he gaze into what will be: the future. When he does, it is with trepidation. It is as if he were caught in an unfortunate location on the wheel of life which, for him, is always moving downward. He is unable, perhaps afraid, to break out of the wheel, unable to loosen the chains that bind him to the portion that life has dealt him.

Delorme's style exhibits much humor, irony, and understatement. It is tough and filled with the lingo of the prison and street. Rarely, he drops his mask and reveals his innermost feelings: fear, psychic pain, despair, disappointment, tenderness for others, particularly his brother and mother, but also for the imprisoned men, especially his Indian "brothers." Delorme is a believer in the unseen, or the spiritual world, and he believes in God, the Great Spirit. Sustaining him has been his bravado—"I can take it. This ain't shit." "Fuck the world!"—and his physical courage. Certain themes echo throughout his story: the stress of survival; poverty and its impact upon his family and the important role it has played in turning him toward a life of crime; the hole, or solitary confinement (he comes back to this over and over); his motto, "Fuck the world," and what this reveals about his worldview and his rebellion; drugs and alcohol as an escape from pain; his intense self-hatred and his self-destructive behavior; and, perhaps most important of all, the prejudice and rejection he experienced as a child, which set the stage early in life for his anger and rebellion that persist even today.

My aim is to present the spirit and personality of Delorme as he presented himself to me—the good and the bad. Although there is something of the trickster about him, his frank and open sharing of his life story seems to signal an honest telling. To the extent that a human being can reveal himself or herself honestly and openly, Delorme seems to have done this, even though, like many good storytellers, he may have stretched the truth in some instances.

So here is his story, grim, shocking, sad, humorous, poignant, irreverent, tragic; it is the life story of a Native American who is a convicted felon. This is no holy man speaking. This is the tale of a man who decided that the only good Indian is an Indian who refuses to conform to the demands of white society.

The first three chapters of *Chief* were produced while Delorme was in prison. These narratives, despite the bitterness, hardness, and anger revealed in them, display no whining or self-pity. However, self-pity creeps into chapter four, "The Old Rebel in the Free World," which was collected after Delorme had been out of prison for nearly ten years. In prison, Delorme was recognized by fellow inmates as a "real convict," one of a few highly respected prisoners who are known for their dignity, physical courage, coolness, and loyalty to fellow prisoners, and such men never show weakness or resort to self-pity. But once he was released into the free world, he gradually shed this prisoner identity and the values espoused by the convict code.

Chapter four, "The Old Rebel in the Free World," lacks the artistry exhibited in the first three chapters. In addition, this last chapter contains several conflicting accounts of events. While taping the conversation which produced this final chapter of his story in 1992, I immediately noticed these problems. Each time I asked him to clarify what he was saying, he changed his story in some way. I noticed that he appeared to be experiencing memory loss at this time. I believe this is the reason, in part, for the discrepancies in this final chapter and its poorer quality when compared with the well-crafted narrative he produced ten years earlier while imprisoned. Shortly after I returned to my home, Delorme entered the psychiatric unit of a state hospital.

In transcribing Delorme's life history, I have used ellipses to signal an interrupted thought or faltering speech. In addition, brackets are used to indicate editorial additions.

Delorme is a fine storyteller, a man skilled with words who shows great insight into his condition and that of other Native American men caught up in crime and the criminal justice system. Driven, hounded, pushed, Delorme has battled white society's rules all his life and continues to resist conforming despite the overwhelming odds. He has chosen to walk the black road. The powers of the bison and the elk have never been his to acquire. Unlike Black Elk, Delorme has been granted no great visions. His vision is a grim and tragic one filled with cruelty, rejection, and poverty. Yet Delorme seeks visions of the other world, as the reader will come to understand, and his spirit is such that, although he is bitter and angry, he hates no one (but himself) and is generous enough to want to tell his story to the world.

Inéz Cardozo-Freeman

1940   Eugene Delorme is born April 9 at the Marty, South Dakota, Catholic mission school.

1941   Family moves to Aberdeen, Washington.

1942–50 Gene's father, a carpenter, becomes a severe alcoholic unable to work; his mother works in cannery and restaurant to support family. Delorme and his brother Donny begin bringing home stolen food. Stealing broadens in scope and at age ten Gene steals a car.

1950–53 Gene and Donny are sent to the Chemawa Indian School in Oregon.

1952   Father sentenced for one year to Washington State Penitentiary at Walla Walla for theft (a case of beer). When released, he moves to Texas.

1953   Gene and Donny return to Aberdeen from Chemawa. Mother moves family to Tacoma, Washington. Gene is sent for several months to Greenhill Juvenile Detention Center, Chehalis, Washington, for theft.

1955–57 Gene is sent again to Greenhill Juvenile Detention Center for theft and parole violation.

1957   Sentenced to six months in the Tacoma jail, then is reclassified to adult status and sent to Monroe State Reformatory.

1959   Returns to Monroe for parole violation and is later paroled.

1961   Paroled.

1962   Returns to Monroe for six months, parole violation.

1963   Returns to Monroe for eight months, parole violation.

1964–68 Sent to Monroe for auto theft; requests and receives permission to transfer to the Washington State Penitentiary. Paroled.

1969   Begins working in a photography studio. Meets Linda. Marries Marie. Daughter, Gina Marie, is born.

1970   Wins two national photography awards. Is separated from Marie (later divorced).

1971–71 Goes into photography business with Linda.

1972–73 Sent to Washington State Penitentiary for six months for parole violations and theft. Paroled.

1973   Works briefly as a photographer. Returns to Washington State Penitentiary for burglary conviction.

1974   Receives work release from penitentiary and spends five months working on construction crew at Western State Hospital.

1976   Paroled. Commits first-degree burglary with a weapon; receives twenty years for burglary, five years for possession of stolen credit card, and three years for parole violation. Sent to Washington State Penitentiary.

1978   Completes high school GED and enters college program at penitentiary. Meets Cardozo-Freeman. Begins taping life history.

1981   Moves to minimum security at Washington State Penitentiary in preparation for work release. Transfers to the University of Washington, Seattle, to complete baccalaureate degree while finishing his sentence. Studies Northwest Coast Indian painting and carving at the university.

1984   Graduates with dual degrees in social work and social justice. University honors him as an outstanding minority student. Begins work as Counselor II for Puyallup Tribal Authority, counseling drug addicts, alcoholics, and ex-offenders. Relationship with Linda ends.

1985   Discovers he is diabetic. Meets Jackie.

1986   Loses job. Lives with Jackie.

1989   Breaks up with Jackie.

1990–93 Brother Donny dies of drug overdose. Gene is in and out of hospitals and jail. Hospitalized (April 1993) in the psychiatric unit of a state hospital in Washington.

CHIEF

Eugene Delorme (*right*) and his brother, Donny, ages three and four.

Eugene Delorme (*standing*) and his brother, Donny, in their twenties.

1

The Seeds of
Rebellion Sowed

I'll tell you a little about myself, Chiquita. I'm a Santee Sioux Indian and I'm 38 years old and I have a nine year old daughter. I'm divorced and currently involved with an older woman that I used to work for. I'm going to school, to college. . . .

If you can imagine, I've got sixteen years in here and a reformatory. I was pretty much raised in institutions. I went to Indian school. I've been to the state boys' school, reformatory. I've come right up, right through the ranks, you know, so . . . but I'm changing; I think age is mellowing me out. I don't know, but I'm busting my ass. Somehow I've got to change it all. I'm getting tired of it.

Duane, my partner, is about the same age as me. We've been in the dope scene, the robberies, burglaries; we just came up the same, you know. We're both from fairly big Indian families, very poor. Ah, poor boys, I guess we got a funny attitude about that. We laugh at that stuff [because] we're older now. We can [laugh now], I guess, but it wasn't funny then, and I think it had a lot to do with me being in prison. But what can I do, you know? All we can do is laugh at it. Can't regret, huh? You can't live and just live and regret, worry about the past. It's done. Future is all that counts now.

As I was saying, Duane comes from a pretty big, poor Indian family, and him and his brothers, they hustled all the time when they were younger, shoplifted when they were, you know, nine, ten years old, learned to steal the same age or younger. Like I said, the exact same in my family. We got out, me and my brother, when we was little, and we would break into a store or a warehouse and anytime we brought food home my mom would be happy about it, you know. I'd make my whole family happy, and we'd be heroes for the day, you know what I mean? So that went on and on. So those were what you want to call impressionable years. I had a lot of positive reinforcement for my stealing, lots of it. So here I am pushing forty, and now I'm trying to break that habit. I know what it [the habit of stealing] is; I know why it is, how to break away from it and [from] accepting all the praise I got from the family for doing something good, right? It [breaking the habit] doesn't have the same impression [as being rewarded for stealing], you know what I mean? Because those other feelings [of reward] are deep, deep in there for some reason. So it's going to be tough.

I was born in Marty, South Dakota. It's not really a town, I guess. It's a mission, an Indian mission, and my mother . . . well, for chrissake! . . . now I never thought of it that way—another institution . . . I was born in an institution! Holy catfish!

My mother, she grew up in a mission school because her folks died when my mother and her sister were kind of young; they were teenagers. They're still together all these years. My mom's taken care of her sister, Ruby, 'cause she's blind. My mom was born on the Santee Sioux Reservation in Santee, Nebraska. My mother was French and Sioux. Her dad was French and Sioux and her mother was all Sioux. My dad was from Canada. He had a large family in Canada, Quebec. They're all French-speaking. He had twelve brothers, and I guess he met my mother when she was at the Catholic school in Marty, South Dakota, where I was born. She was . . . well, her and her sister got separated at an early age. Her mother died when they were about nine or ten years old. Their dad, he couldn't care for them, and he was an alcoholic and a pretty wild guy. His name was Trudell. The Trudells had a helluva reputation back in the Dakotas. Or was it Nebraska? He drank a lot, ran a lot of moonshine. The Trudells were pretty well known back in that area. There's a lot of them. They had a real reputation for taking what they wanted when they wanted it. That's how the Catholic father back there got his mission built. He told the Trudells he needed some wood; all of a sudden the wood appeared there.

My mom said that when her mother died of cancer, her dad, afterward . . . she thought he died from a broken heart, they were so close. After her mother's death, her dad wouldn't talk to the kids, and she, my mother, got mad at him because he just couldn't think about anything but losing their mother and he didn't care if the kids starved. There was her and her sister, Ruby, who was blind, and her brother, Billy. So my mom was out there trying to get food. She'd go out and steal food. My mom was the oldest, so she was the boss. She'd go to the store, steal food and put it in a big bag, and away she'd go, just like a little tramp, she said. They also made money selling rags. She was about twelve then, trying to support her brother and sister.

My mom was a little hustler. When my mother's mother was sick in bed with cancer, my mom and Ruby and her brother, Billy, they used to run around with a little wagon and sell rags. I think Kirk Douglas said his dad used to do that, sell rags. But with their little wagon, that's what they did. And they'd pick up coal and take it home from the tracks. They were regular little hustlers when they were small, just like me and Donny, keeping things going at home. Their dad worked for the city back there. He used to bring a lot of stuff home from the dump, toys and stuff he'd find there. My mom had a lot of stories. My mom's brother, Billy, still lives on the reservation in Nebraska, the Santee Sioux Reservation. He's still living back there with his family, and him and my mom didn't see each other again until a few years ago.

I didn't live in the Dakotas very long because I got pneumonia two times running, so the doctor said they better get my ass away from that kind of climate or I probably wouldn't make it. So anyway, they moved out of there, came straight through to Aberdeen [Washington]. I was about a year old then. Aberdeen is a little town on the coast here, fishing and lumber. It's an old town, and it's just depressing as hell to even look at.

I was baptized Catholic when I was real young [in Marty, South Dakota]. And I remember as a youngster, I remember going to church with my whole family [in Aberdeen]. My dad would be sober. And my sister, I always remember her white dresses. And me and Donny, my brother, were always dressed up in slacks, little suit jackets or something nice, you know. We always had at least a little Sunday outfit that we got to wear to church. And my whole family went and Ruby went. She didn't stay home, 'cause she was nice and healthy then. And she could wrestle with a goddam grizzly bear then when she was younger, and still might give you a tough go now. So anyway, we went to church real regular. I remember going to Sunday school a lot. I didn't mind church then. It was kind of an adventure. I remember we took Holy Communion and I always took my confession serious. I think probably from the third grade on is when I started resenting the church a little more. And, of course, not only that; I think my family was in the process of breaking up then.

As far back as my memory goes, I can visualize my dad just always drunk; to me it seemed like he was drunk all the time. Of course, my brother and I, we sort of bonded like twins at a very young age because . . . I think it had a lot to do with the instability at home, with my dad always being on the warpath, drunk, and him and my mother fighting so much, beating her up all the time and I still don't . . . well, I blame him, I guess, but, of course, I understand it more [now] because he was actually a gentle man, I think. He was a gentle man, a God-fearing man, if you want to call it that. My dad, he didn't do anything but spend what money he had on the wine. He was still a good man; he was a good Christian man. When he was younger, when he first met Mom, he had hopes of becoming a priest then, and he worked with the fathers and everybody, studying theology. Then him and my mom met at the Catholic boarding school and they eventually got married. The nuns built them a house and furnished it and everything for them to live right there at the school. And so he didn't have drinking problems until he got out here to Washington.

Aberdeen was a real rough town, fishing town, logging town. He was kind of small of stature and I think even that may have had something to do with it . . . maybe belly up to the bar, you know. He found good friendship there. Otherwise he was pretty much of a loner. He found good friendships and he got more into it, more into it, and pretty soon he was just a falling-down wino. He was an excellent carpenter, a master carpenter, and a lot of people hired him for jobs, but a lot of time his jobs got half done; he never came back because of his drinking.

Like I said, my dad always did want to be a priest. He was always a religious person. I don't know where it came from. My dad went to the penitentiary in 1953. He and a couple friends broke into a warehouse and stole a bunch of beer, so they packed his ass off to Walla Walla. He got out in 1955, so actually he did less than two years. He got out and went to Texas and got working for a priest back there. He spent eighteen years working and helping them out. And they kept him out of prison; they kept him from drinking. He didn't start drinking again until he came out here again eighteen years later to visit us. Then he died out here in 1976. Me and Donny had already been in prison two or three times. He had seen us kids when we were little, then he didn't see us again until we were grown up. I never knew my dad was so little until I went down to pick him up at this bus station. I seen this little guy sitting on a little suitcase and I walked up to him and I looked at him. I could tell he was a Delorme from his nose, and I said, "You Pete?" He said, "You Gene?" He said, "You Don?" We were just standing over him. He just come up to about here on me.

I don't know nothing about my dad before he married my mother. I don't know where he come from. Well, his family's from Canada. I already told you that. They all spoke French, I know that, and he had twelve brothers, no sisters. He had dark, wavy black hair but he was more my complexion than Donny's, a swarthy-looking fellow, good-looking guy. Dad was part Chippewa and Santee and French, so I'm Chippewa and Santee and French. There's no such thing as a full-blood. The French have blond hair and blue eyes. I'm a throwback. The only other person in our family who ever came up with light hair and light eyes is Rita, my sister's daughter. That's the only one we've had that didn't have black hair. In my father's family, they all had black hair. But my grandmother was a pure blond, my great-grandmother on my father's side. She was the only blond and I was the only blond after her. My mom told me about that. A couple times they were teasing me about my blond hair; they'd tease me about it, but my mom would tell me about the great-grandmother that was blond, spoke French, so as near as I could figure, that's where my light hair comes from.

But my father, just before he got to be too bad a drunk, he would help us. He'd make us swings, he'd make us toys to play on, and he'd take us out fishing once in a while and he'd take us out picking ferns and berries a lot. We'd make a family outing of it. We'd look forward to that. Those were some of my good memories, getting in and out of a beat-up old car, jalopy. We had one of them big old square cars just like them old-time Packards with spoke wheels, and away we'd go, putt-putting up the hill. We'd find a good place, we'd spread our picnic out, and we'd spend the whole afternoon picking berries and ferns. Us kids just played around in the woods. That was some of the good memories that I had of my father. And later on when he got really seriously hooked on the alcohol, he was kind of relegated to the position of a child. My mother always loved him even when he was drunk and he was obnoxious. She protected him.

My dad drank a lot with his brother, Ernie, who used to come down from Shelton. He'd bring his wife and daughters down. He had three daughters. We'd all play together and they'd drink together and Mom and Juanita would . . . I don't know what they did, visit, I guess. And they drank while they were there unless they got into a big fistfight or something and took off. The best thing I liked . . . we used to go to the beach a lot. We used to go to Westport in our old clunker cars. We'd go down to the beach and spend the night, spend half the day and the night playing in the water down there, picking up seashells. Just the smell of the ocean; I can almost smell it now. That was on the good days, you know. They'd start drinking beer down there and they might ruin a weekend, or sometimes they might go without drinking, which must have been hard on them. Probably had a bottle hid, you know. A drunk can have a bottle, but everybody's gonna know it ten minutes later.

During the time my mom was working at one of the restaurants or canneries bringing home the paycheck, my dad was usually hanging around the tavern down in Aberdeen, bumming drinks. If he had a few bucks, he'd buy a few. Mom and Ruby would yell at him when he'd come home acting the fool, getting crazy. But he'd just get home and get all obnoxious, bothering people, [and] eventually they'd get in a fistfight. My mom generally won. It just scared the shit out of me when I was little. Scared Donny, too, I guess. He was always hanging onto me. We'd both be there crying, wondering what the hell to do. We'd be hiding behind the bed crying and screaming, but eventually we got used to it as we got older. By older, I'm talking about two or three, I guess. I'm not sure just how old I was then, probably about two or three. But when there was trouble between my father and mother, us kids, we'd be crying and scared, you know, scared he was gonna kill her or some damned thing. My mom would talk to us about it. She'd say, "Aw, don't worry about it. It ain't no big deal. Your dad's just drunk." Maybe she'd call the police, maybe she wouldn't. They got used to it down at the police station.

My Aunt Ruby, she'd try to get hold of him when they was fighting. She'd reach out for him with her blind hands and try to find him. If Ruby got ahold of him the fight would be over with. She was strong, she had strong hands. Wring his little chicken neck if she'd find him. She'd hear all that scuffling going on, she'd get ahold of him and that would be the end of the fight. He'd usually go running out the door screaming at them, "You two bitches!" Pretty soon us kids started joining in on the fray, then all hell would break loose. Boy, we'd throw pots and pans, dishes, ashtrays. He didn't stand a chance. Had the whole damn family out there, man, so he quit that shit. He wasn't that stupid. He couldn't win that battle. I must have been five or six years old then.

But I can remember my dad was always a Christian, a strong Catholic, a very strong Catholic, except when the wine, the alcohol, took over. Then his personality would change and he would . . . every time he came home he was ready to get in a fight. He wasn't a big man. He wasn't large in stature or anything. When he was drunk, he really couldn't do that much damage. Hell, my mother was a hardworking woman. She was tough and she took about as much abuse as she wanted to take, and then she gave it right back again, plus she had a pack of little wild kids with her that would help her out. Like I said, when we got old enough, we'd jump him, too. I'd be hanging on one of his legs and my brother'd be hanging on his other leg. He'd be screaming, my mother'd be screaming, my sister'd be screaming, and Jesus Christ, we'd have a helluva knockdown dragout fight, twelve midnight, one o'clock in the morning, whenever the taverns close. So he really wasn't able to do too damn much damage after a short while. He'd generally get the short end of the stick trying to deal with that tribe. I felt sorry for him at times.

By the time I was ten or eleven, my father wasn't beating up my mother. No, no. He just got more into drinking, he was more of a drunk. Alcohol got ahold of him better and he was weak and he didn't hang around home much; he'd just come home and sleep. By then he was having severe d.t.'s and seeing snakes. He couldn't quit if he wanted to. He'd be screaming around the house, nobody there, scared to death, bugs be crawling on him and all that stuff. He wasn't into fighting anymore. Years went by, you know. He just spent his time trying to find some more wine. And we'd come home and he'd be quiet as a church mouse off in a corner somewhere. He'd be gone the next morning. So we just kind of went like we didn't even have a dad, you know; he wasn't there to bother us.

I think I felt more relief because Don and I had our say-so even at that early age. We stayed out when we wanted; we came home when we wanted. So it was a relief not to put up with any bullshit from him. When we was little he would beat our asses [with a] switch or something when we'd get in trouble or do something. We didn't like that too much. But the drinking went on. I ignored it. I don't remember having any feelings for it one way or another, except if it was time for a whipping or something, then I'd get scared, wouldn't want to get spanked. I'd seen so many drunks by the time I was ten years old down in Aberdeen, one more didn't make any difference. We was real indifferent to it.

But my Aunt Ruby was great, just like she could see. She was like a sighted person to us. There wasn't any thought about leading her around or anything. She knew the house, knew the area. She could get along, find things we couldn't find, and that's what she did. Ruby and my mom, when they were ten or eleven years old and their mother died, their father shipped them out to a boarding school because he couldn't take care of them by himself. But Ruby and my mom got separated because they sent Ruby to a school for blind people. I don't know how many years she spent there, probably over ten years. But I know Billy and my mother went to get her. They ran away from the boarding school to try to find Ruby so they could all get back together. Mom's got some real stories about those runaway days.

Sometimes my Aunt Ruby cried. I didn't know why she cried. A lot of times I just assumed that she cried because she couldn't see and sometimes she got sad about it. But I don't think so now. I think she cried because there was so many times that she couldn't find enough to feed us, things like that, and it just all come down on her. But, you know, who was I to assume at that age? When she cried, we all cried. It was so sad. She very seldom cried, so when she cried, something had to be very wrong, so we all cried. We'd all sit there together and have a big cry. But I always assumed she got sad all of a sudden because she couldn't see something, but that wasn't it; she was worried about us kids, worried about Dad coming home and beating her up or something. My dad did beat her a couple times. She don't go down easy, though, that's for damn sure. Once she reached out, got a hand on his shirt, he couldn't get away from her and she'd start slugging him. He snuck up on her a couple times and hit her. That didn't make her cry; just made her angry, you know. She'd call him, "You little sonovabitch. If I get my hands on you, I'll break your goddam neck." And I'd say, "Go, Ruby, go!"

But when you're kids, it's pretty mellow. When you're kids Don's age and my age, my sister's age, we could ride it out. Let the adults worry about it. We'd just go on playing while they're fighting. We'd just assumed there was going to be something to eat. It was automatic. I see a lot of kids nowadays, it's the same way; they're resilient. Maybe in my family more so than white kids' families, maybe and maybe not; you can't really say that either, because Don and I had two friends that were white boys and their mother was a prostitute in Aberdeen and she treated them bad and they were always happy and laughing, looking and waiting for me and Donny to come and play. And all four of us would be out all night long. We wouldn't even come home until daybreak.

My family never has broke up other than my dad. He was into the booze real heavy all during the late forties and early fifties. He was a stone wino, apple wine. He hung out on Aaron Street in Aberdeen, and on the east side of Aberdeen there was a tavern over there called the Owl Tavern. He was always up there and I used to hang around. He'd be around the house all nervous and all that bullshit, trying to think of an excuse to go to the tavern. As I look back now, he'd say, "Get your coat on, man." We'd say, "All right, let's go." And we'd get our coats and all three go walking toward the store. And when we had a car, of course, we drove. But his favorite tavern was right up the block a little ways.

We'd go to the store and then we'd go down to the tavern, if he didn't go straight to the tavern. Anyway, he'd tell me and Donny, "You guys wait outside for a few minutes. I'll be right out." And he'd go in there and he'd order a beer or a shot of wine and he'd bring us out a couple candy bars and say, "I'll be right out. I'll be right out," and we'd sit there, and we'd wait and we'd wait and we'd wait. And I'd be peeking through the old smoky, dirty windows, look in and smell all that disinfectant and wine. I can remember that smell. Seemed like bums all the time, hobos. They were fishermen, working men, so they weren't the best dressed, you know. Sonovabitches always scared me. Stick their head out, "Aw, you guys always hanging around." "Oh, my dad's in there. We're waiting for him." "Whose kids are these?" But sometimes we'd be out there for hours. So if we'd see he was real drunk, we'd say, "Aw, the hell with it" and go home. We tried to tell him we was going home, but he didn't pay any attention to us after about the fourth or fifth shot of wine. It didn't take very goddam much wine to get him drunk, that was for sure, and he was gone. And we didn't see him the rest of that goddam day or night unless my mom would go get him or else somebody brings him home. A lot of times the cops used to bring him home. The chief of police lived right up the street from us. His name was Gallagher.

So Don and I . . . even at such a young age, at six or seven years old . . . Christ, a lot of times we were out all night roaming the damn neighborhoods in the dark. And my mother . . . the reason she didn't really even realize it is because she always worked two jobs, so she was always exhausted; she didn't have time to really be staying up baby-sitting us, so she didn't know where in the hell we was one way or another. She pretty much had confidence in us. But my mother never spanked Donny or I. My mother believed in the old Indian ways; a lot of her attitude stemmed from Indian beliefs. Most tribes are that way. Mothers let the boys pretty much run free. There's no physical punishment. There's not a lot of verbal reprimands, either, because we are expected to grow. We're expected to experience pain and learn from the things we do daily, the boys are. That goes back . . . Christ, in ancient history, as far as Indian boys getting out and learning to deal with nature, and deal with each other without having to be pushed around and led and taught like the girls. But my father, he came from a family . . . that's the kind of discipline they had in Canada: beat the shit out of them boys if they get in trouble. The French Catholic influence, I guess, but with the Santee boys, the Dakota Sioux, the boys can do no wrong, you know. They beat the hell out of the girls if they act crazy, but the boys can spit on their mother, or do what they want and run free all night long if they want to. The Indian girls are brought up strict and they're quiet.

My sister . . . who understands girls, you know what I mean? She's older than me by two years. We fought, we argued a lot. She was a tomboy. She played with us a lot out in the woods and stuff like that, but she was a little older and it didn't take her long to get that in her head. We wouldn't never let her go with us anyway when me and Donny would go places.

My mom, she was a strong Catholic and she believed . . . she accepted the fact that there was not going to be any divorce because it would be a sin against the church. So even though my dad was an alcoholic . . . he quit working . . . what she did was relegate him to the status of one of the children. I guess she had made the decision that, "Okay, well, I'll just have to take care of him, too, drunk or no drunk. He'll just be one of the kids." She couldn't get divorced, so she had to keep him. So she always worked two jobs. As early as I can remember when we was young, she worked at a

restaurant. She cleaned at night, which she thought was a lucky job because every morning when she'd come home early in the morning, she'd
have these gallon jugs full of the leftover food, leftover soups from the
kitchen. And that would be our food for the day. And so we were lucky in
that respect.

About 1945–46, when I was about six years old, I used to go to work
with her sometimes, and I'll be a sonovabitch, when I was six years old, I'd
run for the cocktail lounge and steal drinks while Mom was working in the
other part of the restaurant. You see, my drinking started very early. Anyway, she would get off work, sleep for about . . . oh, hell, I don't know . . .
three or four hours . . . probably not much more than that because she'd
have to go to work at the cannery where they did fish and crab and things
like that. She'd work at the cannery for another eight or nine hours, then
she'd come home and spend time with us and we'd have supper. It still
seemed like we . . . I don't know . . . it seemed like we had some memora-
ble evenings together. We listened to radio programs in the early days.
They had spooky radio programs on, and all of us would be snuggled
around the radio on the davenport and getting the shit scared out of us little kids.

Mom and Ruby . . . Ruby would cook us a big supper, whatever she
had. It might be biscuits, it might be hamburger gravy, it might be just
white gravy on biscuits, or we'd have something left over from the restaurant, or Mom might have got paid and we'd have something good to eat.
But anyway, I don't remember worrying about anything. And what kid
does? Of course, parents are struggling and you don't really realize that
until you get older. But my mother was such a hard worker. She really
didn't have any problems as far as getting a job, you know. I guess now I
would think about it as people taking advantage of her, because women
didn't get paid very good in the forties any damn way. But she just worked
her damned ass off.

Donny and I got in a lot of trouble. I mean we were always getting
picked up. They didn't necessarily send us to jail, but he and I were always
into something. No matter what it would be, we enjoyed it. I can't remember exactly when, but by the fifties I'm pretty sure that we were on

welfare. That was after my mom got hurt in an automobile accident. But I think they gave us eighty or ninety dollars a month to live on, something like that. Anyway, it seemed like a lot of money to me, kind of made do. Mom would always manage to make sure that we had enough money to go to the movies, which didn't cost much anyway. There actually was a Bijou Theater in Aberdeen, and another theater called the BNR Theater where the teenagers went. 'Course, Don and I weren't teenagers; we were little assholes. I can remember pretty vividly enjoying the movies.

For the most part, Don and I created our own recreation, our own excitement. Our excitement was, of course, nighttime activities . . . breaking into warehouses, big empty warehouses that had Ford tractors, things like that we could start up and drive around. The buildings had great big floors. We got into a big warehouse one night where one of the car companies in town had stored their new cars. This was a big, empty cannery with a lot of floor space, a lot of floor space. And all them brand-new cars has keys in 'em! And all them cars had gas in 'em! Oh, my God, have mercy! Don and I and two friends of ours called the Murphy brothers in Aberdeen that was part of our little gang, little punks . . . my God, we got those cars started. It was like one of those crash eliminations. And these were brand-new cars. Boy, we ran 'em off the goddam dock and into the river, into the Wishka River, and we smashed them all into the walls, we smashed 'em into each other. Boy, that was fun! Oh, my God, I'd love to do that again. Right now!

That's what we'd do at night. That's what we'd do on Sundays when the businesses is closed. See, I think that particular day when we did that to those cars, it was a fun day; it was like going to the park for us. I mean, other kids went to the park; we broke into places and played. I think that was a Sunday because I remember that it was daylight. We got that big end-door up to the dock opened, and this one Murphy kid drove that brand-new car straight down that dock and it went flying off that dock and he rode it clean down into the river, climbed out the window, and swam up to the dock, and he jumped into another car. Talk about a gutsy little punk! And I remember his mother; as young as I was, his mother used to give me a hard-on. She was a whore in Aberdeen and she was a good-looking woman. I loved older women, young as I was. Goddam, oooh she was nice!

So we spent our childhood in Aberdeen. Even now it's a small place; only about twenty-five to thirty-five thousand people live there. I don't remember a real lot from those days. What did we do? We played. There was white kids all around us who we didn't always get along with and it wasn't personality, because we were probably too young then, but just because we was Indian. We got attacked by the white settlers around us there. It's a anti-Indian town, anyway, as is every town, I guess. But I never felt comfortable around white people, white kids. Even now it bothers me. I've got a little more pride in myself now, in my race and my heritage.

I guess I was awful uncomfortable around white kids because that's all they got down there is white kids in school and I didn't even remember ever meeting any other Indian kids. There was a high school, a junior high school, and a rotten-assed Catholic school that we all went to and they were all on the same street. I sure hated that Catholic school. We started third grade in that school. We went to the first and second grade in the raggedy-muffin part of town. My mom put us in a Catholic school because she thought that the discipline would help us. My ass! My ass! I'm still angry! It didn't help. She made a *big* mistake in life there, putting us in a Catholic school full of white kids. We were the only two nonwhite kids in that whole goddam school, St. Mary's in Aberdeen. Them fucking kids. I hope to hell I never have to go through an experience like that again! That was a miserable goddam time in school. I sit here and trip back about grade school days and how my brother and I fought our way through it. In the old days we battled all the neighborhood kids. They bumped our heads with rocks every time we was going home from school, or we got bushwhacked, getting called names.

I think back to those days and it makes me uncomfortable, probably because I felt so uncomfortable alone, especially in school, the first and second grade. I tried to squeeze as far back in the room as I could. I dreaded recesses! I dreaded school! It was a nightmare when the damn teacher would single me out to read or do anything, because when everybody would look at me, I just felt dirty, I guess. I was told that; even the adults down there, maybe everywhere, they just don't mind calling a little kid a "dirty little siwash [savage]," "dirty little blanket-ass," "Why do we let them goddam Indians in here?" or something like that in the stores and the taverns when I'd go looking for my dad, or in restaurants.

Jesus Christ, Don and I could've got busted for a murder beef being in that goddam school, because we took their shit for about a year. Them fucking kids, dirty little white bastards, shit-eating goddam dogs, used to fucking . . . my mother used to have to walk to school, when she could, when she wasn't working, just to escort us home, for chrissake! Just like them blacks in Alabama when they put 'em in them white schools. The National Guard had to escort them to school and back. Well, that's what they had to do for us. My mother had to escort us little bastards to school and back because these little white sons-of-bitches would beat me and Donny up. Every goddam time school was out, they'd wait out front and throw rocks at us and beat us up.

I remember this one fucking white punk, this older kid, he used to ride by on a bicycle and he'd either hit me with a belt or a stick or a rock. Damn! I wish I could find . . . I wish I could still find that sonovabitch somewhere! He used to follow me and Donny along on his bicycle, and my sister, too, Mary Jan. And he'd spit, you know. He'd get in front of us on his bicycle and he'd spit and he'd say, "Lick it up, Delorme, lick it up, you motherfucking Indian punk." "Lick it up, Delorme," and he'd spit again. Dirty little sonovabitch, and I never was able to get back at him. He'd call me all kinds of rotten Indian names. It was his game. Every day he always used to do that. He was big. He was too big for me. I was scared of the punk, you know. My mom used to come and meet me at school once in a while. She worked at the cannery and so she couldn't come too often. Give me a little protection, you know. Listen to me, Chiquita, . . . crying like a baby!

See, we got . . . Don and I . . . we made a plan and we got ourselves kicked out of school. But we made a plan and we terrorized the fuck out of some of them dirty little Catholic sons-of-bitches. We had burglarized a real fancy home in Aberdeen which really wasn't very far from St. Mary's School, only a few blocks. A real fancy home. We burglarized that one day; nobody was there on a weekend. Me and Donny got into the house and it had a . . . I don't know what the hell you call it . . . antiques or something, a collection. Anyway, we took a couple of these big old Japanese samurai swords that he had on the wall. So what we did, we took 'em down by the school and we hid them in the bushes right at the edge of the playground, you see, because every day at recess . . . Don and I had separate recesses because I was two years older than him. Recess was a goddam terror, see, it was like a half hour of terror for me 'cause they wouldn't let me play no games, they wouldn't let me swing on the swings. I had to go stand by a goddam nun just for protection during recess every fucking day. I couldn't even play. Them little white goddam bastards would run me off the swings, they wouldn't let me do nothing, they wouldn't let me in no games. I was just an "Indian punk" and "fuck you" and all that shit, even at that age, see.

So anyway, Don and I, we made a plan. When it was my recess time, which was about an hour before his, he come out of class [to go to] the bathroom, but instead of going out to the bathroom, he ran out to the yard where I was at out in the recess yard. This ain't the joint; this is the fucking school! Catholic school! So Don makes his escape out of his fucking classroom, he meets me out in the fucking playground, we go to the fucking head of the playground yard, and we grab our swords. Man, did we kick ass! We terrorized them motherfucking nuns, we terrorized them fucking kids, and they're *lucky,* lucky we didn't cut a motherfucking head off, 'cause I was sure trying! Man, I swung so fucking hard with that samurai sword that some of them goddam kids, if I'd a hit them, I'd a chopped their goddam heads clean off. Boy, we terrorized them motherfuckers! They had the police up there. He took our ass out of there. Them motherfuckers were scared after that.

When we came back to school, them motherfuckers didn't have nothing to say, know what I mean? I mean, you gotta do something, see. And I can see now why, when you grow up like that, you get so goddam angry that what you do is like Don and I did. We had to take the *illegal* way. So everything, all these steps in our lives are illegal because people are terrorizing us; people are fucking with us. The only way we can get back is

. . . and then we built, we built our steps to prison, you see. We can't do nothing legal to get satisfaction. We have to do things illegal. We have to terrorize people. You gotta let them know "If you fuck with us, you're gonna get hurt." And all that does, of course, is stack the negative weight on our side so we end up in prison [while] they end up successful white assholes. We end up in prison, you see. And I'm still . . . I'm still angry, Chiquita. I'm still angry. I can accept it now, but you know, I think back . . . it makes me angry because I know that events like that in life drove Don and I to prison, to waste our whole fucking life in prison.

Anyway, by the time we got in school, my dad was already drinking pretty heavy. He was always at the tavern. I remember him and my mom fighting a lot. My mom took over the job of making money and bringing the food home. We were five or six years old and then the little business she had at home folded. We had this two-story house and in the basement my dad and mom built a little shop to make crab pots. They would finish the crab pots. They employed five or six people. This guy down in Westport, he had crab boats and he'd take the crab pots. And we was making pretty good money doing that. Then the business folded up. It was hurt by a guy that went into the line pretty heavy.

My brother and I, even at that age, we just did what we wanted and what we wanted to do was just play when we wasn't in school. There are lots and lots of canneries and logging companies and lumbermills down there and our biggest thrill used to be to break into the offices or the lunchrooms when they were closed on Sundays and running around in them. It was kind of a kick being where you wasn't supposed to be, I guess. Of course, we also come up with something to eat, too, every now and then. We were just kind of like the mice in the place. We had our own special holes in the buildings that we could squeeze through, so as the mice would be coming through, we'd be coming through, too. We'd run around in there and play and finally we'd get tired and go home.

We didn't hang around the park or play baseball or things like that. We just never did. It was a habit we got into because my brother and I, we avoided groups of kids like the plague. We just had each other as company and the hell with everybody else in the world, 'cause anytime we got

around a group of kids they always ended up stomping us, anyway, because we was Indians. And I think their parents taught 'em that. "You see
an Indian, beat him up." Or "If you see an Indian, a dirty little Indian,
bonk him on the head with something." Goddam it, I'm not dirty and
never was! I used to think I was, though. I used to feel that way around
other people. I never enjoyed the company of other kids or did any of the
things that they did because it was like suicide to walk into the city park.
Even at recess at school it was a cold whipping. Recess at school, I ended
up standing with the girls or something 'cause I couldn't get into any
games. Couldn't get any ball to play with. Somebody would take it. If it
wasn't the kids, the teacher would come and take the damn thing away
from me and give it to them.

So we just had to putter through those years and I don't remember
anything really fun about being a kid. I was in a hurry to grow up so I
could pay back some of those bastards. They picked on me, they picked on
my mom, they picked on everybody in my family it seemed like to me. The
cops were always beating up my dad when he was drunk. I was determined to survive long enough to get big enough to do something to them
all. That's what I wanted to do. Of course, I never did. Maybe I'm just
lucky that I never did, but I was always on the verge for a long time. The
potential for violence was always there. Definitely!

Catholic school was the worst. Them nuns, boy, whipping! If they
weren't doing it, the priest was. I don't remember how I acted but I know
I probably acted like I was deaf and dumb, 'cause I'd never talk. I stood
quiet all the time. I'd stay by myself all the time. At recess I'd either try to
stay in the room or go sit on the front steps of the school until the bell
would ring, then go back in, and that's what I remember.

We had a couple of white kids who were poor slobs and lived in the old
Junky Jones houses like we did. There was this one real estate guy who
owned every rundown junky house he could find and they called him
Junky Jones. So that used to be a target for the other kids, too. They'd say,
"Ha, ha, ha. You live in a Junky Jones house. You live in a Junky Jones
house." I never did figure out if this guy was real or not, but I knew I lived

in a Junky Jones house. It wasn't the best place in town, I'll admit that, but it was a roof over the old head, you know what I mean?

Well, some of the white kids that lived in Junky Jones houses lived pretty close to us, so we started running around with a couple of brothers and we formed this little gang, and I remember things started getting a little better then. By then there was four or five of us, but we was ready for anything then. We went around looking for the little chumps to beat up. Boy, I'll tell you, that was right down my alley, too. I had a lot of bones to pick with a lot of people. So when I was old enough to know what a goddam stick was for, I sure as hell jumped at the chance of using it and getting back at a few sonovabitches.

So we got off into a regular little gang called the Night Owls. We'd sneak out of the house. Well, me and Donny didn't have to sneak out; we'd go out of the house, 'cause they didn't pay no attention whatsoever. My mother was involved taking care of Ruby, my blind aunt, and my younger brother who was a baby then, and my sister and my dad, who was a full-blown drunk, a wino. So I mean they didn't really miss me and Donny. It was better. It was easier on them that we were able to take care of ourselves and hustle our own food over at our friends' house. We'd eat there, we'd eat here, and we'd steal food or we'd break into a restaurant. So we had stashes all over town. We'd bring a lot of food home, too. We'd bring gunnysacks with canned goods and meat home and it was party time. We might come tripping in . . . hell, me and my bro might come tripping in around midnight or one o'clock in the morning, and if we'd bring some food with us, by God, everybody would get out of bed and eat. My mother didn't tell me to go steal. She just didn't tell me not to go steal. She was just working her butt off every night cleaning the restaurant, bringing home a couple jars of leftover soup and bones and this and that that were left, you know, that the cooks left, and she'd bring them home, and so it was almost automatic.

I mean, we were hungry and almost everybody else in town was always hungry, so when Don and I, instead of thinking of toys and things to steal, we started finding stores and different places that left food out on the back

docks, like potatoes and stuff like that. So we started hauling home food
to help out. But she didn't say, "Don't do it." Everybody in the family was
happy. Everybody'd get up and eat and it helped out a lot. And we felt
good about it. We felt proud that we were doing something to help. I
think I told you before, Chiquita, we was like Robin Hood stealing from
the rich to feed the poor. In our case, it was our family because after my
dad started drinking and quit bringing home any money it was strictly up
to my mom, and women didn't make so much. They were lucky if they got
a minimum wage then.

My mom's worked all her life. She's still working and she ain't never
made more than minimum wages. I don't think they had any minimum
wages in those days, 'cause she didn't make a helluva lot of money. That
was her best job. But one day she didn't go to work because she had a car
wreck, collided with a jeep head-on, and that put her in a hospital, crushed
her chest. So it was rough for a time then. My mom was injured prior to
the fifties, about 1947, and after that is when we went on welfare. She was
in the hospital for months. God almighty, she was driving a little car . . .
she collided . . . she fell asleep or something on her way to her second job
or her first job and she was injured real bad and she couldn't go back to
work after that, see, not for a long time. Eventually she did finally go back
to work, but it was a long time and . . . I mean, she always struggled, she
always struggled; she was a typical Indian mom.

Of course, I know white women struggle, too. I mean, I'm Indian so
I'm talking Indian. I really recognize that strength in all women, that
strength to provide for their children no matter what they have to do, and
I envy that strength, you know. Men don't do that, I swear to God. I can't
help it; I look at people and I watch people and I know that women have
. . . somehow they have a method of reaching inside themselves and finding that power, that power of God to keep going on and find what they
need to provide for their children, to come up with the strength to work,
to do things they don't want to do. And my mother was always that way,
always that way. She'd do any goddam job, anything that they offered, just
to bring home a few bucks.

My family was used to scraping. My old Ruby, she could make a meal out of anything. Give her a handful of flour, boy, and a little bit of salt and she'd come up with something for us to eat, that's for sure. My dad would shoot some sea gulls and we'd eat them sea gulls. He didn't have no gun. He'd shoot them suckers with a slingshot. He made a slingshot out of plywood and then he'd shoot 'em with these steel ball bearings. Knock them babies right out of the air. But he used to trick 'em. He'd sprinkle bread crumbs or something out back, then he had this little hole cut in the wall of the house and he'd hide in there with his slingshot, see. And when one of them big old dumb birds would come and land on there and start pecking at that bread, he'd knock them babies over. That's our Indian chicken, you know. We never ate any of the dogs in the neighborhood, but I know that they probably thought about it, you know what I mean? We never had a dog. We always had a cat, but I'll tell you one thing. Before these four kids would starve, that old cat would go into the stew pot, you goddam right.

But we had a little something to eat every day. I don't remember going a day without eating, even if it was just plain biscuits, baking powder biscuits, or fried potatoes. That was what it was most of the time. We'd have gravy on them baking powder biscuits. That was pretty standard fare around our house, and I still like it. My favorite food is still hamburger gravy and toast, or hamburger gravy and biscuits and fried potatoes. I love 'em. I love eggs, too. For a while we had some chickens. Well, we was fat then, when we had those chickens because we had eggs. We didn't kill the chickens to eat 'em unless worst got to worst, then we rubbed out everything and ate it.

I was just thinking, my aunt is so important. She's so important . . . this whole thing . . . my Aunt Ruby, my mother's sister. She was blind and they grew up together from the time they were small and their mother died. I told you a little bit about her, Chiquita, not too much. We used to call her Mom, too, because when my mom worked, my aunt was the one that cooked for us, cleaned for us, washed all the clothes and everything by hand, gave us baths in those great big, big buckets on the kitchen floor. She'd heat the water on the stove, give us our bath, take care of everything while my mom worked. So my mom and her sister raised us and so, you know, I've got very fond memories there. I can't imagine life without her, except now, of course, that we're older, but I mean when Mom had to work and take care of us, Jesus Christ, how would she have managed without her sister then—somebody to take care of the kids while she worked? That would have been pretty damn tough.

There's a lot of things that I remember about our family. Family outings, which was just my mother and my Aunt Ruby and the rest of us kids. We had some of the funniest-looking cars. I mean *old* cars. We used to go for rides on weekends. That was in the Aberdeen area. We'd go up into the hills above Raymond, Washington. We'd just sort of go from Aberdeen to Raymond and we'd go down to the ocean a lot. Mom would take us for rides to the ocean [or] up in the hills, and damn, that used to be nice! I sure remember that. I mean she would manage to spend time with us. And like I said, Ruby was just as important in our lives as my mother was; she was our mother, too. We had two mothers. Ruby pretty much raised us kids while my mother worked to make the money to feed us, and although she was blind, it's not something you'd ever think about, because she was so able to get around and do things. She'd be down in the basement chopping wood, killing chickens and plucking chickens, cooking all the time, getting us off to school, feeding us supper, getting us to bed at night. My mother didn't have to worry about those things. All she had to worry about was getting her ass to work and getting some sleep and dealing with my drunk dad. And so we were pretty busy, a pretty busy household.

But we had a lot of good experiences as a family, I think. We didn't know . . . we might have been different from other people, but they were good experiences. Hell, I even enjoyed the bare-assed Christmases we had. We might have a Christmas tree sometimes and then we'd get all our Christmas gifts from the Salvation Army. And my dad belonged to the Elks. And he belonged to AA in Aberdeen, too. And they would have Christmas parties and we would go to them and I remember those Christmas parties at the Elks. My dad might be a drunk, but they still gave all us kids presents and we had good things to eat and it was lots of fun.

I think when you're young like that, those family problems between your mother and dad, you just don't tend to notice them that much. Or maybe I'm wrong. I don't know. I'm not sure now because it didn't seem to be a big deal at the time. We just kind of went on regardless of whatever my dad did, regardless of whether he stayed drunk. Seems like half the time they were down at the tavern, which wasn't that far away from our house, trying to lead him home. Hell, my mother couldn't even go in and get him because there was a law against Indians going in taverns. They recognized my dad as more of a white person than an Indian, [but] they kicked my mother out because she looked more Indian. That law didn't change until the fifties, when Indians were recognized as, I don't know, as citizens or whatever the hell it was, and they were allowed to go in taverns. I know she had to put up with a lot of indignities like that during those years.

My dad would try to take her out with him. She might want to go with him sometimes just to kind of keep an eye on him, and they'd kick her out of the goddam tavern and let him stay there, and he didn't have the brains to leave; he'd let her have to leave and he'd stay in the damn tavern. What an asshole! She put up with that. She wanted to go down there, I don't know, just to keep the peace or keep an eye on him or some damn thing. She was always afraid he was going to get beat up or run over or killed, or some damn thing. So when he was up to the tavern, she'd send us kids up to check on him if she'd be too tired to walk up there and put up with his bullshit, so we'd go up and peek through the doors and see that he was still sitting up to the bar yet and wasn't laying on the floor. We might hang out front for a while. If he'd see us out there or if we let him know we was there, like I said, he'd bring us out a candy bar or something, then we'd go home after a while. That was a trip.

We lived on Curtis Street and it was a dead-end street with a mill down at the end. Our house was kind of a two-story white house, an old, old, old house. The bottom half was a huge basement. There was a bedroom as you came in the front door off to the left and as soon as you stepped in you was in a small living room. It didn't seem that small to us but I guess it was small. It had a wood stove for a heater in it, and straight ahead from the front door was the kitchen and it had one of the old-time wood stoves in it with the heavy iron lids and the overhead warming boxes and a big oven.

There was a wood box sitting beside it, and crammed in the little kitchen was a table. And we had an icebox with blocks of ice in it. Most people had refrigerators by then but we still had the icebox. Then right off the kitchen to the right there was another tiny bedroom. That's where my aunt and us kids slept.

The house didn't have a huge yard [but] there were plenty of places to play for a kid. It was pretty far back from the road. There was a long two-plank sidewalk that ran all the way back and the sidewalk always floated when it rained. We'd have to round up the boards afterward and put 'em back, see. It wasn't that far from the river, maybe five blocks. Behind the house and across, there was a lot with berry bushes which was huge to us at that time. And we went and picked berries out there all the time. And my folks made money picking blackberries and selling them.

The general area belonged to a lady who lived right next to us. I think she was a Croatian lady. And there was an old witch, an old witch that lived next door to her, and she used to scare the shit out of us. We'd always hear stories about this old lady. She always wore black and she had a black veil on her head all the time, and people used to tell us, man, [that] she killed kids and she had kids buried under her house, and shit. Well, one time we found a little cat skull under there and we swore to God that it was a little tiny baby's skull, you know. We just went screaming and yowling. I remember that we had some great times with it [the story] because a lot of times we went sneaking around her house and trying to peek in her windows to catch her butchering some little kid or something.

Our main playing place was a yard and a big chicken coup. We had some chickens, too, and our landlady had chickens. Our landlady used to put up with us all the time. She had a pretty little daughter. I had an eye for the women even then, Chiquita, didn't I? Man, I'm talking a long time ago. How old was I? I was four or five, six years old.

But I started to tell you about our other neighbor that we spent time with. That was our chief of police, Gallagher. He lived a couple blocks up the street. We ran around with his son, a little fat freckle-faced boy, and he was part of our gang. An "Our Gang" type of thing, you know. All the little neighborhood brats, we all ran around together, and we used to sneak in people's garages, play in the fields and all that shit, and yell like a bunch of tomcats when we got to stay out after dark. And he used to take us for rides in his police car. He liked to let us kids sit on his lap. He'd drive us around the block and he'd blow the siren for us and come back home again. I remember they had a player piano in their house. I used to like to go in there just to listen to that player piano and watch that roll go around. Oh, I thought that was so neat, you know. We'd take turns sitting there, playing a song, and we'd keep up with the keys as they'd be going. That was a big thrill.

I was telling you about this section of a little hill that stuck out and we used to play on it. It seemed so high, like we was on a thousand-foot cliff with a sheer drop to the bottom. There was a huge sandstone boulder that stuck out on this thing. A street ran below it and off a little ways, so the whole bottom was actually sand if you dropped down or fell. But this boulder, there used to be a trick to going around it where it jutted out to the corner. If we went from one corner to the other, we really thought we'd done something, you know. We'd been across the damn thing a hundred times. Someone else had carved a little foothold in it.

We used to get a kick out of playing in the hills all day, and we'd make our way across this boulder and edge our way across and put your belly against the rock. For some reason this particular day I froze up. I mean froze up. At first my foot slipped [when] I reached out my toe and I thought, "Oh, Christ, I'm dead." And I started screaming and hollering and raising all kinds of hell and this little girl and my partners were trying to think of a way to get ropes. And Donny's screaming, "Hang on, Gene. Hang on, Gene. I'm gonna help you." And I said, "Oh, my God. Get me down from here!" And this little girl, she wasn't a helluva lot bigger than me, here she comes. Oh, I was glad that she had the balls to climb up there. I really was. Everybody else probably thought it was funny, but here she comes. She comes up there like Tarzan. Not like Jane, like Tarzan. She's going from root to root and berry to berry. She swings out over there. Here she comes, and goddam, she reached right up there and all my partners are watching. She swings out and grabs me around the waist and takes me down. Ha, ha, very embarrassing. Very embarrassing, you know, for an experienced guerrilla fighter like me [who's] been up in the woods every goddam day. But we took off and we went outa there. Ha, ha, she wouldn't never done it again in a million years and I'd never got stuck in a million years again. But I never went across it again, either. Believe me, I stayed away. If the rest of them wanted to go that way, I'd go another way. There were other ways to come off that hill without going across that thing. I never liked heights, anyway. I can't even jump off a diving board.

But I went back there in 1975 and I looked at that and at all them old houses. I went from one end of town to the other. They was all gone, all gone. And like I said, they all belonged to Junky Jones, so they were all in various stages of decay anyway [when we lived there]. If it wasn't for us, nobody would be living in the damn things, so you couldn't hardly expect them to still be there.

But anyway, when we crossed the bridge to the other part of town things got worse. That's when times were toughest. Pickings weren't so good. My mom worked at a cannery then for a while and my brother and I, we had been picked up quite often by the police and threatened with foster homes and this and that, and it never did scare us much. They used to say, "Aw, you're gonna end up in Walla Walla"—you know, Walla Walla State Penitentiary—things like that. I never believed 'em, but it hit pretty hard, I'll tell you, and it's pretty clear today right now, too. I firmly believe that that had a lot to do with my eventually meeting their expectations because at that age, of course, when adults tell you that, especially the chief of police or other policemen, that you're going to the penitentiary, then something's going to click in your mind and that's going to be your ulti- mate goal, regardless of whether you know it or not. I won't get into the psychology of the thing, but I was very aware of it and I'm fighting it even now.

We stole, we went on to bigger things, my brother and I. Like I said, we had our little gang and we ran around and did a lot of crazy things. You can get pretty crazy at that age. We burglarized everything in town, I think. I don't think there was a store in town we didn't get into. We stole bicycles constantly. We even stole a car now and then. Seven or eight of us dingy kids would jump in a car and away we'd go. God, the driver, which was generally me, would have to be sitting on a pillow. Couldn't even reach the foot pedals hardly, but we'd go screaming down them highways, full speed ahead. Cops would be chasing us. One time they chased us for a long ways. Boy, they fired a couple shots in the trunk of the car before they finally got us pulled over and they looked in the car and seen all these dingy kids. There wasn't one of us that was over ten years old. They chased us about ten miles in an old Chevrolet we stole. We didn't even know who was shooting at us. We knew the sirens were blowing and we were going to give 'em a run for their money, man. "Step on it, boys! Al Capone and his mob." They dragged us all screaming and kicking out of the car, took us by the ear to the old police station and we spent a couple days in the juvenile hall over that. But we got out, we went home. We made the paper on that one. We had our picture in the paper, all those dumb-looking kids in the paper.

I guess I was ten years old before I started stealing bigger things like the cars, breaking into buildings, schools, causing a helluva lot more damage, a lot more damage. People started getting a little bit more serious. My brother and I have always been inseparable. At the time we ran around with a couple other brothers, white kids. Like I say, this was a small town. It's close to two rivers, close to the ocean. Those two rivers don't really close the town in, but it cuts right through the town and so there's a lot of fishing boats. We used to steal a lot of stuff off the boats. That got us in a lot of trouble. We got picked up dozens of times prowling around at nighttime inside a building or some damned thing. But we always got to go home. My mom would always be down sniveling and crying. Of course, in that size town they know the police department pretty good, damn near everybody in it. Like I said, we used to live pretty close to the police chief, so we kind of had an in there, you know. So anyhow, they knew the family. They had picked up my dad so many times for being drunk or beating my mom up that I imagine they didn't even keep count anymore. Most of the time they'd just take him and let him go somewhere down the street someplace and tell him not to go home until he sobered up, or stay away from the house until the next morning.

As long as I can remember, Donny and I were together like two peas in a pod and we cared for one another and we somehow survived our early childhood, you know, playing on railroad tracks, playing on the river, where somebody might see a little kid that young playing like that, they would freak out. Donny and I always looked out for each other. We just did everything together. Somehow through the years we were so close, fighting back against society, and fighting back against other kids and other people, and fighting back against poverty and hunger and doing what we had to do, you know. If we had to go steal food, we stole food, and we just always did that. And then, later on when we got to be a little older, like teenagers . . . well, we went to boarding school together down in Chemawa, the Indian school in Oregon. We went to the Greenhill Juvenile Center here in Washington and a lot of times when he went to jail, I went on purpose, you know, so he wouldn't be there alone. And we were just always back to back against everybody, everything.

Anyway, my mom worked hard trying to take care of us, so I expect that had a lot to do with the things that happened to Donny and I. Even so, I don't ever remember any kind of discipline from my mother. Each time we'd get arrested she'd just be happy that we'd get home. And she'd say, "Boy, you guys are lucky this time." But that was all. More than anything she was just happy that we'd be heading back home again after a long day at the old police station.

So it went on, never really changed our ways because we didn't have anything else to do. We didn't make it much further than the fourth grade in Aberdeen because they finally got tired of us and arrested us on burglaries. We left a trail of candy bars about three miles, candy bar wrappers from this cannery we had broken into. We stole all the candy bars out of all the machines, so they just followed the trail of wrappers on down to the riverbank and snatched us up. That time things didn't come out too good. They give my mother a choice: they would either put us in a foster home or she could send us off to Chemawa, which was an Indian school in Oregon out of Salem about six or seven miles. So she said, "Well, I'll send the boys to the old school." She'd been talking about doing it for several months, that maybe that would help. So that helped make a decision there and the welfare [department] bought us each some duds, bought us each a box to put our clothes in and some new coats and things, and we was off running.

I forget where they got the car to take us down there but we got down there, anyway. The family took us down and they went back to Aberdeen. That was tough. Tough! Oh, ho, ho, I do remember that! Sonovabitch! Yeah, that was a rough go. I wasn't happy at all. That was the first time we'd ever been away from home and we knew we weren't gonna go home for a while. We never did get along with other kids anyway and this whole school was kids. Gosh, it seemed like thousands of them, at least a couple thousand. But we were loners. I remember there was a lot of crying and bad feelings the first day or two. So about the third day my brother and I packed our stuff and out the window we went. We said, "Well, we'll just start trucking, man. We'll go across here and through a couple fields and down a couple roads and should see Washington over the next rise." So we hit the road about the crack of dawn. We never knew we had more than 150 miles to go. Needless to say, we didn't make it. The state patrol picked us up and took us back.

So we was there and eventually we got used to it. It was a lot of discipline. I remember a lot of counting, a lot of standing, walking in file lines, and a lot of fights. Of course, that was an Indian school and I had to be the only kid in the goddam school that had light hair. I had real light hair when I was younger and my brother Donny, he was a normal-looking Indian—you know, dark hair, dark eyes. I had to have blond hair and green eyes. I still have and Indians are a pretty goddam prejudiced people anyway. But eventually we got to like the place and we got into the routine of things in the new school.

It took a while to start making friends but we did, and even started liking it. We weren't used to strict rules and regulations. That was a problem until a few sessions with a Ping-Pong paddle on our bare butts. I was in grade school and one of my daily chores was tending a few stupid sheep. I lost that job because I was riding them like horses and one died; end of the herder's life.

Don and I always managed to find things to do. I'm sure that's because we were antisocial and really didn't care about rules. So we didn't worry

about boundaries; we quickly found a way around everything and anything. One thing that comes to mind was the way we could hustle other
Indians. Every year a special train brought in several hundred kids from a
Navaho reservation. They ranged anywhere from ten to eighteen. Most
really didn't know English, of course, and we spoke no Indian, but sign
language served us well when trading for silver rings and belts.

We always had money. Too much for little guys. We pulled a couple
profitable deals. During summer vacation there were only a couple dozen
of us there. We didn't get to go home because the local cops in Aberdeen
didn't appreciate our talents. Summer at school meant we all lived in one
building coed. I had a girlfriend. She was also a half-breed and suffered the
curse of blond hair and blue eyes. This is not cool at Indian school. We
were quite a pair. I can't remember her name but she was several years
older than me.

I had the money, which I picked up from several sources. The big one
was when Don and me robbed the post office of several hundred bucks. I
hid the money in the sheep barn. Don and me also sold, bartered, and
traded the various items we picked up. We traded food and clothes to the
reservation Indians (Navaho) for real silver rings, belts, and costumes. It
was the first year and we learned very fast.

The second year I picked up two new girlfriends. Neither could speak
English worth a shit but we worked it out. One was thirteen and one was
sixteen. I had turned a devilish twelve years old, and that is no shit. We
were together most of the time, of course. Don was there also but wasn't
interested. I bought them a lot of pop and candy, that's for sure.

I was also an altar boy at the church and I used my position to secure
more money from the donation baskets. I would separate the bills and
pocket a role of tens or twenties every Sunday. This is the way we were
able to pay for Mom to come visit. She didn't have the money to travel so
far and it being the Christmas season, it was only with the help of God that
we were able to not only pay for the round trip but sent her home with
some money. Sure as hell felt good to us.

I had problems during the first few weeks or months because of my
light hair and green eyes. Lots of fights. I was called "white trash." That

was fucked up because when I was home and went to public school, I was called names like "dirty siwash" or "dirty Indian."

Well, anyway, we spent two years and one summer there. We enjoyed ourselves once we fell in with the cool crowd. I was friendly with a few of the older students, which was a real advantage since they were able to travel into Salem, Oregon. Once on a field trip we saw the state penitentiary. I sure as hell didn't think I would end up in a prison for half my life.

One of the things I think you have heard about, Chiquita, is the efforts of government schools to eliminate the tribal languages. I expect this is one of the reasons for the mass moves of Navaho Indians because they remain close to the earth and tribal customs are strong. I can't speak one word of my own language. Hell, I never hear Sioux spoken except at some powwows. The only ones who speak Coast Salish are the elders, and few of them. Coast Salish is the language of Northwest Coast Indians. This includes the Puyallup Tribe and thirty-five other Washington tribes. They're stretched all the way from Vancouver, B.C., to Oregon.

I never was worth a shit in school but one thing I could do was read real good, so I was often chosen to read in plays or other school events. I saw my first television while I was there. I saw Eisenhower, the president, on his train. The tracks passed right through the school and he made a brief stop. One thing I remember was the time they brought Don and me all the way to Tacoma to have our tonsils removed. It was the first time I saw a large city. Also, Mom was able to come and see us there. The hospital was the old Cascadia, a government Indian place.

Cascadia has a real history. It was taken from the Indians by the state in the sixties and turned into a correctional facility for young kids. The Puyallup Tribe took it back by force in the early seventies. That was a real show—armed Indians everywhere, even on the rooftops. The police and federal agents lined the road and fence around the hospital for days. Eventually the hospital was legally returned to the tribe. It was a touchy confrontation. The Puyallup Tribe has quite a history of police confrontations over fishing rights and human rights.

I also attended my first Indian powwow at the school. I saw the costumes and dances from the different tribes for the first time. I had never before seen so goddam many Indians in one place either. The holidays were always good for lots of food and other special things. Eventually Don and I were allowed to go to town by ourselves. About all we did was look around town, maybe buy something, go to a movie, or just bum around. Anyway, Don and I learned a lot about life and surviving while we were there. I believe the school set a pattern for us which we followed all the way to Walla Walla. Institutionalized. Hell of a word.

We came back to Aberdeen in 1953. My dad, of course, he was still off into the wine bottle. That was the year my dad went to the penitentiary. My family was living in a haunted house. I'll tell you about this one deal. This was really true. I definitely am into the spiritual thing. I believe in ghosts. I believe in the afterlife, probably because of things that's happened to me and because of things that I've seen and heard. I'm interested in psychic phenomena and I make it a point to study it. I do get one publication which is a psychic-phenomena paper published in England. I'm connected with a spiritual church in Seattle. I don't know that I'll go up there when I'm out, [but] the majority of all their services are seances and they spend a lot of time in contact with spirit masters, as they call them. Anyway, I've had experiences with those people, too, and got a message from my younger brother who died in 1964, which caused me to pause and think. That's nothing new. Wasn't my first contact. That was my most recent experience. This was last year.

Keith was back over here last year. He used to be a convict here a few years ago and he was weird then, for chrissake, and he had a tough go while he was here because of his strangeness, needless to say, both with convicts and officers alike. But we had a seance here last summer and we had it upstairs here in the multipurpose room just off the education room. And he puts on a blindfold. If you know anything at all about seances, then you'll know about the little cards that you fill out with questions for a loved one that you want to ask a question of or get in contact with. And then they take the cards and, of course, you blindfold him [Keith], and the cards are all folded up and he just starts going like crazy, you know, talking to spirits and grabbing cards at the same time and answering questions. It's just amazing. And all of a sudden he'll jump and look up, and if your imagination is good enough, you'll get a picture that there is a spirit standing next to him and talking to Keith, and he relays the message. But anyway, that's the way it works.

And the message came through from my little brother, and there's no way that this guy knows anything about my younger brother or that I even have a younger brother. My other brother wasn't there at the time. He was up at the Indian club [in the prison] and didn't know about this. And I still say to this day that I didn't have Donny over there [at the seance] because I didn't even know that I was going to go up there. I was just kind of drawn up there and I just kind a moved in on it, you know. But still I got a message from my brother saying that . . . telling us that he'd been trying to contact us for a long time and couldn't find a way and he was happy and wasn't truly dead, you know, in the sense that we think of. And he passed the message to me that I could have what I want if I would just keep making the effort to change my life, and that I could have some of the things that I wanted and that things would be better. And that was the message I got.

I have always wished that there was a way to get through to my younger brother and send him my love and [say] I was so sorry that he died when he was eighteen, because we never had a chance to get to know each other like Don and I knew each other, because he was younger. We started going to prison and all that, so we didn't get a chance, and I was only out of the joint four days when he died. So I was still sad about it and I was guilty about it all these years and I just felt bad, you know, so this message was important to me, real important to me. And I immediately went over and I told Donny. Donny feels the same as me about it, of course, and I told my mother on the phone.

See, my family has always been into that because we have been bothered by poltergeists and it's been something else. I've learned that it could have been caused by my sister and her adolescence. But in Aberdeen . . . let's see . . . the house that we lived in on the east side, that house wasn't never haunted that I can recall. We talked a lot about ghosts and things there when we was younger and we always used to really have fun. We'd be sitting around at nighttime in the house with the heater stove in the front room, and then us kids would just sit around and my mom and Ruby, they would sit and tell all the ghost stories and scare the hell out of each other. And we'd build this up and then we'd listen to these spooky programs on the radio at night and by bedtime, I'm telling you, the house would be full of boogeymen. So Ruby wouldn't have a hard time getting us kids to bed. She'd always say, "Get to bed or the boogeyman's gonna get you. The black hand's gonna come out from under the bed and get you." To this day, I'm scared of that sonovabitch!

Aw, Christ, the things you go through, I'm telling you! I never did that to my kid and I wish they'd never done it to me, as far as the boogeyman is concerned, because, goddam, I'm still scared of the dark! I never could sleep in a room without some light on. None of us could, and I still can't. I can't stand the dark. I suppose I'll get over that, but why in hell should I, you know what I mean? I just reach out and it's pitch black, for chrissake and . . . to tell you the truth, my girl, everybody's left the library and I'm here right now alone and I swear to God I've got the creeps. I usually go when everybody else goes. I usually don't stay with you like this, you know, so I'm making a helluva contribution right now, Chiquita, so I hope you appreciate it.

Well, like I said, the house on Curtis Street in the 1940s, it wasn't haunted. But when we moved over to the main part of Aberdeen to another house, the last house we lived in [in] Aberdeen, up to 1953, that place, it had an upstairs and a downstairs. We lived in the downstairs. It was an all-gray clapboard house and it had a rotten foundation, rotten everything, and it was weathered from the wind and the rain and salt. It didn't have any yard to speak of, just some mangy old crabgrass. The apartment upstairs had a couple windows facing out to the street [on the side] which you could call the living room. The downstairs where we lived was built pretty much the same. It had two bedrooms, I think, or else there was one big bedroom, a dining room, and a kitchen and a bathroom. And there was a long, creaky old stairs that went up to it and the whole thing had an enclosed porch. The enclosed porch was the main entrance for the upstairs and was also our back door. The back door unlocked and opened up onto this one little porch. And there was a door that let out to three or four steps down to the sidewalk, which ran around the corner of the house and out to the street.

Next door to us was a store owned by some Hungarians or Czechoslovakians or something. It was painted yellow. In the upstairs apartment you could look across the roof of that one-story store building and the space between the two buildings was probably ten or twelve feet. We had a tiny front porch with a front door in our bottom apartment. My people lived there for a long time. That was during the years that Donny and I were at Chemawa. Before we went to Chemawa we lived on South Alder Street, and it was another crummy little house full of bugs and I hated that house. It was cold all the time; you could never keep it warm. We lived off an alley in this one-story white crackerbox shack of a house and all the windows in it were cracked. It was always cold and real dirty. We lived there for probably a year, long enough to have one of those Salvation Army–Goodwill Christmases and before we got fancy and moved over to this other dump.

But anyhow, they were experiencing strange things at this house while we was up at Chemawa and they started telling us about it. They were always telling us about what was going on around the house. They kept hearing footsteps and things upstairs in the upper apartment, see, and they were trying to figure out what it was, of course. They all thought it was a ghost, and of course they had the whole damn neighborhood convinced it was a ghost after a while because, I mean, everybody went along with the idea. It damn near sobered my dad up, so chances of it being a ghost were pretty damn good.

But the day my mother brought us home from Chemawa everybody was there at the house to check it out to try to see if they could catch what was doing this. And they spent all day long nailing windows shut and putting flour all over the floors and all over the window ledges and taking the light bulbs out and nailed the windows shut. Like I say, it was the second story. On the way down the stairs they set a whole bunch of traps 'cause when it was dark, boy, it was dark. There wasn't a whole lot of streetlights and that upstairs was just black. So all the way down these rickety stairs they put these beer cans and they put black thread and they worked their way out of the place, you see, so that if there was anybody walking, there would be a shoe print. You couldn't avoid that unless you floated in the air. You had to make prints.

So that night they told us what everybody was gonna do to catch whoever it was that was sneaking up there, or if it was a ghost, well, they'd know it. They had it timed, too, and I think it was about ten or eleven at night. We were sitting in the bedroom, me and Donny. Ruby was sitting there with us and she was saying, "It's almost time, it's almost time." And everybody in the house was real quiet. And there was about five or six different kids over there, guys and girls, and my dad. And he was sober special for that night. And my aunt, she was ready with her old stick, and she just grabs hold of somebody's old shirttail and away she'll go. She'll run into anything, you know.

And goddam, I heard those footsteps! Sounded like the guy wore 15-D's. Footsteps were going from room to room up there just as plain and clear as day. They kept walking and when it got to the back bedroom—you could tell, you could walk around our apartment and follow the footsteps, see—man, everybody took off out the back door and ran up those steps and they had all the flashlights. They went up all these steps and they had all these traps set and all the beer cans started coming down. They got up there at the top of the steps and they figured, "Okay, you sonovabitch, come out of there." And slowly they worked their way from room to room. They checked all the flour on the floor. No footprints. They checked all the windows. Closed. No footprints nowhere. Not a soul up there. So it was pretty convincing that that didn't scare the old ghost away. He came back night after night and walked up there.

So one morning early—I seen this myself—I started out the back door. It seemed like we heard somebody coming down the steps. I was going out the back door and this other door was still closed, so I opened it and I seen this little form of a little guy. He looked like a little guy all hunched over. He was just going around the corner of our house. And I ran back in; I was screaming, "I saw him. He's a bum or something," and they ran out there and there wasn't nobody between the houses, nobody on the sidewalk out there. Just disappeared into thin air.

But the haunted house that we was living in, it was our last house in Aberdeen. My mom said, "I'm packing everybody up and moving to the big city, Tacoma." And we went. I was almost a teenager by then. I was twelve years old.

2

The Rebel Emerges

Needless to say, we didn't like Tacoma either, and we were all set to leave when we got there. We lived in a housing project. We was on welfare, of course, and I was ready to start seventh grade. Donny and I, we cooled back for just a short while, then we started up all over again.

As soon as we cased the town, we started adventuring around, looking for something to get into. Didn't take us very long to find something. My brother was first. He got busted breaking into a store. He went to Chehalis at Greenhill, which is a state training school. When he headed there he was twelve years old, so, 'course, it was only a matter of time and I went several months later. I was thirteen. They got me for breaking into a truck and stealing cigarettes. I don't remember if I smoked or not. I don't think so, but everybody in my family did, so another kid and I broke into a big semi and took a case of cigarettes. We got arrested for that. It wasn't my first arrest in Tacoma. We had had some trouble, but I can't remember what we was arrested for. But we had been arrested several times. This time we went to Chehalis.

So that was my first gig there. It was all right, I guess. Wasn't too far from home. Anyway, my folks could get down there, and old Mom, you could always depend on her to come and visit. I stayed down to the state training school, Greenhill, for the better part of a year that time and I escaped. I escaped several times while I was there. I was involved in just everything you could be involved in that wasn't right: setting fires, breaking windows, just generally raising hell, you know. Otherwise, I could've got out of there in ninety days. I could've been home, but I stretched it out. Didn't look like they were going to let me go, so just about every eighty days when I was sure they wasn't going to let me go, I'd just let myself go. I'd boogie on out. Away I'd go, get arrested. Got in a lot of trouble in those escapes, got in an awful lot of trouble because . . . I don't know . . . you just get a little bit wilder. You just feel, "I can do any goddam thing I want to 'cause it just doesn't make any difference." And I was pretty much up on the law concerning juveniles, I'll tell you that. I was pretty much aware of the limits of the law, so I knew that they couldn't do a helluva lot to me. So all the burglaries and robberies that I pulled, I knew they wasn't going to do anything to me other than send me back to the training school once I got caught. So I went pretty wild.

Like I said, I stayed down at the state training school, Greenhill, for the better part of a year that time and I escaped. It was planned, you know. I heard that one way for us to get out was to get put in the county jail, get transferred to an adult status. If you got in enough trouble [at Greenhill], they'd get tired of you and they'd transfer you to adult status, and it was guaranteed that when you went to court you'd get probation. I mean, because it was your first time since you was an adult, you'd get a break. You had a couple breaks coming and then you'd get out, see, [but] they can hold you as a juvenile until you're eighteen. So it's harder than hell; they don't give you a date for getting out when you're a juvenile. They just keep holding you.

One time when I was in the hole at Greenhill and I thought they left me in there too long, forgot me, I took a razor and started slashing myself. I wasn't trying to commit suicide. I just wanted . . . I don't know . . . I just started cutting on myself. I cut myself on my arm and I just kept going with a razor blade, and I changed hands and I went on down to there, and then I just kind of started hacking. You see, I was pretty young, fifteen.

They took me out, finally. They came in and seen me sitting there with a lot of blood on me and I . . . they took me out. I went to the hospital and they bandaged me up. They put me back in a cottage and . . . I got a little worried myself, you know; they didn't come in there fast enough [and] I got a little dozey. But those kind of cuts, they clot, and I'd quit bleeding and [so] I'd have to get myself to bleed more, get the clots off because I wanted a big puddle on the floor. I didn't want these drips all over it.

Jesus Christ! They left me in there [in the hole] a month! I was in there so long they even forgot to feed me, they forgot to feed me. That just settled it for me and I said, "Man, oh man, they just forgot about me." It's just a little itty-bitty room they put you in and they lock this door, then they go out and they lock another door until they can't even hear you shout, really. You've just got a little old dirty bed in there. Isn't a bathroom or nothing.

They threw me in the hole because I ran away. I said, "To hell with this. I'd rather go to the hospital." I figured if I did that, my mom and them would raise hell and [they'd] figure [there] had to be some reason I did that, because my mother didn't believe anything at all. I'd bitch about getting beat and stuff like that, [but] nobody believed it. They don't believe kids. They don't believe adults, either. The authorities were the ones that were doing it. I never bitched to them. I didn't know anything about other authorities. I figured if they did it, that's the state, period. And I thought the only way I could get out of this, I guess, is if my mom really gets mad and does something, [then] maybe they'll take me out of here. And I told them, "Well, if you do it again, I'll just kill myself and you got to answer for it." So they just kept me in the hospital for a day or two, sent me over to see the nut doctor; got done with him and I was perfectly normal. He said, "It was a tough way to do 'er but I guess it worked, didn't it?" I said, "It worked. It hurts, but goddam, I'm out and I won't have to go back in." He said, "No, you don't have to go back in. I'll make a note of that." Because I'd been in the hole a lot and it wasn't helping me, just made me want to run away again. I wanted to go home, didn't want to stay there. Stayed though. I figured, "It ain't worth it, man. Couple days home, what the hell? I don't seem to know how to run, so I might as well stay here. Get caught every goddam time I leave." So I stayed a while.

While I was there [at Greenhill] they built a new building which was going to be a maximum-security building. At the time, they didn't have a maximum-security building as such, just a couple little cells in each cottage, which was one long building which had cubicles in it. They usually put four guys in a cubicle, so there was no locked fronts or anything on it. They did have an open tier that looked over to the bottom deck. Well, it wasn't that hard to get out of the place if you wanted out. You could kick that door down, and several of us could jump the guy that was on at night and take his key. There was no fence around this place and that's the way we usually got out. We'd just take his key and just trap him in the office and away we'd go. So when they got this new place built, it had cells.

When it was getting close to opening time on this building a few of us were getting a little nervous, you know, a few of us guys that had the heat on us. So they came around and they made a little bullshit speech, telling us, "No, we're not gonna decide who goes in there. Nothing will be held against you until the building is actually opened, [but] from that time on, you'd better watch your p's and q's because then we'll decide." Well, this turned out to be a lie. It was just a ruse to keep from having a mass escape. Some of the guys were keeping their own score, you know, and just about decided that they were prime candidates, because we knew that as soon as they got us in that building it was going to be a rough go, see.

Well, we believed them, so we just kinda kicked back and started straightening up our hands a bit. Son-of-a-gun, one night, here they come. They had everybody lined up downstairs and they said, "Delorme, Larson, and Gordon"—the three of us in that one building that were kind of ringleaders—they said, "Get your stuff, your mattress. That's all you need is your mattress and let's go." We thought they was going to move us down to Green Cottage. Even then they were lying, because this was a routine we used to go through. There was three different cottages built in a row for different age groups. So every now and then they'd take two or three guys and you'd move up a notch. Well, it was a little bit better being down in Green Cottage than being where you was at. You're moving up to Green Cottage, you know, so we said, "Okay." We got our stuff and they started marching us down the little breezeway there. So we come up to the Green Cottage door and we started to stop and they just kept pushing us, "Just keep on walking." We look down to that new building, we see four bulls out there waiting, blocking the breezeway in case we tried to make a break. And that was our last chance and we goddam near did it, too. But they were out in force that night. Boy! They were expecting us to try something, so I kind a held my mud, kept my cool.

They were in such a goddam hurry to get us into a cell for a change, they moved us in before they even had the lights put into the place. They didn't have the beds in; didn't have the joint painted yet. All it was, was a roughed-in place. They had the fronts on the cells and that was it. So they took us in that night in the dark, brought flashlights in, took us up, put us each in a cell. We laid our mattress on the floor of the cell, kicked some of the concrete and dust out of the way that was still laying all over the place. You know how a building is that's not even finished. We said, "Well, this is it." We started laughing and joking, of course. Nobody's going to act like it bothers 'em, for chrissake, not in front of other people. But I knew. I knew that we was in for a tough go. I know that they'd done put the wraps on my ass for a while.

Well, we just kinda stood there in the dark talking to each other from cell to cell and hollering in the dark to see who else was already there. We'd catch a voice and we'd say, "Hey, Willie, hey, it's Dave." "Dave who?" "Dave Bailey." "Aw, you sonovabitch, when did they bring you over here?" "Oh, about an hour ago," and all that shit. So we was just playing a game on who'd be next. We all knew. We'd rattle off a name, man, and wait for that door to slam open down there. About every other guy that would come in, they'd be dragging him in because he'd be fighting all the way. We'd be laughing, boy, watching to see who the hell it was that come by, see who was right, who was wrong. So this went on half the night, dragging guys into that building until they damn near filled it up. So we christened the place.

Took 'em about a month to get the damned thing in order. They kinda rushed a little bit. Put the beds in; the beds were bolted right into the wall, metal frames with springs in 'em. So at least we got up off the damn floor. There was absolutely nothing in the cells, no bathrooms, no nothing, no sinks. They gave us shorts to wear. They didn't have any heat on in that building. A matter of fact, all we had was a pair of shorts to wear and a tee shirt. They even give us socks, some kind of little booties to wear. So that was our uniform, and one blanket, no sheets. They didn't want no one hanging themselves, so we had one blanket.

And it was pretty miserable there for a while, but we got off on it, really. We said, "The tougher they make it, the better it is," you know. We'd tell 'em to fuck themselves every time they came through and throw shit at 'em, throw rocks at 'em. That was a mistake [they made]. They didn't sweep the cells out first, because they left all those chunks of concrete and pieces of metal and stuff like that that the workers had left in there. So the next morning the shit started. We started right off the bat, boy. Soon as they came in there to feed us, we started throwing chunks of concrete at 'em, bonging 'em in the head. When the workmen came in, we attacked them, so they refused to work. When we run out of stuff to throw, we'd spit at 'em, and pissed over the tier at 'em. We managed to do a lot [of damage] even though we were locked in cells. There just wasn't that much more they could to do us. We kept that up.

We decided among ourselves, "Well, if we don't want to sleep on the floor at least let the workmen come in." We took the food just so we could throw it. So we got our bunks. We let the workmen come in. We'd kinda hold back in the corner like dogs in a cage, let 'em move us around. While they'd finish one cell, we'd let 'em move us to another one. That was our exercise. So it was months I was in there. I escaped outa there, too, in a blaze of glory one night. We planned it for a few days. The only way we could get out to the bathroom was the night man would take us out one at a time. He'd take us and walk up to the end of the tier with you. He'd stand there while you went to the bathroom and then he'd escort you back down and lock you in. Well, we had a couple guys that were pretty good size, pretty crazy, too. One of 'em had stolen a pretty good-sized crescent wrench and had it hid.

So we started that night about eleven o'clock to go for a piss call. So the old man that was on, he come down and he took the padlock off and took the guy over to the bathroom, and when he was coming back down the tier, the kid hit him on the back of the head with that pipe wrench, damn near killed him. So he took his keys and started letting the rest of us all out.

So we were out. We were still locked in the building, but we were all out of our cells, and all that was left for us to do was get through a double door that was downstairs. We had the master key on his rings and the padlocks were on the outside. You weren't supposed to be able to reach in and open 'em from the outside; somebody coming through the front door was supposed to. But this was that square-wire cage, so they didn't design it with kids really in mind. We took the smallest guy there and he was able to put his hands through those little squares and unlock those padlocks. You know, there's no way an adult could get his hands through those squares to fidget with the outside lock, but this little teeny guy could, with hands like a little girl.

So we got out and we burnt the place up before we left. One of my friends got killed in that fire. He didn't get out of his cell and some of the furniture downstairs was set on fire. This was three or four months into the building, when they started making a little house downstairs so some of us could come out once in a while and watch TV. So we set the furniture on fire. Set anything we thought would burn. But the black smoke from the plastics, from foam rubber and stuff, boy, it smoked. Whew, it was smoking so bad by the time we finally busted through that front door we couldn't hardly see where we was going. Guys were starting to fall out then. We couldn't put the fire out, either. It was going too bad.

We come out through the door and they were waiting for us, and we had clubs and sharp-pointed sticks and things. We battled our way through 'em and got away. We got away from in front of the building any-way and we came out of there. Damn near all of us were barefoot. I had a pair of jeans on and a tee shirt. Didn't have any shoes. Temperature was about ten degrees. It was wintertime, and let's see . . . there wasn't any snow on the ground, but it was cold, frosty. I know everybody went different directions, but the majority of the guys went the same way I was headed and that was around the corner of the building.

The quickest way off the grounds was past the administration building and I went running down through there as fast as I could. Came up to the small electric fence. There was two or three guys standing there trying to decide what the hell to do, whether to go over it or around it. You could go around it, but it was a long run. So someone was trying to talk the other one into getting up enough nerve to see how much juice it had in it, do something with it. And I come running by there and I squeezed underneath it. So that kinda broke the ice there. Then some of them jumped over it and the other ones crawled underneath. It was just put there. It wasn't to pen us in. I think they let cows out in there, you know. So it was mostly to try to keep them cows out in that field and from coming up that long entrance way. It wasn't high-voltage stuff. It was just enough to give you a little zap. You know how electricity is. But none of us knew anything about it, so we didn't know if it had a thousand volts or ten volts. You'd just spot those little glass conductors and you'd know there was a little juice there. So it worked on us, actually, just like it worked on a bunch of cows. You just stand there like a bunch of dummies and look at it. You had a little incentive to go by it, though, 'cause they were screaming and running after us.

We went from there and we crossed this field and we pretty much lost sight of everybody in the dark. I was running, going like hell across that field, and heard somebody holler at me, "Hey," calling me Eskimo. That was my nickname in there. So I stopped, checked out who it was. Two buddies of mine from Seattle stopped to rest or some damn thing, waiting to see who was coming. I don't know what they was waiting for, but they was sitting on the ground there.

So the rest of 'em were going crazy running every which way, and we sat there and decided to get our shit together and strike out in a separate direction. Let them take all the heat 'cause they were bunched up like cattle heading for the town. So we figured, "Okay, let's skirt the town and then we'll find some place to get a car, scoot on out of there while all of them dings are getting caught."

In a small town like Chehalis, we figured all the police would be all over there, plus the officials that worked at the joint there, so we went up on these railroad tracks. We were walking down the tracks and we seen a light coming, someone bopping a little flashlight, so figured it was one of them bulls. We ducked off the tracks. Just our luck: where we jumped was a swamp, so there was no other way to go except to cross that swamp. And it was cold. But we started staggering through that swamp. The water came up to our chest. The grass and the weeds that came up through were another couple feet above that. We couldn't see a damn thing. We hung on to each other and tried to take a straight line. We didn't have no idea what it [the swamp] looked like. We never seen it during the daytime; it was off the grounds. So we just hoped for the best. We wasn't particularly afraid of drowning. What we were afraid of was getting wet and freezing to death, you know, and we wasn't even cold yet because of all the running we'd been doing and the excitement.

So we started to cross the swamp. A couple times we tripped over logs in the water underneath and backed up again. But in the dark, you know, we kinda run around in circles about a half-dozen times. It didn't seem like we was ever going to get out. We knew damn sure it wasn't that big a swamp, so apparently we wasn't walking in a straight line. I got a little worried about that. Where in the hell is the end of this goddam swamp? We just didn't seem to be coming up out of the damn thing.

We had to walk real quiet. By then we could hear voices. They should of been getting a lot lower. We could hear 'em up on those tracks. And the light shined on us a couple times; not on us but around us. We just stood stock still, you know, and we inched along, inched along, and they finally got tired. None of 'em wanted to get off into that water, so we kept going.

Finally we come out on the other side. I been back there since that time; that goddam swamp is just little. It's not very big at all. But we got on the other side and we got through two or three fields and the first thing we came to was a big old mill. We run around there and my teeth were starting to chatter and my feet were cut by then and hurt. We hid under the mill for a while. It was quiet and we knew nobody was working there, but we decided to look around and see if we could find a car anyway. We could hear the sirens downtown already, so we went to the end of the building along the shadows and we moved our way along to the front of the place. That damn near was the borderline of the edge of the town. There wasn't anything there, not one vehicle, but off down the street I spotted what looked like a dairy or something and there was a couple cars there around the building, so somebody was working.

So we got in an old Chrysler sedan and we hot-wired it, put the old tin-foil trip on it under the ignition. In those days the starter was separate from the key and you could just put your key right in and attach three leads in the back. You could put a big wad of tinfoil in between those three screws that hold the wire, and that tinfoil served as a contact for all three and you'd be ready to go. You'd hit the starter and you was off and running.

And so we cruised outa there, took a few back streets and got outa town with no heat. They were real busy downtown stopping cars, going through the main streets stopping cars. We got outa there and went through one of those small towns. We was goddam near froze to death by then. The heater didn't work in this car. We gotta get some clothes some damn where, you know, so we stopped in Centralia, Washington, and we started taking turns running down the street trying out car doors to see if we could get some blankets or some clothes out of some cars. We didn't come up with anything, so we took off and hit the highways again.

We went to Seattle and went right through my town, Tacoma. Headed to Seattle, was gonna go to this guy's sister's house and hide out for a while, but we got caught. There'd been an accident on the Seattle-Tacoma highway and a couple deaths involved, so there was a lot of heat there, a lot of cop cars. So we come up the road and it was just cracking daylight then. We come screaming down the highway. We thought it was a road-block for us or something, so we just stepped on it, man, went as fast as we could, went flying by the accident scene going eighty miles an hour, so they threw the heat on us. A couple patrol cars peeled off and come after us, and it was a little chase. I mean the competition wasn't too tough.

They caught us pretty easy. They got us about five or six miles up the road, I guess. It couldn't have been more than that. We went quite a ways, it seemed like to me. We made a bum turn, turned out at this gas station. It looked like it had a road behind it, so we screamed off into this gas station and when we got behind it, goddam road didn't go anywhere except down off the bank and off into this cow pasture. So the guy had us pretty well hemmed in there, arrested us and took us to the youth center in Seattle.

We cooled our heels in there for about two weeks while they decided down in Chehalis whether to take us back or not. They did. So we went back down there. They didn't do a damn thing but put us in the hole. Stayed in the hole ten days, got out, and was ready for action again, back to normal. The man that got hit that night was still wearing bandages on his head. You could still smell the smoke. Things were a little bit quieter. Everybody was caught, though, that had got out, so nobody got free except for a few hours.

Everybody managed to do some damage somewhere. Richard, this one kid, he was fourteen or fifteen; he was the one that died in the fire. Smoke killed him. That kinda threw a little heat on the place, you know. The public started asking what the hell they were doing with us, what kind of building was that, and all that bullshit. No kind of safety devices in there, no fire extinguishers, no way to get guys out of their cells. There was a fire that proved there was no way to get you out. One guy that did work there, he did try. He got burned on his hands, suffered smoke inhalation, trying to get the guys out. He got several other guys out of their cells before they died, but Richard was last. He couldn't get him out. He give it a helluva try. That fellow's name was Cage, Mr. Cage. He was a pretty good man, a pretty good man. Everybody liked him.

It was about a month after that, like I said, that they called me out of the cell one day and I went over to the administration building. I was thinking about escaping along the road there. I was thinking I was gonna break loose and run, and I don't know why I never did it, because as a rule that's what I would do: soon as the guy loosened his grip on my arm a little bit, I would pull loose and take off like a gazelle across the fields and start the chase again. That was my plan.

As soon as they said they wanted me over at the administration building for something and [that] somebody would be sent over to get me, I'd say, "Aha," and I'd start saying good-bye to everybody and say, "I'm going." I'd watch real close out the window to see exactly who and how many they were going to send to get me so I could weigh my chances. I was hoping it would be a fat guy who couldn't run very fast.

Wasn't that long a walk between our building and the administration building. I got over there and went up into the superintendent's office. I walked in there and there was my mom sitting in there, big smile on her face. I said, "What the hell's going on here?" and they told me, "Well, sit down." I sat down. He says, "Well, we're gonna try something with you. You're not making a helluva lot of progress down here, that's obvious, and so the only thing that I can think of to do is send you to the county jail. But I got a feeling that unless you make some drastic changes, that's going to be what's gonna happen anyway. So as far as I'm concerned, my responsibility is over with." He says, "If you got any things you want to get, get 'em. If you don't, get the hell out of here." And he says, "Keep going. Get out of here, knucklehead, and I mean it."

No, he didn't say that, but I walked out of the place anyway. My partners were looking out the window that day. They couldn't believe it, boy, seeing me walking out of there and I was waving and whistling and hollering, talking plenty shit, man. My mom was smiling. Got in the old car and back to Tacoma, man. Didn't have to run off or anything. So that's how I got out of Chehalis finally. That was the summer of 1957. I went into Chehalis in 1955.

When I got kicked out of Chehalis, I went back out to a gang I had been running with, and we did a lot of fighting and we did a lot of stealing. I quit school in the seventh grade, as did most of the others. We called ourselves the Rebels, and that's what we was. There was six or seven of us. Jimmy Chuck—his Indian name is Many Dog Hides—he was one of the craziest ones, a real skinny kid. He had a couple sisters, couple brothers. His whole family was always mad at him because he was always in trouble.

And Jake, his cousin, and a guy named Bernie. Another Indian, myself, a white kid named Harry, and his brother, Gordon. That was it.

By that time we seldom went home. I think I'd turned seventeen. We used to go home to sleep once in a while over at each other's houses, and eat, but we all lived on the lower east side of Tacoma. It's a ghetto. Maybe not as bad as the big cities, but all in all lots of people there was on welfare. All the people we associated with was Indians. They lived down there because they were close to the river where they do all the fishing. And the big Indian hospital was there. It's not a hospital now, but it was then—Cascadia. Well, these guys that I ran with in this gang, we was really committed to each other. About as committed as you could be at that time, so we were really just like one. All we did was live for kicks. I never even started the eighth grade. They tried to get me into some kind of school in Chehalis, but that didn't work out. I was into a school building and I was there one week. I viewed that school building as a means of escape one day and I got out of there and got away. So they never invited me to try the school again. I never did finish much schooling. The rest of the guys all quit, too. We'd all been in jail. Every one of us been in jail numerous times for drunken fighting or some kind of burglary. Mostly fighting.

We didn't pull off any kind of organized capers or anything. We just lived from day to day on whatever we could bum. Bus come by, we'd even bum money from the bus passengers. We used to terrorize the buses so much that they decided to just eliminate that damn bus stop and went right on by. Just making it a generally pretty rotten neighborhood, thanks to our efforts. And if we couldn't get anything there, we'd move up the hill. There was gangs at McKinley. There was gangs at Sixth Avenue. There was gangs all over. But we were a little bit more serious in that we were more dangerous than the normal gang because we didn't just fistfight. We'd take a shot at a dude and we'd cut him up. A lot of other guys didn't really get off into that much violence as we did. So when we did come around to somebody else's neighborhood, it generally remained pretty quiet until we left, because when we came, we came prepared—baseball bats, knives, guns—and we'd come up and break into places and leave with some kind of money and go back down to our little hideaway.

We made a lot of trouble that summer but we didn't go to jail too much. We did go to jail for drunken fighting at restaurants and different places. They'd snatch us for doing some damned thing. We'd have parties and the cops would always end up coming and dragging us off, but we'd always get out in two or three days.

In the summer of 1957, we were going to dances. I used to have a car 'cause I was always stealing cars. I'd go to Seattle or someplace and steal me up a car and bring it back, change the plates and drive it for a month. Didn't get caught that often. In fact, didn't get caught for that. So it worked out. So we had a car we all kicked around in and we went to all the dances. Go in the parking lot and take our beer with us. We smoked and we drank. The only thing we didn't do was shoot dope, none of us. It wasn't because we wouldn't, but because they really weren't doing that then. There wasn't that much around.

They had a dance at the Red Mill late that summer. In those days taverns closed generally at twelve o'clock and this dance would go on until two or three in the morning. By the time everybody came out to that dance they were drunk, and they'd come from several towns around. We spent more time out in the parking lot than we did inside at the dance. We had our cars back in a sort of circle. We all stayed kind of off in a corner in the back of the parking lot, staked our claim. We had our women, we had our booze. Anybody that came near that we didn't know was subject to attack.

One night we had a helluva fight going out there. We had a fight with some guys from Sumner, a helluva battle. There was about twenty or thirty of us. We recruited others that wanted to get down and fight with us. I was carrying a sword. It was longer than my leg. Somewhere along the line I took that sword out and I hit a guy with it and about that time a cop stepped around the corner, so I dropped it and I ran and kind of got lost in the crowd, but he kept his eye on me and he snatched me up and handcuffed me to a tree. He couldn't think of anything else to do with me because my partners were following along and throwing stuff at him and giving him a bad time. He called for reinforcements and some state patrol showed up, county guys and stuff. It wasn't a half hour and we had a full-scale riot going. Destroyed at least seven cars. Kicked all the windows out. A lot of injuries on both sides and, goddam, I never could get loose from that tree! They caught my brother and two other friends of mine and they didn't have them for long because the rest of the fellas took 'em back away.

So anyway they got me out of there and put my ass into a police car, took me out through a little back road, got me into Tacoma under escort, and took me to the county jail. I was seventeen. Of course, they knocked the shit out of you first. Took me into this little back room and they said, "How old are you?" And I told 'em, "Well, I'm seventeen." And the cop knocked me down and he said, "You look eighteen to me." So he commenced to kick the shit out of me. They never asked me no questions. They just kicked the shit out of me 'cause they were a little hostile. A couple of their boys got scuffled there in the hassle and I was the only one they had they could get back at, and they charged me with inciting to riot, first-degree assault, everything they could think of. Anyway, the assault charge was the only one I was worried about, because it carries a mandatory sentence and a mandatory isn't that good to get. A normal sentence you could get five years for burglary and you get a third off, so you do three. If you get a five-year mandatory sentence, you do five years. You can't even get a third off. You get that for violent beefs, assaults and armed robbery. Anything with a weapon.

But they needed a witness in order to convict me, so I went to court for inciting a riot, but they really couldn't stick that on me, so I only ended up staying eight days in jail for being drunk and a minor. I was handcuffed to a tree, so I hadn't hit no cops or nothing, so they couldn't charge me with none of that bullshit. All I did was stand there and yell. I especially started yelling when my partner tried to cut down the tree with me handcuffed to it. Boy, you should have heard me scream then! I said, "Jeez, what are you doing with that hatchet, man?" My partner saying, "We'll get you out. We'll get you out." "Goddam, you'll kill me if this tree goes down!" Oh God!

Took me eight days to heal [from the riot]. Took me longer than that to heal from the beating them cops gave me, and I think that had a lot to do with them not pressing charges, because when I went to court my mother and them were screaming about the cuts and bruises all over my face. Both my eyes were black, my nose was all smashed, my lips were all smashed. My teeth were knocked loose, my ribs were kicked in. That was all by the cops in Tacoma. County sheriff did that. So my mom was screaming about that, demanding an investigation, and the judge asked me about it and the cops were in the court, too. They were more than a little worried. When it happened, they were pretty excited, same as we was, so I told the judge, "Well, it happened out there at the dance. Some goddam drunks came up and hit me with a bat. Beat me up."

I didn't rat on the cops and so I think that was the main reason they didn't press the charges. They didn't bother me after that. The fact of the matter is they started saying Hello, and started getting pretty friendly that day in court. I took the heat off them sonovabitches. If I'd told the judge, I'd probably had about a half dozen of 'em for assaulting a minor, but I figured you live in that town, you know, there's no use starting that. It's all a game and that was just my loss. That's it, I lost. That's part of the game. Someday my day would come. I always thought of it that way. I'd have fantasies about blowing cops away, but that kind of went away. I'm not mad at anyone in particular. I've had cops save my life. I've had cops save my brother's life, so it balances out eventually. You just kinda keep track of it. I keep track. I keep score and I can't say that even being in prison I've been beat that much. The only beating I've suffered in prison is the guards that work here or worked at Monroe.

But anyway, after this riot thing I got a little bit more rowdy. During the summer we broke into a supermarket up on the east side. We had a stolen car then. I drove the car up through the doors of the store, smashed the door down, and backed out, and then we loaded up with beer and away we went.

Two days later they trapped me as I was pulling into my mom's house in the alley to unload some of that stuff which I still had—beer, wine, and cigarettes. I seen the cops blocking the bottom of the alley. Another cop pulled in behind me, so I took off and I drove right off through the yard beside the houses and between them and got onto the next street, let the car go by itself and leaped out, and I took off running. I ran down to a res-

ervoir that was being built and I ran alongside of it, got through a couple
of gullies, and I got away for an hour or two, but they caught me. I was
walking down the street and they spotted me.

I got sentenced fifteen years for all this shit and [with] the other
charges that were on me, they classified me, of course, as incorrigible. I
was still seventeen. Incorrigible, delinquent, and psychopathic, so consequently I was transferred to adult status, which meant they could take me
and give me an adult sentence. So at the end of the year the old juvenile
rampage was over; I had to start paying the price from then on.

3

County Jail, Monroe, Walla Walla, and on the Street

Once you get through the juvenile court you are in trouble. So with the fifteen years for the burglary I was pretty much on my way to state reformatory, even though I was seventeen. I got probation on it. It didn't last very long, of course, a matter of a month. I was arrested several times while I was out on probation for fighting and for theft, investigations, suspicion, arrests, and this and that, so they finally took me back and I violated the probation and they sent me on to Monroe.

I did six months in the county jail in Tacoma when I was seventeen. That was a real trip there. It was a dungeon, a dungeon. But I had it pretty good, as usual. Didn't upset me very much. Just someplace that I couldn't leave for a while. So I just kicked back, kicked back and said, "Okay, here I am. I ain't going nowhere. Six months." And I did the time the best way I could. I played cards, had weekly visits, eventually made trustee, came out of the tank, and, oh, you do the same as you do in prison, only maybe not quite as much of the hustling. But you hustle like hell to make your time as easy as possible. Pick up an extra mattress or pick up an extra blanket, get a little extra food.

I had the distinction, of course, of being the youngest guy in the county jail in Tacoma and I was pink, you know what I mean? When a kid's pretty nice, pretty good looking and soft. I got teased a lot, but I never, I never ever had to fight all those sexual advances and things like that. I had a lot of friends doing time in there, so even if I got threatened by somebody bigger, I had friends that were ready to fight with me. So I never did have to go through that bullshit, although I seen it happen to other guys.

That county jail, of course, came before Monroe. Let's see, I spent six months there. Well, like I said, I got violated [violated parole] because I got in a lot of trouble again. I was involved in several car thefts, a couple burglaries, fighting, drinking, so I went back to court and they sent me off to Monroe.

Before Monroe, I had to go to Shelton [prisoner reception center]. I always felt hate when the pigs came to take me to Shelton, being shuffled around like cattle, standing naked while I waited for my turn to bend over so the pig can look up my asshole. That type of skin search is the very last thread of self-respect going down the drain. They do it knowing they are not really looking for anything except a small show of resistance from one of us, and when it does come, it is pitiful and embarrassing for everyone except the pigs. They love it and pile on the man with fists and clubs.

There is something about being naked that makes you just a piece of meat, even less than an animal. That's when the inner hate begins and it doesn't go away, because being a fish at Shelton is a constant stream of abuse and disrespect. It is six weeks of brainwash designed to internalize your embarrassment and disrespect for yourself at letting men treat you like shit without doing anything to hit back, even though it is physically impossible to do anything. The slightest resistance results in punishment all the way down the line to Walla Walla or other joints. If you've never been through it before, it's a bitch, and it just gets progressively worse.

The new fish gets on the chain, goes to Shelton, gets off the chain, and the bulls come march you on in and they start unchaining you. There you sit on a bunch of wooden benches. . . . They got a great big box in the middle for everybody to throw their stuff into like Jews in concentration camps. I always relate everything about this experience to Jews, because when I see films about what happened to them, it reminds me in the worst way of Shelton. You all stand around naked with the bulls shouting at you. It's a dehumanizing process.

While you're at Shelton, they give you all dark blue coveralls and they're all different sizes. You might get one that's too little; you might get one that's just huge. Then you go to the barber chair and they cut your hair off. A dumb haircut. You know how hair is to most of the guys. That I wipe out of my mind so it won't bother me before I even get there. I'm always ready for haircuts so I won't get mad. I cut my own hair rather than give them the satisfaction of cutting my hair. Even though I might want to grow my hair, I don't. But new people don't do that; they don't know. Or they might say, "I'm not letting them cut my hair." You hear that all the time but you know in your mind what's going to happen. But if they don't want their hair cut, they run everybody out of the room and run in and grab the guy and force him into the chair and handcuff him to it, and then they really cut his hair off with big splotches sticking out all over.

Shelton is where you hear people crying. And that's where you start that other mean process. There's absolutely no compassion there, because the fish are already practicing to be tough. I've cried, too, even as many times as I've been through there. The last time I was at Shelton I cried because one night I was just sitting there thinking about Gina, and that got to me 'cause I had promised her that I would never go back, and here I am again. It really got to me.

The thing you'll always remember is the chains. They have heavy chains almost like a tow chain and it wraps around your waist twice, and they've all got these padlocks and it's got a big ring in front, a big silver ring, and they've got handcuffs through that. Then your hand goes through here and they're handcuffed to the ring. Then after everybody is chained up like that, they've got another ring on the side and they run another long chain through all that so you're all kind of close together, and they make ten-man chains and put you on the bus. All the time you're on the bus you're scared that the bus driver is going to have a heart attack and go in the river, or the bus will catch fire. You see, anytime you're helpless, all those thoughts come to your mind.

When they come and take you off of the chain, you make sure that your people don't know when you're leaving, because it's not something that you want them to see. You wouldn't want your people to see you, 'cause you hide this stuff from people that you love, anyway. You don't tell them what's going on too much. It's bad enough for me being in jail. Hell, my mom'll freak out if she sees me all chained up. She'll think that's the way I've got to run around all the time, and besides, I can't give her a little wave. I'd just rather go, because it's just a short while that you're chained and then you're unchained again.

When I go to the hospital down here in Walla Walla, the strangers, I don't care if they look at me, but not my family when my legs are chained. There's no use being ashamed of it. The chains aren't going to go away. Right? So you kind of start playing the role they expect you to play, giving everybody dirty looks and things like that. They can tell where you come from and you know what they're thinking about you, so you just kind of fall off into it, and maybe it's the same way we do when we get out of prison a lot of times. We play the role we're expected to play. And we *do* play it. I did that last time they took me down to the hospital. I got off on it a little bit because I couldn't hide the chains. People were looking at me. Scared the little old ladies. Actually, the little old ladies were the only ones that would talk to me. One minute you want to say, "I won't hurt you." You want to explain about your chains, but you don't have to with two guards standing there. This whole play takes place in silence. The only sound in the carpeted waiting room is the muted rattle of my leg chain and the handcuffs. Everyone seems uneasy and most people try not to stare.

The last time I made the run to the local clinic, I was standing in the waiting room looking at the people. There were a few empty chairs, but the looks on the faces were hoping I wouldn't sit down. Finally a lady asked me to a chair beside her. She was one of the two little old ladies in the room. I spent the entire ride down telling myself not to be embarrassed and not to fight the chains so I wouldn't trip and fall flat on my face. If you do trip and fall you have a very hard time getting up because your hands are not only cuffed, but a waist chain holds the arms and hands close to your waist. No balance. You have to be picked up and put back on your feet if you fall. That can be embarrassing. There is something special about the way a person walks in chains. It is a slow, even, shuffling pace, so the guards are always waiting for you to catch up.

I have developed a feeling through the years that this whole prison trip was sort of a personal fight between me and the state or the system. It's been my belief that the powers want to break me down and make a mindless robot out of me. But first they have to defeat me, kick my ass until I scream for mercy, fuck with my head until I can't hang on anymore. What I tried to hang onto is the beliefs I had. Right or wrong, I was stuck with them and I defended them. Only *I* will let those beliefs, attitudes, and bad habits go, and only when *I* decide to do it.

The major point was that I thought I couldn't let my real self be seen while under *their* control, or it would show weakness and giving in to what *they* wanted. Each time I came to prison I was sad, completely burned out, and feeling like "Aw, fuck everything." I wanted to just let go and ride with the current, even if it meant following their rules, God forbid. But once we came around that last bend in the road and the joint sprang into sight, every cell in my body said, "Here we go. Get your shit together now or forever hold your peace." I would say to myself, "Fuck this. I'll make it again, no matter what comes down."

The joint has a mind of its own to me. It was built to destroy people like me, and I took real pride in having ridden through so many times untouched, unchanged, and still saying, "Fuck the world." I was afraid to let go because I didn't know any other way. I hadn't learned enough about life to even imagine that I could begin to take control in a different way. I was fully institutionalized and thought I had this tiny bit of freedom to hate, and to think my own thoughts. So I moved my world to my head and somehow was able to be happy in the thought that I was free mentally. I never saw the wall or the towers after a week or so. I wasn't crazy, of course, but I took satisfaction in the thought that I was holding onto something *they* hated and wanted: my ability to smile and think my own thoughts. That is what the price would be: I would lose these if I let the joint break my ass.

And so anyway, I got to Monroe and all my partners were there already. I went to Monroe, February 1958. All my friends were there already, the old gang, the Rebels. There were already four in the joint. My brother was coming up the ladder. He was in Chehalis by the time I went to Monroe and he was on the old escape trip. They already had him in maximum security in Chehalis at Greenhill. He was also eventually classified as a psychopathic delinquent, consequently sent to Washington State Hospital along with three of his partners after a pretty wild escape from Greenhill one night. So I mean it was only a matter of a year and he followed me to Monroe.

Monroe is just like a . . . it's just like this place, exactly the same as this. There's a little more confinement, really. Physical setting is pretty much the same. You have a high wall and you have seven or eight towers placed along the wall and four cellblocks, including segregation and the hole. And they have school. They just had high school at that time. And they have the shop area, which is inside the wall down at one end of the joint. And the administration building and stuff is at the other end. So like I said, it's a maximum-security place.

That was the first adult institution, other than the county jail, that I had been in and it didn't really scare me. I mean, you're always nervous, you know. But the feelings . . . when I went there, I was in the fish tank where they keep you for six weeks when you first come in. You don't go right into population. You're kind of out on the fringe and you have a separate cellblock you live in and you have a separate yard that you go out to, but you can look through the fences at the other guys and spot a friend, or whatever.

Of course, when you go out to the yard all the rest of the guys in the joint, they always stop and look at you, so you know exactly what a monkey in a cage feels like because you have the other convicts in the joint standing around the fence peeking through and sizing you up and looking you over. Looking over the crop, you know, checking the crop out, and they'll be whistling and jeering. And if they spot a guy who they know from the county jail is a rat or something, they'll point him out and make sure the whole joint knows about it, and start screaming and calling him names and making sure we know about it. And if we've got a little girl with us, a homosexual in the bunch, they'll be whistling, calling names and shit, and so we go through that when we go out to the yard the first time. But pretty soon you get over that because they get tired of looking at you and the new guys just go about their business, which ain't no business at all, sitting around on the concrete.

So that was a freak joint. But I had the same feelings when I was a kid when I had to go to a new school. That's about it. I was just as much afraid of a new school, of changing school or classes, as I was of going to prison. And I really, really hated school! I never . . . God, I hated it! 'Course, now I love it, but now I'm older and I understand a few more things.

At Monroe I had a lot of friends there. Like I said, the whole gang was there and they were out of the fish tank, and they stuck together in a little clique out there. They were throwing me over cigarettes and things like that, telling me what cell to ask for, so you'd be pretty much close to where they're at, so you could kind of be with each other. You can't get away from each other really, when you're in the joint, but when you're in [adjacent] cells, you're kind of apt to be a little closer because you're always passing things back and forth and talking about girls that we all know, and our friends are the same, so you try to be together on a tier, or no more than one tier above or one tier below, because then you could pass something on a string. You just put it on a string and throw it out over the tier and it swings down till your partner catches it, whether it's a note or whether it's coffee or whatever.

The parole board gave me four and a half years to do at Monroe. The top end of my sentence was fifteen [years] for second-degree burglary, so I started out doing four and a half.

All of Monroe is closed custody. They've got farms and things like that you can go to, of course, which is minimum custody, but it comes a lot later. I didn't think much of the time. Four and a half years didn't seem like a very long time to me. I was so young, you know; it didn't seem like no time at all. I'd be there and I'd be gone. That would be it. Just chalk it up. I planned to do a lot of growing and learn a lot of new tricks while I was in Monroe. In fact, I was looking forward to coming out a helluva lot smarter crook, a big-time criminal, you know what I mean? That thought appealed to me.

I, regretfully, was not interested in school or learning a skill or a trade or anything else. And so I puttered along month after month after month. I turned eighteen in Monroe. The only thing I got into was the boxing program because I was kind of, well, normal size. I thought I was kind of skinny, myself, but I got into the boxing program and I put a lot of effort into that. Learned the best I could. Had a few fights, won a few, lost a few. I got very good at it and to me boxing became . . . oh, I don't know what it became . . . it gave me more confidence in myself. A little pride. I was real good at being able to learn it and not being clumsy and clutsy like some of the guys were. They never seemed to be able to learn the moves, no matter how much they practiced. No matter how hard you tried to show 'em, they never learned and they just constantly got the shit beat out of 'em. But it didn't take me long to learn the new moves that are important to boxing. If you can't learn, man, get out. If you want to keep going, you'll just be punch-drunk. But I got pretty good. The thing is, I didn't quit after a little while. I didn't quit after a few months or a year. I kept at it year after year and I kind of seriously considered becoming professional because I was young enough to spend these years learning, and then go out and use it to make some dough, because there was nothing else I could do. I hadn't even gone through the eighth grade, so I had no profession.

So I kept boxing. I got better and better. I didn't get hit. When I did get hit, I didn't care, which makes you pretty tough to fight when you don't give a shit whether you get hit or not. As a matter of fact, you'll take three or four shots to get one in. People don't like to fight that kind of person, you know. They act like they like getting hit. In a way I did. I wanted to look like a boxer. I wanted my nose broke. I wanted scars. I wanted to look that tough-guy look. I thought scars from punches looked pretty neat. Rocky Graziano and some of those guys, I thought they looked pretty goddam neat with their scar tissue and shit, so I didn't dodge no punches, you know what I mean? I fired away, boy, I got good and mean. The sound of swinging fists and hitting, you're firing it, man. And I was pretty skillful if I wanted to be. If I didn't want a guy to hit me, he'd never hit me, because I could move and I was pretty goddam slick, you know, and I didn't give a shit. I just wanted to bulldog him half the time, unless the guy was real good and a real sharp heavy hitter. Then I cleaned up my hand a little bit and started boxing, you know, because this guy, you can't play with him.

When I was at Monroe I kind of fought my way through there. I attempted to go to school there once and I didn't like it and quit. I had a lot of trouble with the pigs there. I was always in trouble for sniffing carbon tetrachloride. But I got pretty well loaded on that, I'm telling you, and I was constantly at that bottle, sniffing. I'd get it from my partner who worked in the dry cleaning shop there, which has an easy access to it. Me and my brother—like I say, he caught up with me in about a year—well, we was always sniffing. That's all we did. We didn't smoke dope or use. There wasn't any drinking to be done, really. But we did use that carbon tet, so we were in the hole an awful lot. Five to ten days in the hole and come out and go back to your normal routine until you get caught again.

What they're trying to teach us is "Naughty, naughty. This will happen if you do that," and threats, you know, and physically being locked away or beat up or whatever. That'll work on a child but it won't work on adults. They don't scare me none. "You don't scare me none. I'll do what I want to do, when I want to do it, and I'll have what I want out of it any way I can get it." That's the way I've lived.

So the hole at Monroe, it's just an isolation cell down away from the rest of the population. It's quiet, as isolation is supposed to be. But anyway, that didn't bother me any. I liked to get out, though. You get so goddam hungry down there! Shit! All they do at Monroe is twice a day they give you what they call a fritter, and man oh man, it was like meat loaf but it had . . . Christ . . . it had wheat germ in it, it had cornmeal in it, it had ground-up carrots in it, mashed potatoes in it. It even had pieces of macaroni in it. They take a whole bunch of stuff, just like you cook for the pigs, you know. You take a whole bunch of stuff that's left over from lunch and you mix it with some kind of meat loaf stuff, and they make a big patty out of it, a hamburger patty. Only this was a fritter patty. They even had celery sticking out of it or lettuce mixed into it. Jeez, I'm telling you, they'd just be dripping with grease! Oh God, they tasted horrible. They stunk! But old me, the old chowhound. Some guys used the fritter for a pillow, you know. I liked 'em! They were horrible, though, but if that's going to be the bulk of your diet you better get to liking it. Right? Right. So I liked 'em. Just like hockey pucks, I'm telling you. But that's all you eat down there twice a day. And apparently they're nutritious. But we did almost starve to death, you know.

Well, like I said, I did a helluva lot of hole time, segregation time, in Monroe. I think I'm probably kind of proud of being called a psychopath and incorrigible at that age. You kind of live up to it. That was something, you know. It was better than being called a nothing, wouldn't you say, Chiquita? So at least I got an official title from somebody and that gives you some identity. At least on the books you had some identity. Oh shit, I'm a psychopath, what do you think? They keep telling you that. It just falls in line with what I had said once to you before, that whatever people called you, big people, even at that age I looked at that as . . . even though I was eighteen and supposed to be an adult and all that . . . I still looked at the guards, the doctors, and administrators as big people, you know, 'cause I didn't feel big. *They* were the big people to me, so whatever they said, you know, must have been true! And if they said I was incorrigible and I was psychopathic—at that time, psychopathic really meant something terrible to me—I must be a cold killer or something, so I took it to heart. And if they said it, especially a doctor, then it must be true. And so, I guess, I really tried to carry out the part. I didn't try to be Mr. Nice Guy, I'll tell you that. I didn't try to be a tough guy, either, because I know I wasn't. But not weak, either. So just kind of an image to work at, and it got me through Monroe. And I did more time than you usually do with sentences like I got.

At Monroe one time me and Donny were sniffing glue, getting loaded as usual, and all of a sudden the door clicked. I looked out the tiers, here they come, about four or five of them, drug me out. They already had Donny. Drug me out, took me down to the segregation tiers in another part of the building, and stripped us down in the shower room [and] started shaking us down. One of those sergeants was running his hands through my hair really rough, so I just plowed . . . boom . . . hit him in the mouth, right in his cigar, knocked his ass down. It didn't take a quarter of a second and they all piled on us like he did it on purpose. Beat the fuck out of us, drug us from there back and through to the back hole that they had condemned for twenty years, threw us in there. Had no heat, no lights. It was funny. I had to laugh going in the sonovabitch. I was beat up so bad, [yet] I still had a laugh because the guy had to brush cobwebs out of the way of the fucking doorway before we could get in the sonovabitch. They threw us into this fucking cell that had those big padlocks that they hook on. There's a little hole and you look through the door and that's all the light you get. No blankets, no nothing, naked. I was in my early twenties.

They let us out in about ten days. It was funny. We started hollering. Me and Donny were hollering at each other, talking, and pretty soon another voice spoke up, said, "Gene. That you?" "Yeah. Who's that?" "Bob, Bobby Miller." [I] said, "You sonovabitch. I thought you went home." "Hell no. I been back here sixty days." Then another guy hollers up, "Fuck you, Delormes." That was another friend of ours named Robby. We thought he went home. The whole gang was sitting back there in the hole. They'd disappeared their asses. They were glad to have company. We just laughed and hollered all goddam day long.

I wasn't scared. I was just angry. Just angry. I just wanted to hit somebody. Those cops, you could only hit just once. That's it. You're done. I mean you're beat. We know that to start with, but if you can get in one punch, you feel good. You're going to get thirty back, but you feel good anyway. They were holding me by my neck. All I could do was piss, so I pissed at the one in front of me. I spit at him, tried everything. He slugged me in the stomach for pissing on him. The other one smacked my face for spitting. They all knew us. We still laughed and joked with them when they come took us back out. Took us to court and the court people asked, "How did you get all them bruises?" We said, "Aw, we was sniffing glue and fell down the stairs and shit." We lied about it because that way they treat you better. It's part of the convict code. That's why we got out of the hole in ten days instead of thirty or forty, because we didn't tell on them. Hell, we could've been in there ninety days. But Sergeant McLeavy, the one that got in on it with me, I could've gave him up in court. I could've told on him and he would've got busted in rank or fired. There was several of them there and we didn't say nothing. We said we fell down, fuck that, so they come let us out. No, you don't tell on them. You got to live with them because if you tell on them, they can lie about you every fucking day. Parole board comes, they write out a bad report. So the convict code covers that shit, too.

I made one escape attempt from Monroe, [but] I got drunk and passed out and they caught me before I ever left the grounds! That was several years later, 1961, the first time they ever let me out of that joint. Let me think . . . yeah, from 1958 to 1961, and I was finally out to the farm, which was minimum security. I only had thirteen days left to do and I went in the hole. I got in the hole with three or four other guys on an escape attempt, of all things. Back in the hole! Ninety days back down in the hole again. I was sick! I did thirteen days in the hole and they let me out, and after ninety days I finally did go home.

But it was rough, tough, getting out of there [Monroe]. There was reasons why I did it [tried to escape]. I rationalized quite a bit. I did truly think about it; even in a drunken stupor I weighed my odds. I weighed my odds against staying out on parole and staying out on escape, and I knew I probably wouldn't make it very long on parole because I'd be capering, you know. As a matter of fact, I resented somebody's suggestion that I should quit already, because I was just getting started. And I hadn't even started the big stuff yet. So I was anxious to get to the robberies and the big shit, and drugs, which I hadn't tried yet, so I wasn't going to quit. I wanted my piece of the action. Hell, I hadn't even stole many cars yet. They talk about "quit stealing," [and] I hadn't done nothing yet. So I figured, "Okay, if I escape I'll be more careful. If I escape, I won't have to go to no parole officer. I wouldn't have to answer to anybody. I could just keep moving and slipping and sliding and dodging, do what I wanna do and probably at least stay out a lot longer than I would if I was out on parole." And actually that might be true. It doesn't look that farfetched to me, even now, although I definitely want to stay out now, of course. I would not hesitate to take parole. But that was my reason at that time.

I needed a few drinks to bolster my courage because it was very involved, you know, grabbing a pig at night and tying him up and what that
entails, which is completely unnecessary, completely unnecessary, any
kind of physical violence, because you can just walk away from the farm.
There's no fences. But we wanted a little head start, you know. We figured
we'd get a head start and take his car, too. The only way we could take his
car, of course, was with his car keys, and the only way we could get his car
keys was by taking them from him. But it all went down the drain. The five
of us, we all drank too much and we all passed out on our beds. We had
our street clothes, our escaping clothes, on. The guy come by to count us
about one o'clock in the morning and spotted all of us dingbats laying
around on our beds in street clothes, and he just quietly went around and
we all woke up with handcuffs on us! He caught that crew. You dumb
sonovabitches! So he carted us off to the hole. Ha! We all laughed.

But we come out all right. I got out of Monroe in 1961 on parole, went
home. Kind of nice to be home. I hadn't learned a damn thing from the
experience. Who does? I was only out ninety days. Ninety days and I was
on my way back to Monroe.

You cram a lot of living in that short time. I had a girl friend, got drunk,
did this, that, shot a little dope, all in ninety days. I did a lot in those ninety
days. A lot in that . . . during that time out I got involved in what started
out to be a burglary, a house burglary that a guy told us about. He said it
was a cinch deal, a snap, a breeze, that we could go out there to these people's [house]. They had a nice place down by the bay in Tacoma and there
was pretty ritzy little houses all along the bay. People paid pretty good
money to live there. So normally you say, "Well if they're living there, they
must have the bucks." So we says okay to this deal. We decided, "All right.
Right up our alley, boy, and easy, [an] easy take." So we picked a Saturday
night. And remember, this is on the word of some kid that had been out
there. Well, he said that they'd definitely be gone on Saturday nights.
They'd definitely be over in Seattle somewhere partying, so we could rip
this joint off easy. All we was after was a big stereo outfit they had. That
was our target. That, and anything else that was laying around would just

be gratis, something extra to throw into the old pot. So we drove out there.

We stayed downtown first, drinking. I said it was a Saturday night and my brother and I and this other Indian kid, we went downtown and we got drunk, and we sat around the bars and we drank and drank and drank and I was carrying a gun. Why? I don't know. Just something to do. Made me feel big or some damn thing. But anyhow I was carrying a gun. I had no intention of using it, no intention at all. So we waited until the taverns closed, then we figured okay, it's pretty damn close to midnight. So we said, "Let's boogie on out, man, and take this joint off now."

So we drove out there in my car. I had this Oldsmobile, so we went out there in my car and we didn't foresee any kind of trouble. This was supposed to be absolutely easy. So we got there and it was all dark and we had a little trouble finding the joint. We kept looking and looking. The kid had been there before, so he vaguely remembered, but when we got out there in the dark there was several houses that looked alike, you know, set out over the water. We finally zeroed in on one because it had a Thunderbird in the garage and they had a Thunderbird, so we figured this is it. But the car being in the garage didn't ring any bells. We was kind of drunk. So I went up and I do my old burglar trick. That was knocking on the door real hard. That's just standard procedure on a burglary, you know. You check. You knock on the door and you ring the bell and you knock on the door. If somebody answers, then the caper's closed. I mean you just ask 'em some dumb question and then you take off and go find some place where there's nobody home. That's standard procedure for the old burglar.

But in this case, I'm standing there with a gun in my goddam hand, pistol, and I kept knocking on the door. Well, I figured they weren't gonna answer, so I was trying to get in the door, and goddam if somebody didn't open it. Sonovagun! The guy opened the door and instead of taking it on the old heel and toe and getting on down the road, I went and stuck this gun in his face and I grabbed him and I took him out on the porch and I talked real softly to him 'cause I figured somebody else was in the house. I told him, "Let's start walking and don't make any noise." Told him, "Lead me straight to wherever your partner's at." I figured if this guy's home, his partner's home. So he says, "Okay."

The guy was shaking like a leaf already and we went into the bedroom and his partner was sitting up in bed, a fellow about eighteen or nineteen years old. By that time my brother had came in and so me and my brother were in the house with these two fools. *We* were the fools, you know! But they were fools to open the door. That's the only way they were fools. So anyway, things commenced to get worse and worse. I was starting to think, "What in the hell am I doing, for chrissake?" But then I thought, "Well, to hell with it." But I was pretty goddam mad. Strange, I got mad at them for being home, for causing it to turn into being an armed robbery like this. [Armed robbery] is not my game. It's not my game to be capturing people and holding them like that, but, I mean, it was done and that's what I figured. I went through that much trouble, so I might as well go ahead and finish the damn thing.

So we tied them up in the bedroom and I stood guard over them and, jeez, I don't know, we didn't hurt them but . . . I don't know, kind of a cruel streak came out. There's something funny about that. You tend to get a little cruel there when you got people so completely at your mercy. And I can even feel ashamed of being that way now because it was the only time in my life when it happened and because I can put it off to the . . . when you're drinking that much you don't do much of anything that's rational, anyway. But we started terrorizing them.

I suppose I started it. I started teasing 'em and terrorizing 'em and scaring 'em, putting the gun to their head and threatening we was gonna kill 'em and put 'em in a bag and dump 'em off into the bay. That didn't set too good with 'em, of course. They started yowling and squealing and screaming and begging, and that went on and on and on, for chrissake. We didn't molest 'em, you know what I mean. But in the meantime, while I'm in the bedroom holding these guys, my brother and this other kid cleaned the joint out. They had a bar, so we took a bunch of booze. We took the stereo and we took clothes. Oh, we took all kinds of jewelry and things they had. Finally we took their car to carry stuff in because we had more stuff than I could carry in my car.

We finally left after about a couple hours. We left 'em tied up on the bed with neckties and we took off. Well, apparently they worked loose pretty fast and called the police. So like dummies we were driving around. This was across town from where I lived. This is Browns Point in Tacoma, and I lived over on the east side just off Portland Avenue, little old east side. And we had driven over there and were looking for a place to unload this stuff. After we got over to my side of town with both cars, my car ran out of gas up on Roosevelt Hill. We were headed to a friend's house, a big housing project that we lived [in] at one time. I was headed there to unload the stuff, but my car ran out of gas and it had the stereo and all the stolen goodies and stuff, so I said, "Jesus, I can't leave it sitting here." So we decided, well, we'd better make a run down to a gas station and get a can of gas and come back.

Well, we took off, my brother and I. We left the other guy with my car. He was smarter than we was. He was an awful lot younger but he was still smarter. He was the only one that wore gloves and he was the only one that knew better than to ride around in that red-hot Thunderbird.

So we went down to the gas station. We took a five-gallon can of gas with us. We were headed back up Portland Avenue and I took a turn and went up to the top of this hill, McKinley, and I was coming down. There's a real steep hill you gotta come down, so I came over this hill and I guess I was on the wrong side of the road. I was plastered, you know, and there was a police car coming up the hill. I damn near run him up on the sidewalk, so the chase was on. He turned around and come after us and he was going like a bat outa hell, and I was going as fast as I could get that damn car to go. And I had the lights out and I was headed . . . this street dipped down between two hills, Fairbanks Street . . . so I went from one hill to the other. This street that we was on ran from McKinley Hill and it went up to the top of Roosevelt Hill. That's where my car was.

The police were chasing me, so I stepped on it. I knew the neighborhoods real good and there was fog up at the top of the other hill, so I figured, well, if I can beat 'em to that fog we can abandon the car and take off on foot. So I was going at it a pretty damn good clip, fifty, sixty miles an hour on those little streets, and this cop, he stayed right on us. As I said, I had the lights off. So we got to this next hill, Roosevelt, and we were in the fog then and goddam if I didn't hit this parked car, flat out, too, ran into the back and it just totally wiped us out. Both cars were burning and we were trapped in our car and my brother, he was really smashed up. He took that windshield in his forehead, the dashboard and every goddam thing else that he could hit, he seemed to bounce off of. Well, me, I was relatively unhurt, a couple little scratches and other than that it wasn't too bad.

But it was getting hot. All you could see was fire around the car. So I told my brother, I says, "Man, this is it for us." I says, "We're either gonna have to jump out of this car and go through that fire or we're gonna burn alive right here." I said, "I'm gonna count to three." I said, "I'd rather jump out of this car and get shot than stay here and burn to death." So we counted to three and we hit the doors and rolled out into that fire. I caught fire, so my clothes were burning. My hair burned off and clothes and I ran past this cop. He was just so amazed to see me come running out of that car a ball of fire, I guess, he didn't know what to do. My brother was screaming. You could hear him halfway across town when that fire hit his ass. He couldn't get his door opened. Finally, it was just by a miracle that he got the door open by accident and fell out the other side. So he got out, but he got burned pretty bad.

In the meantime, I had crossed two, three yards and I had thrown all my clothes off that was burning and I crouched down behind this house. I was trying to see into the car because I heard my brother scream so hard that . . . well, my heart just sank. I thought, "He's dead," and I had to get back there and see. I couldn't see in the car because there was too much fire. The doors were open, but we had that five-gallon can of gas in the back seat of the Thunderbird when we hit that parked car and it spilled over. It didn't have a lid on it. It had spilled over so that the whole five gallons of gas was on the floorboard of the Thunderbird and when we opened the door to that car, that sonovabitch really blew up.

Well, anyway, I went down a couple of yards and I made my way back up there to take a look and see what the hell was going on, and I couldn't see. All the neighbors were out there and I was trying to see the expressions on their faces to tell whether or not he was in that car, because I figured they'd have a pretty horrified look on their faces if he was in the car burning. But they were all looking up on this lawn, and so I seen the cops up there bending over something on the ground, so I knew that was Donny and I figured if he ran that far then he must not have been burned that bad.

So then I took off, boy, hell-bent for elections through the bushes and the gullies. I finally ended up down in the bottom of this gully. Down at the bottom there was a stream and I was down there in the dark. It was three-thirty or four in the morning and I put mud all over my face to make it feel better. Old Indian trick. I put all this mud on me, and I had about six blocks to go, so I climbed up the side of this gully and I skipped down to my girlfriend's sister's house. She let out a scream when she opened the door and seen me standing there. The old mud man, you know, mud all over and no hair on my head. It was all burnt and smoking. And I asked her right off the bat, I said, "I think Donny's dead." I told her where the wreck was. I asked her if she'd get in the car and drive up there and check it out. So she jumped in the car and took off and she run up there to see him and when she got there, there was all kinds of fire trucks and all kinds of police cars, and she said she seen them take him away in an ambulance and the car was still burning. So that's all she knew.

And they all started checking the next morning. Of course, I holed up there in the bedroom, and she was a registered nurse that worked over at St. Joseph's Hospital, so she started doctoring me for the next couple days the best she could and, luckily, I just kind of sat there and toughed it out. I didn't go into any shock or anything. My worst danger, of course, was getting infection.

Well, things started looking bad. It looked like I wasn't going to make it. I said, "Oh, the hell with this noise." I had a friend of mine drive me out to [a small town] about thirty or forty miles from Tacoma. So we went out there and I went into this little clinic. There was a doctor and a couple nurses there, receptionist. So I just said, "The hell with it," and we went in there, me and my partner, and we just captured the place. We just went in and took everybody hostage and locked the place up. There was no customers when we went in, just the staff. But we locked the joint up and held those people in there in the infirmary, and I made them all work on me and do what they could and give me shots. The doctor kept telling me I had to go [to] the hospital, there's just not much he could do, but I told him, "You better do what you can do, pal, because this is probably your last chance and this is my last chance." I was just bullshitting. I wasn't going to hurt him, but I was pretty desperate, you know, and I had one thing in mind, and that was to stay well enough on my feet that I could get back to Tacoma and stay free there long enough so I could go up to that hospital in Tacoma and break my brother out of there and take him with me if he pulled through.

He was in real critical condition, so I didn't dare take a chance on moving him. Of course, I had all the plans made on how to get him out of there and I had two good friends and I had a girlfriend that was prepared to go all the way with me, with the nurse's uniform and the wheelchair and things that we'd need, the doctor's coat and the doctor's tag and stuff, and to walk into that room past them police and take him out of there. We would've took him out on a table and took him down and put him on a wheelchair and away we'd a went, see. But we didn't dare move him because we had to let them work on him to get him out of that critical stage at least, or else we'd be killing him. There was no fear of them taking him to jail right away, not in that shape, so we figured there'd be plenty opportunity to go and break him out, but things didn't go my way.

It was about four days and I got arrested. About four days after I was out, I contacted a friend of mine that was out of the joint here. I'd been in Monroe with him, and damn if the dirty little sonovabitch didn't turn me in! After he drove me from my aunt's house where I was hiding again, he drove me to the house of another friend of mine, a Chicano kid that I'd grown up with. His name is Speedy. I knew I could count on him. Speedy had, without me knowing it, the night before went out and stole a brand-new car and got money because he was looking for me. He knew I needed help and he was going to take me down to California and hide me out with friends of his.

So I got over there and this asshole dropped me off there and when he left, he told the first cop he ran into where he had dropped me off, so they grabbed me. They went into that goddam house like Al Capone was in there. I was a little bit desperate and I had a notion to grab three or four of them kids that were in the house and hold them hostage or some damn thing. You get crazy and you don't know what to do. Well, finally, because of the kids screaming, and my girl was in there, so I said, "Well, the hell with it." I was pretty sure them cops were going to use this opportunity to blow me away, so I told those people to get back in the bedroom somewhere and be quiet, just get away from me. And so I stepped out when they came in. Well, they didn't shoot me, but I thought they would. They carted my ass off to jail.

So there I sat. My brother stayed in the hospital for eleven weeks and when I was first in jail, a couple days there, they used my brother against me to try to make me confess, see. They used to come out in the middle of the night. They'd get me out of the tank in the middle of the night and say, "Well, we got some bad news for you." First they tried to say, "Well, we talked to your brother and your brother confessed and he's not going to make it and he didn't want to die with this on his mind and he wants you to confess." And I said, "To hell with you. I know my brother. My brother ain't a snitch and my brother wouldn't even talk to you assholes." Which turned out to be true. Come to find out later from my brother, he said every time he opened his eyes and seen them goddam cops there, he says he'd just [go] back into a coma and he'd just stay in a goddam coma until he knew they was out of the room. Then he'd wake back up again.

But in the meantime they were trying to drive me crazy, and they kept telling me, when that didn't work, they'd come back the next day. And they told me he was going blind and he was going to be crippled and just everything rotten you can think of, you know, just to try to break me down, which didn't work. I said, "Well, if he goes, he goes. And if he goes, he can go without telling you guys a goddam thing 'cause I ain't telling you nothing. It will be a mystery."

They had us on kidnapping charges and on robbery charges and auto theft. Everything they could think of. And I held tough down at the old jail. I just stuck to my story. "I don't know what the hell you're talking about," I said. "I got a few burns on me but that's no shit." I said, "I was in a car fire. I was working on my car and the sonovabitch caught fire. That's how I got my burns," I said. "I don't know how Donny got his burns." But they wouldn't let me make telephone calls. For the first twenty-one days I was in jail they wouldn't let me use the phone. They wouldn't let me see my mother. They wouldn't let me see anybody so I could find out Donny's true condition, you know, because there's one thing the Tacoma police know, that me and Donny, we're like identical twins. We're that close. So their first thought was to play us against each other. But that doesn't work because we know each other too good, you see. I know exactly how my brother's going to act when he's in jail, and if they talk to him I know what he's going to say. And he knows what I'm gonna say.

Well, what mostly did happen was a lot of plea bargaining and a lot of wheeling and dealing on the side. They had the goods on us pretty goddam good. They'd picked up this kid that was with us. I'm not sure how they got him, but they picked him up and they finally had to let him go because they couldn't get either one of us to implicate him. I told 'em, "Yeah, I know the guy but I don't have any dealings with him. He doesn't run around with me." So he got out.

But through a series of closer and closer deals and working with one detective and knowing our situation realistically—that they were going to get us either on an armed robbery or kidnapping charge—they started wheeling and dealing the best they could. So I agreed to give all the stolen material back, which amounted to several thousand dollars' worth of stuff, and I had Speedy take care of that end of the deal. He had hidden everything for me so they didn't have any evidence. They started looking for my car. If they had found it, they would have really had the goods on me, but Speedy knew that, too, and he found my car first and unloaded it. But for a break on the armed robbery charge, I agreed to give all this shit back. And anyway, we kept working it out until we ended up getting charged with auto theft and that was all. And the kidnapping charges all went out the window because the whole crime was questionable.

If the police started getting suspicious, I just started playing right along with it. The newspapers had great big headlines with our pictures on the front page: "Human Torch Runs From Car" and all that bullshit. "Two men Critically Injured in Bizarre Armed Robbery," this and that, see. But the newspapers and the police made a real mystery out of this thing. They suspected that these two guys we robbed had deliberately hired us to do this, somehow, because they tripped themselves up, see, when they turned in the list of stolen goods. They added in there a three-, four-thousand-dollar diamond ring, which we hadn't even seen. So that was just baloney. They were trying to take advantage of their situation and make some extra bucks out of the insurance company, you know, so this cast a shadow of doubt on 'em, and so I took advantage of that, boy, right to the hilt. And I kept playing them cops along like, "Yep, you're really close," and this and that, and by the time this whole trip got to court, those two guys that we robbed, they didn't know what to do. They were scared of getting charged themselves by then. So when it came time to stand up and identify Donny and I, they said they'd never seen us before. So the judge threw the armed robbery charge and the kidnapping charge right out of the courtroom, but we got stuck with auto theft, which was one helluva a break, I'm telling you. We goddam near shook hands right there in court when them two guys turned around and said, "No, that ain't them." I goddam near jumped for joy.

But anyway, we got ten years apiece and we were back on our way to the joint again. And we were about half-assed famous from the newspapers on all that shit, a lot of coverage on it. That was the winter of '64. And a lot of our friends thought we were dead because it was a pretty bad wreck.

We got back and the parole board gave us ten years, too. Ten-year minimums. We went back to Monroe first and they started giving us a hard time as soon as we got there on the chain. They told my brother and I, "One of you guys is going to segregation and one is going to be out in population." They said, "There's no way that we're going to contend with the two of you together." So Donny and I decided, well, we'll take turns in segregation. And I said, "How about transferring us to Walla Walla?" because they don't act that way at Walla Walla. "I think they're prepared to handle us."

Generally, to live like that at Monroe you have to do something to get in segregation, but we didn't do anything, man. We just had a reputation, you know. They figured if we got together out there in population, we were gonna raise hell. They wouldn't be able to handle us. So my bro, he took the first run into seg. He stayed down there ninety days and I was out in population ninety days. And in the meantime I had talked to the captain and everybody at Monroe who had any kind of clout, and I promised that in exchange for coming to Walla Walla, I promised to be a good sonovabitch there and not get into any trouble. So for ninety days or so at Monroe, boy, I walked the straight and narrow line, I'll tell you. And I never got in any trouble.

So after ninety days they brought my brother out of the hole. In the meantime, he didn't give 'em no kind of hassle down in seg. He was quiet as a church mouse. And they didn't know what the hell we were up to, you know. I tried to make it plain to them that we would do anything if they would just get us out of Monroe and send us to Walla Walla. We felt that we were grown up and we wanted to go away from Monroe and they didn't like that. Our attitude was a little different, you know. We were . . . well, you'd have to call it hard core, incorrigible. We figured, "To hell with you sonovabitches. We're a couple of desperadoes and we don't want any part of your goddam therapy programs and we don't want any part of school. We know what we are. We're a couple of bad motherfuckers, so ship us out of this sonovabitch or else we're gonna burn the goddam place down and kill somebody in the process." That's about the way it went.

So they did, they sent us to Walla Walla, and we commenced doing that ten-year minimum here at Walla Walla. And we got along great here when we came in. We got along good and we zeroed right in, found the top dogs in the joint and we got steered right in the right directions. I mean most everybody knew us from the newspapers, and they knew our reputations as good convicts and everything from other people that had done time with us in Monroe and jails and this and that. So when we got to Walla Walla we was accepted real good. It wasn't hard to get a cell. We walked around here and we weren't worried about anything, you know. We had friends that were ready to back us up and we made plenty of new friends.

Don and I were both happy-go-lucky. We weren't sour-faced, surly type of convicts. We were the younger type of convicts. We were both in our early twenties and, like I said, we were easy to get along with. We made friends real easy. We treated our friends good. We tried to treat everybody the way we liked to be treated: with respect. And we laughed, we joked, and we were doing hard time because we did have a lot of time. We were facing ten-year minimums and that means that we were young enough, if we made it look like we had changed, we could get out of that. And the old-time convicts, of course, they told us the same thing. We listened to every word they said because we knew that they knew how to do the time. And they knew how to get time taken off your sentence. So that's your schooling, you know. We really went for that when we came in here.

This prison was a lot different in 1964 than it is now. They didn't have any programs. Security was a lot tighter in the wings. It doesn't look like it's changed that much, but there's been a lot of changes. At that time those tiers were being used just for cell houses. But it's not so now. We didn't have an entire wing for protective custody then like we do now. There weren't that many rats and it wasn't that violent in here. Once in a while there was a killing, but it wasn't that often. Now we have an entire cellblock with nothing but stool pigeons and there's like 125 rats in that building and they stay in there, eat TV dinners three times a day.

I had come back to the penitentiary with the big minimum, the ten-year minimum for auto theft. Generally, you would expect to get three, two and a half to three, of that ten from the parole board, but in our case, my brother and I, we got the full ten. And we did it—it wasn't too bad—three years and six months of it.

I think I was back once before that but just for eight months. See, I came back here two or three times and got short sentences. I came back once for eight months and I came back once and only got six months. Those were more for traffic tickets I had in Tacoma than [for] anything else, a couple minor violations on parole, like moving without permission or something like that, and I ended up back here.

But the long one we did, my mind was a lot different then, Chiquita. I didn't really give a shit about anything. I was more into just trying to be a good convict, follow the convict code, learn to respect my fellow prisoners, you know, that sort of thing. That seemed the most important thing for me at that time because my life was just from one institution to another up to then, and after that, and so you know what's more important.

I didn't belong here; and you know that when you are inside, you are just so mixed up, yet there really isn't any way that you could stay out for long once they let you out unless some miracle or big stroke of luck happens. It would take a hell of a lot of luck, I'll tell you, to stay out on parole for any amount of time. They know. Hell, they know when you walk out the gate that you're gonna come back nine times out of ten. And it does work out that way, too. The guys walk out for a month, two months, three months, six months if they're lucky, and they're back here again.

During that time here I occupied myself by boxing. I had a good heavy routine so I spent several hours of every day training over here in the gym, and that keeps you busy and it takes a lot of energy out of you that you don't know what the hell to do with anyway. I got to the point where I really couldn't sleep at night and I had to come over here [to the gym] and really work like a dog in the ring and on the bags, going through my routine, you know. If I had to miss a day, I didn't like it at all.

And there's a certain amount of prestige or respect that you get from being on the fight team if you're any good. If you're not, then it's kind of a joke, but I always did good, real good. I enjoyed the sport. I wasn't afraid to get hit, you know, once I understood the game and had enough experience. That's where you get the edge on a less experienced person because they don't know what to expect. And you know that with the gloves on and with the training, and you have a little confidence in yourself, you can relax in that ring and a guy really can't hurt you and you can do a lot of damage. And so I did that. And while I was trying to stay healthy that way, for some reason I started sniffing again. I got started at Monroe, you know, the inhaling of fumes from different chemicals like carbon tetrachloride and things like that.

I continued that little game, pastime, over here and hit 'er a pretty heavy lick a couple years. The effect on me was I ended up here in the mental ward for a couple months pretty well screwed up in my head from that stuff and . . . I guess I've never really read the jacket on their diagnosis of what happened, but they called it something like . . . oh, what the hell was that? It was some dumb-assed, bogus diagnosis. It was chronic schizophrenia, and that's not the case at all. More than anything else, all it was, was poisoning, overloading the system with the chemicals. The high in it comes from kind of a lack of oxygen. But in any case I ran around here hearing voices, seeing things, and just generally getting more and more run down, you know, constantly fighting it, so I did end up in the mental ward—the third floor they call it here, the ding ward, booby hatch.

My friends got me up there. Well, you know, for a good reason they were concerned about my welfare, so they kind of tricked me, got me up there, got me checked in. So I sort of twiddled my fingers and talked to myself up there with the rest of the nuts. I fit right in. You couldn't pick me out of that crowd, I'll tell ya. And so one day, luckily, it just sort of went away; I got slowly back in control.

My description of what was happening to me at the time was like . . . my mind was like a three-dimensional crossword puzzle and all the parts normally would be together, but in this case all the parts become disconnected so that, Christ, at any given time there was dozens of things going on at the same time in my mind. There was voices from without and images and voices from within. Hallucinations, bells, whispering, ghosts, everything at once all day. And at nighttime I was talking with the Grandfathers, the Elders. As I saw them, they were like elders; they were wisemen. They wore robes and I could see them and they were trying to help me. And I had been trying to talk to them, anyway, but I could see them, you know. And I had several terrifically vivid things happen to me.

One time a great big burst of sunlight came through the side of the cell block when I was laying on my bed. It looked like the walls of the cellblock exploded all of a sudden, and I sat up real quick on my bed and this great big eagle, big golden eagle—and he was shining like he was made out of gold—he flew in. He came in, just streaking in. He just hit me in the chest with both his feet and he took my heart out and flew away. I thought I was going to die, but I didn't. And it was kind of a moving experience, it was so vivid.

It was getting too heavy, those things [that] started happening to me, and at that time I was getting pretty serious into religious questions, you know, the meaning of life and what it was all about, and I spent many hours over here in the library reading, reading, reading, and ordering texts from the state libraries, like *The Church,* for instance, and *The Book of the Dead,* which scared me so. In the state of mind I was in I found it hard to read because, for some reason, it scared the hell out of me. There was pages that I refused to read, and there was pages I read; I mean entire pages that I read and it would be so profound and have so much meaning for me and seemed to include me, you know, like I was in the book, somehow. And I remember this specifically: one night I was reading. I read a page. I was reading further up in the book and if I closed my eyes and I concentrated real hard to try to ask the Grandfathers, the Elders, what I should do and this and that, well, they told me to turn to such and such a page. So I did, and I read that page and it seemed like it was talking about me, you know, and it scared me. It was a good forecast for me, and so I showed it to my partner and I told him some of the things it said and how it pointed out to me some of the truths, and he read it and he said, "I don't see anything like that here." So I took the book back and I looked at it and it was completely changed. None of the things that I read were on that page anymore. They were nowhere in the book. And so that's what I mean, that I thought that it was getting a little bit too heavy, the little mental breakup I said I had.

I should back up a bit here because it did start off from a lot of my digging into the psychic world. I've always been interested in psychic things, parapsychology and spiritualism. I feel close to it. Things have happened to me in my life that make me believe that I am a little closer to this other world and I'm fairly close to knowledge that isn't available to everybody if I have my mind in the right state and if I ask and make contact with the beings and entities that are there to offer us help. But I guess I just wasn't prepared for some of the truths that I seen, and using that stuff makes you . . . when you're sniffing—it's what you call it, sniffing—I'll tell you exactly what it does. It just puts your mind in a state of hypnosis. And that's why people talking to you and different sounds create suggestions, and your mind visualizes what you're saying and what the sound is. It'll create a picture to go with a specific sound, like a bell or something. I may hear a bell ringing and when I'm sniffing, just that fast, I'll see . . . I'll actually be there, just like I was transported somewhere. I may be all of a sudden walking out [of] the school, out the doorway of the school because of the sound of that bell, and this little trip may last ten seconds and something else will happen.

We [Indian prisoners] used to have a lot of fun doing that. We'd sniff until everybody's mind and face looked blank and we knew when we were ready. And then we'd take turns reading a story out of a book or something while the other three guys in the cell listened. And they listened with their eyes closed. And they'd be laughing and giggling, and all the time while I'd be reading the story they'd be visualizing three different things, three different stories. Their minds would make up the pictures as I went along, so when we understood how this worked more, we were able to play with it and kind of ad-lib. I think I'd make stories a lot more descriptive and funny, try to make them funny so they didn't know when you got scared. And we really looked forward to doing this.

That reminds me of something that happened once. I made me a knife one time to sell it. I figured it would probably bring me ten bucks and I really made it nice, a double-edged stiletto, real sharp on both sides. Then I cut out a wooden handle on it and wrapped the handle in leather. It was really nice. I made a sheath for it, and I'll be a dirty sonovabitch—I got busted! The pig ran into me on the tier. I was walking down the tier talking to some of my partners and they were all loaded in the house. They were getting down with the 201 (carbon tetrachloride) and I had a couple little snorts, of course. I was kind of acting like a fool on the tier; you know, rowdy and carrying on, and this pig waved to me to come up to the end of the tier. Wanted to shake me down. So I tell him, "Aw, fuck off." I just kept on talking, see. I didn't move.

My cell was right next door and I kept rapping and I had that shank in my belt. I'd been carrying it around like a dumdum, but we was having some tough times in here, so I started packing it for a while, but I should have known better. And so he kept hollering at me and finally this pig starts trotting down the tier and I says, "Oh, shit, the motherfucker's gonna try to roust me, man. He's gonna put the arm on me." So I took the knife out of my belt and I shoved it through the bars and these guys are all freaked out on the juice (carbon tet), old joy juice. We used to call it moon juice, too; it really sends you to the moon. I ain't bullshitting.

So the pig's trotting down the tier. He's got an eye on me and I tried to slide the shank into the cell and when it went in, nobody saw it. I did it so fast it just fell onto the floor in there . . . clank! And one of the guys freaked out and kicked it back out of the cell and the sonovabitch came and landed right back in between my legs! And here comes the cop. Oh shit, he caught me cold! So he run back down to the desk and he called the old goon squad over and, man, I'm trying to get my goddam head cleared up enough so I can come up with a fucking story real quick. And there wasn't too much of a story I could use. I mean, what can you say? A fucking shank. A shank's a shank and this one was monstrous.

So here comes the old gooners. They come on down, man, gaffled me up and put the cuffs on my hands. Away I went. Then they shook my house down and they found the knife's sheath laying right on my bed. Then they went to the back of my cell and found another tube of that goddam sniffer, that son of a gun. Whew! I thought I was in trouble. But as luck would have it, I put out a good story, man. I just had time to tell my partner what I was going to say so he could run around real quick and tell the other guys to back my play. I told 'em I had picked that knife up intentionally from some guys in the cell that were loaded and I talked 'em out of it 'cause we didn't want anyone getting hurt and in the process I got caught with it.

So people were screaming and hollering after I went to the hole. They went right over to Control, several guys, and they were screaming and hollering, putting the story down. I had told the same story when they took me in, so I was out the next morning. I was tagged but I was out. I got a reprimand and warning for a thirteen-inch shank, which was pretty phenomenal! But anyway, jeez, I never played that fucking game again. I stayed strictly away from those knives since I really don't want to use one. I mean, hell, why carry it? But I'm telling you, I wasn't slipping and sliding too cool that night. That time the pig slid up on me and got my ass.

So, to get back to what I was saying before, like I said, we had seances in this state of mind, when we was sniffing, which, of course, was just strictly hypnotic-type suggestions that we put on each other during these seances. We played with the ouija boards and things like that. And so you can see where that would take you, because you do need a certain amount of strength to withstand some of the forces that pull on you and affect you when you're dealing with the psychic world, the spiritual world, the world of the spirit. There is a lot of forces there, good and bad, you need to understand. You need to be able to pull your mind out of it if something is beginning to happen that you don't like. You need to be able to understand it immediately and not only explain it to yourself but to hold yourself back and break all contact with it. And that's not possible when you're in the state of mind that chemicals will put you in.

So, anyway, it was a pretty rough go. It was real tough in the mental hospital, the prison mental ward, mostly because I was afraid. I wasn't afraid of the people around me; I was afraid of insanity. I always have been afraid of insanity. I think I fear that more than death. Why? I really don't know. Maybe because of things I've seen. I just don't know. Can't put my finger on it, but there's something about it that really scares me. I think we could tie [that] back in with [the fact that] I'm afraid of anything and I'm uncomfortable and I don't enjoy anything that I can't control. That's why I don't like drugs that affect my mind. I don't. I absolutely won't bother with drugs that affect my mind, that I couldn't control. This sniffing, you can control. I mean it may not sound like it, but it's controllable up to a point, and some guys go on and do it for years and they don't suffer the same affects that I have. And I've done it since and this hasn't happened to me. But I also know better than to play those kind of games when I'm under the influence of that type of thing.

But I spent a couple of months on the mental ward. I cried, I hollered, I bitched, I screamed, and I was afraid. I was afraid of what was happening to me because I was rational enough to understand and see insanity for what it was. And I lost track of time, so that my first thought was that I had been up here for twenty years, or [that] I had just come up here, but I couldn't tell the difference. I asked, but I was afraid to ask what I thought. But eventually my system kind of flushed itself out and my nerves got better and I was able to start seeing things in the proper perspective a little better, and I worked myself out of there. I didn't need the help of the doctor or anything. I did see him once because of something that had to be done. That's his job, you know. He has to see you, he has to make a report, so I was on my best behavior when I did have an interview with him, because as crazy as I was, I knew I had to really get it up for him. Above all, it took all the strength I had to hold everything together, you know, just like holding a whole bunch of ropes together, holding all the ropes and not letting them get away. Well, that's what I had to do with the pieces of my mind, the fragments that were floating; I pulled them all together just long enough for the interview with the doctor so that I made a pretty good impression on him, so he put down, I guess, that I had a case of nerves, really.

Even when I was interviewing with him, my little faces and things were peeking out of his desk at me and voices were whispering smart-aleck answers to me, and I just ignored them all and put them back like they were little pets that were irritating me and I didn't want anybody to see them. I just pretended I didn't see them, pretended they weren't there. But when I got out of that office, boy, I just exploded! I was dingier than a shithouse mouse the rest of the day. Couple of months and I was out of there and I was back on the track.

Of course, during that time my friends, my brother and all of them, sent me notes, they sent me cigarettes, and they came up to visit me. And they reassured me, you know, and things like that. That really helped a lot. And my brother, of course, I'd hurt him. I'd scared him. Like I said, we're like identical twins. But it all came out good in the end, you know what I mean? Can't hold a good man down, Chiquita. So I come out of there as an outpatient and that was in 1965, I think, or '66; I think '66. I've been an outpatient ever since, one of the best.

I went to the forestry camp one time in here in 1966, after I came through the experience that I was telling you about with the bughouse thing. Once I got that cleared up I went to Waushal Honor Camp, which is about two, three hundred miles away from here. It's in western Washington. It's in the hills, beautiful country over there in Vancouver—east of Vancouver, west of Vancouver, I don't know. But anyway, it's twenty, thirty miles outside of there. And at the camps, they're a lot nicer. They're like logging camps, I guess, except the barracks. They're made for permanent residence. They used to have big dormitories where about seventy-nine guys slept in rows, beds on each side, no lockers, radios and things like that, where you work in the woods and have a lot of different crews going a lot of different ways each morning to work.

And I got out there away from the penitentiary, with the beautiful trees and the beautiful blue river that ran right by the camp, all the green grass, and if you can believe this, Chiquita, I'm telling you, there were deer. Four, five, six at a time would walk right up to the camp, on the grounds, and walk right up to you and eat out of your hands! The deer, I've never seen anything like that, and I was really flabbergasted the first time I seen it. The guy told me, "Here, offer them this. Just hold your hand out. Put this in your hand," a little piece of candy, hard candy, and man . . . 'course, I seen them coming across the highway. They jumped over the fence. There was about eight of them that time, fairly good sized deer. They walked right up to us, just walked right up. Christ! My idea . . . I didn't know if they was going to attack us, if they was going to bite me, if they had teeth, or what they were about, but I held my hand out with the candy in it. And this one lady deer, I mean doe deer, she walked right up and took the candy right out of my hand! But I never forgot that.

And then we had two, three little baby deer, little fawns, that we'd find when the crews were out working. They'd bring them back to camp if they'd find them abandoned or their mothers had got shot or something like that. And we'd raise them there at the camp. And somebody would be taking care of them like a pet dog, feeding them with a baby bottle. They like to run, boy! They'd just run and run and run and then they'd come back. And you know when you're sleeping and you wake up, there's a little baby deer licking your hand. They like to lick the salt off your hands. Or they're laying on your bed when you come back from work.

There's squirrels in the camp, pet squirrels, pet raccoons. It's really something else. Can you believe it, Chiquita, when I first went there I didn't like it? I was trying to come back here? I went in the office about two days after I'd been there and I requested transfer back to the penitentiary. I didn't like it when I first went there. I'd never been so goddam lonesome in my life 'cause it was so quiet. I felt like I was out on the Mojave Desert. Oh, for chrissake, that's where I am now! But I mean, being in here for so long got me so damned used to being in a crowded cell and just elbow to elbow with guys all day long in the dining hall—there's hundreds of guys in the dining hall, noise, noise all the time, you know—that when I got out to that forestry camp I thought it was the end of the world. I swear to God, I damned near cried, I was so lonely. I was homesick for in here! Jesus, that's unbelievable!

I told my partner, I says, "Listen, man, I can't handle it. I've got to get out of here. I'm a city boy. I ain't used to all this bullshit." I hadn't seen nothing yet, you see. You got to remember that I hadn't seen all those deer and stuff and the beautiful sky at nighttime with no smoke, no smog, because you're kind of up in the mountains. You're up four–five thousand feet. It's higher than the cities. But I wanted to go back. I said, "Oh man, I miss my brother. I miss my friends." I said, "I don't give a shit if it is the penitentiary, I want to go back anyway." I said, "If I can't go home, then the hell with it, I don't want to go halfway home." And to me, camp was just another penitentiary, and it was halfway home. Besides that, it was too goddam quiet and I couldn't see any possibility of any excitement. No riots, no fights or anything.

I promised my buddy—he said, "Do me a favor, man." You know, he wanted me out there too, because we was longtime friends. He was an Indian, the only Indian there. So he said, "Listen, do this. Give yourself two weeks, man. That's all I'm asking." He said, "If you still want to go back, to hell with it, I'll go back with you." So I said, "Okay, two weeks and not a day more and then I'm getting the hell out of this place." Shit, two weeks later they couldn't drag me out of there with a truck. I had adjusted. I got a fishing pole, I started fishing, I started seeing the animals. I opened my eyes and I started seeing things in the woods.

I think the Indian really came out in me then 'cause I loved it up there. God, it was so nice. Sure, it was still part of the prison system, but Christ, the pressure wasn't there. Eventually, after you'd be there quite a while, you're back to your smart-aleck ways. Then you start bitching about little tiny rules, things like that. But there's no comparison, for chrissake.

The night sky used to really knock me out. I used to go sit out on the stairs on the back porch of the dormitory, and I used to take coffee and go out there when it was dark and lean backwards and just stare at the sky for hours. I just couldn't get over it. The one thing that would make me kind of sad—and that's the night sky if it's real pretty and clear—I get homesick then because, you know, I think that proves to me that we're not from this earth, really. I think our home is way, way out there somewhere, miles out there in space. It's one of those twinkling stars is where we're from, you know, because mankind has always looked towards the stars. We have striven through history to get off the earth. A beautiful summer night looking toward the night sky gives us homesick feelings. We're animals, so we have to have migratory instincts and I think that's why we look to the sky. Mankind always looks to the sky; all our efforts are to the sky, to space, our curiosity, our feelings. We want to go home. I think if we went home we would be off the earth. Nothing seems natural to us down here. The earth kills us, you know; the gravity kills us. The elements kill us. Everything is tough for us. We have to build houses and we have to wear clothes. We can't breathe under water. We can't fly in the air and we can't run on the land like animals. And we haven't the strength—without guns, we couldn't survive—we don't have the strength and the cunning and the skill of the animals on earth. That's my own philosophy of it.

I compare . . . I keep making comparisons, you know. Man is an animal and I wonder why—Why are we so different? Did we give all this up in order to be a little more intelligent? Were we once able to run like a jaguar and have the strength of a lion at one time? Could we swim under water like the dolphins? Did we give all that up in favor of intelligence? I don't know. I don't think we're from the earth. I think that sometime in history that our ancestors came here, settled here, and they still study us, check on us. And we're going home, baby. We're going home. I don't know. Just a daydream, huh? I set my sights pretty high, don't I? It ain't that I don't love the earth. I love the Mother Earth, and I love the dumb old people in it, too, but . . . what the hell.

I want to tell you about the Indian guys in here. Reservation Indians are very quiet and don't mix with the population. They are slow to make friends and are drawn toward each other. These guys are defensive and generally uneducated, seldom reaching the eighth grade. Their beliefs clash with urban [Indian] values. One of the things they have in common is booze. Reservations are very isolated places. Some places have electricity, although some don't, but they do see TV. Their view of the world comes from TV, or the advice and stories from the old people. So it must be very confusing. Reservation Indians come in for violent crimes like murder. Seldom sophisticated crimes like paperhanging [forging checks] or armed robbery. Murder, committed either in a tavern or at a party while blind drunk, is the usual story. Their religious beliefs run from none to very traditional. Indian religion is kept quiet and is practiced almost at the drop of a hat. The ceremonies are not elaborate—a pipe, a drum, and eagle feathers are the tools. The medicine man is for special occasions.

Indians pray together more than just Sundays. Indians pray alone in their houses while holding the eagle feathers. They speak to the Grandfathers, the ancestors. They praise the Mother Earth. They honor the four spirits of the earth: wind, earth, sun, north for the land of the Snow People; the eagle, the four-leggeds, the winged people, the fish people, all the animal brothers and sisters. These beliefs are somewhat removed by the forced attempt at assimilation into the white culture that the urban Indian goes through. We [urban Indians] relearn our truths from the traditionals, but we do not live the way our religion teaches. The Indian path is one of beauty, not one of death and destruction.

The urban Indians are on that fast track and move too fast for our reservation brothers in the prison. The reservation Indian suffers more from the closeness of the prison. He does not accept the prison and resists the rules, just as all Indians have fought control and genocide by the white man in power. We learn from each other, but more often than not, we lead each other into the jaws of the monster.

The reservation Indian is so far removed from education that his learning ability is affected. It is a very hard chore for him to enter the completely white-oriented school in the prison and make any progress. When he tries to work in the prison industries or the vocational school, he will get into trouble because he will discover that there are chemicals that, when put on a rag and inhaled, will eliminate the pressures of the institution and the world. He will discover that he can see visions if he continues. The Indian believes that these visions are not only of the gods, but very often, since they are a product of the self-conscious, they will carry a man back to the plains, the buffalo, a war party, buckskins, and blue sky. So he is hooked.

The urban Indian also searches for these visions, so both groups are constantly in trouble with sniffing glue, as it is called. It is seldom glue, but that is what is always written on the tag. Both groups are very proud, or at least they try to be. Very sensitive and defensive as hell. The Indian is not very far removed from the violence of the old days, in my observation. It takes very little booze or chemical to eliminate what small bit of control there is.

Before I got out of here on that one long jolt, during that time I spent quite a bit of time in the hole. I hit the hole here probably a good half a dozen times for ten, twenty-day sentences for drinking and for sniffing, for just getting loaded. No fighting or nothing like that.

The hole here and at Monroe, they're the same thing, really. Physically they look alike, too. They're designed the same, styled the same. Apparently the same assholes built them. The cell in the hole is, oh, I don't know how big it is. I think it's five and a half steps long. It's about three and a half steps wide; that's how big it is. No, it ain't even five and a half steps long because they got it blocked off. There's one cell that's got a bunk in it with a mattress in it. It has a sink and a toilet in it and they're designed, built, as one unit. You kind of use it as a chair, too, and the sink is at the top where the old-time toilets at home would have the water tank. Well, these types, where the water tank would be, would be a sink, and it has push buttons for the water. And then the extreme outer part of the cell has a solid front. It's a wall and it has a door in it, a wood door, and it has a window on it. It's like a door with a window and it can be opened or it can be closed. When they close it, it's called "being put on blackout." They check the lights, shut the lights off in the cell, and then they close that outer window and no light gets in the cell. So you're in blackout, you know. If you're talking too loud or you give them a bad time about something, then that's how they get back at you. They put you on blackout for a few days. That's when I was down there and that was a few years ago. I don't know if things are the same or how they operate now; I don't know whether they put people on blackout now or not.

It's not all that up-to-date. It's still crummy, still fucked up; but inside the wood front of the cells you have a space, maybe two feet, and then you run into the solid bar front of the cell itself. It's damn near like a little chamber in there between. You come through two doors for you to get in a cell. Actually your cell has two doors. One door slides open and the other one has a key and it opens and swings out. Normally the cells . . . like out here . . . the bars are, oh, maybe four inches apart between bars, so there's enough [room] to put your hand through. You could put your fingers through and wiggle them around [in the hole], but you couldn't put your hand through the bars.

The last time, I was down there twenty days for being drunk. And it was a little different 'cause I was in M S B, in minimum custody. I worked in the kitchen. We had a party down there, made some pruno out of blueberries. We made twenty-five gallons. I think I must tell you what pruno is made out of: potatoes, old fruit (raisins, oranges, apples, grapes). It's just yeast and sugar, and you put it in a warm place and let it sit for three, four days, then you get her down and scrape the stuff off the top and you start drinking it. It's not bad; it'll get you drunk, does the job. Anyway, a bunch of us guys in the kitchen got plastered.

I was cooking out there at the time and we had the stash up over the grill, in a grease trap up in the grill. There's a big enough area up there to put a cooking pot in, so we put it up in cooking pots. Well, anyway, we got pretty rowdy. We started throwing food around and we got in fights, throwing flour and sugar around the kitchen. The guys in the bakery got drunk and they came out and attacked us with flour, so we started throwing grease, handfuls of lard, around at 'em and the goon squad came out and got us all and they chucked us into the hole. I was in the holding cell for a day and went to court and got twenty days and my partner got twenty days. I had about thirty days left before my parole, so actually it was a kind of a celebration, because I was celebrating getting out. And so this meant going back to the parole board for a disciplinary hearing and not getting out when I thought I was. As it happened, I got ninety days extra time. I got a ninety-day flop, as they call it, so it amounted to sixty days because somehow they counted that thirty days I had left into that ninety. My partner took the blame for making the stuff and he got six months flop, which didn't mean shit to him because he had two years anyway and he figured he'd work out of it.

When you go into the hole, one thing about the tier, A deck, if you tell somebody they got to do ten days on A deck, then that means you're going to do ten days in the hole. Some joints, they call it sleepy hollow or the growler. Here it's just the hole or A deck. It's a tier. All the cells are on one side. Then it's kind of creepy, really. It's so quiet down there, you know. So the first thing I always notice about it down there is how quiet it is. There's fifteen, twenty guys down there, but you don't hear any noise, see, and that's because they're considered quiet cells. Quiet cells in that no noise comes out of them, really, because of those fronts. They're designed to muffle the sound. So then when you're locked into one of the cells, it's really quiet. About the only thing you can hear is yourself, so you spend all your time talking to yourself any goddam time. It doesn't take long. I talk to myself anyway, so when I get down there it's just natural. I start right off with a conversation. You sing a lot and shit like that.

But when you go to court, well, it's all over in one building called Big Red, or the kangaroo court, or wherever they take you to where they give you five, ten, twenty days in the hole. They take you out there and they take you through five barred gates before you walk in your house in the hole. And you get down there and they give you a baggy old pair of coveralls to wear. They take your shoes and all your clothes away. You can't smoke in there. You could conceivably get a paper and pencil to write a letter. There isn't a guarantee it would be mailed but . . . they don't give you any mail while you're down there. You eat regular. They don't withhold the food [but] they knock off dessert; you get anything else, but you can't have cake or ice cream. You get enough to eat, not like eating nothing but fritters at Monroe.

But you go on into the cell, you take your old coveralls and shit . . . Bible, too . . . go in there and they slam the doors shut and you start doing that time. Immediately you mark off that day. You don't count that day and you don't count the last day that you're going to be in there because that last day you'll generally get out in the morning. So you start off counting eighteen days from the time you walk in the door, and that's the same way you count your time in the joint. If you get a lot of time, some guys don't bother to count the last six months because they figure they're that short; that's so close to being out, six months, that you might as well not even count that in prisons because people are doing so much time there. But six months is a long time in the county jails.

Soon as they slam the door, you get your eyes adjusted so that any bit of light that's in there is enough to read and stuff. There's a light on one wall. There's two ventilators. One takes the air out, the other takes the air in. That's about it [as to] what's in there. As a rule, one guy might try shouting around right away to try to find out who else is in there, but it's too goddam hard; you can't hear nobody. You sit in there and get your ears used to the silence and shit. Nobody talks much. It's such an effort to talk and hear each other by shouting because everything muffles the sound, so you have to scream forty times to understand what the other guy says. It's not exactly conducive to long conversation.

But there is a little trick [to doing time in the hole]. In between walking the floor, singing to yourself, you can do what I used to do. I used to take toilet paper, get it wet, and then make little balls out of it. And if I had a pencil, I'd draw a bull's-eye on the wall and I'd just start walking, and every time I walked—I'd do it the long way around—every time I went to one end of the cell, which is only four, five steps, I would deposit one little toilet paper ball on the bar, sitting on the crossbars, then walk back down.

I'd make another one, then I'd walk back over and I'd sit that one on the bar. I'd stack up about thirty–forty of them, then I'd stand out there and I'd throw 'em at the bull's-eye and they'd stick on the wall, you know, and just do the whole trip over and over again all day long!

One time I did ten days here in the hole for being in possession of carbon tet. I bought a little bottle of it for two–three packs of cigarettes, a little pint of it. So I'd be happy as hell, boy. I'd come sneaking back to my house, go in the back there, then I'd pull the curtain across, sit back there and turn the radio on and get the rag all set up and pour it onto the rag, sit there and start sniffing it, you know. You hold it right up to your mouth and you inhale so you take it right down. Man, you get loaded, whew! It really fucks your head up. But it seems like, especially when I was alone, it seems like I'd no more get started when the man would be here. He'd come walking by and if he asked me a question I was busted because I couldn't answer, I couldn't tell him my name, you know, so they'd take me to the hospital and they'd say, "This guy is loaded." I was fucked up.

Generally, by the time they walked you over to the hospital your head's cleared up a little bit. So it was good for ten days [in the hole]. Ten days on the shelf, as they call it. Well, I had that ten days once, you know. I did it. I hated it. Had me going crazy by the end of that ten days. I was pacing. I was so goddam nervous, wanted out of there, you know, that solitary shit. [By the] time you come out of there, it's like getting out and going home or something. It's a joy to come out here and come into the goddam wings and get back out here with the living again. It's like, just like being in a vault or some damn thing. I just will never get used to it. You could get used to it, say, if they just forced you to live down there. Some guys do. Guys have been down there for months and months. But it makes it nice to come out, I'll tell you that.

I did that ten days and got out. I got out in the morning, came staggering out into the goddam sunlight, holding my eyes and dying for a cigarette and a cup of coffee. And I came out of the wing and got into my house and the man says, "Hey, it's good to see you back," and all this bullshit. I say, "Yeah, that's cool." And I went down to the house and I wasn't in the house ten minutes and this dude comes trucking down the tier. He's a friend of mine. He comes trucking down the tier and he says, "Hey, man, you want to get down or what?" I says, "You goddam right." So he pulls on in and gives me a snort. He gives me another little bottle with carbon tet in it. He had about half a jug left he was going to stash with me. Same stuff, the old carbon tet. So, man, I went in the back of the cell, the same trip! The dirty sonovabitch! I no more than got started and here comes the goddam sergeant! Caught me cold. Got me! So away I went. I was back down in the goddam hole again.

I went to court the next day and got ten days more! I said, "Oh Lord," I said, "give me a break. Let me stay out a day or two at least." They said, "No. No way. Ten more fucking days." I said to myself, "Oh, God, I could do ten days, but you got to let me stay out a while." Two, three days and you get your head back in shape and get yourself psyched up, you know, then you can go down and do it, see. Christ, they put my ass back into the same cell again. God, I just had a feeling. I says, "No, I can't do it." Of course, I shoulda never said that either, you know. You can do that to yourself. You gotta, right off the bat, you gotta, immediately when you're caught, you gotta start working on it, you know? Removing yourself from the fact of what's happening. It's the same with pain. Getting your mind set up, knowing that's what you gotta do, gotta put up with, and then you can do it, no matter what they do. You have to tell yourself, "I can do it. It ain't shit. I can do it and it don't bother me a goddam bit." But I got a little weak, Chiquita. I was pretty disoriented anyway from the sniffing and so I wasn't functioning that good. I thought they were trying to kill me or drive me crazy and thought they might succeed this time. And so I was down there again.

Let me see, that was in the morning I went down. They give me the ten days in the morning and by one o'clock that afternoon I was out. Yeah. I kept telling the bull when he came down, I said, "Hey, you know me, I'm serious, man, serious business, man. I don't think I can do it." He says, "Aw, you can do it, ten days." I says, "Naw, I'm telling ya. I'm telling ya, I can't do it. You got to cut me some slack." I says, "I want to talk to the lieutenant. I want to talk to the sergeant. I want to talk to somebody." I says, "I got claustrophobia," which I do have a little touch of, but normally I've always been able to hold it down and not let it bug me that much. You have to [control it], you know. It don't bother you in a big cell because you can come and go. You go to chow, you do this and that. I know if I really need to, I can get out of the cell. So it's completely different. But down there, being in the hole, it kinda brings those things out in you and you lose it a little bit. So at noon they brought the chow around . . . well, even earlier than that. It started when I went into the cell and they closed the door. Already my nerves were starting to jump. I was starting to spin circles and shit and I thought they turned the air conditioning off. I kept standing up on the sink, checking the air conditioning. I couldn't hear any air. I couldn't feel any air, so I thought I was going to smother and I started sweating. I remember that, sweating and walking the floor and wondering what the hell I was going to do.

So I guess they must've took me serious and they notified some people on the mental health tier that they thought maybe I could use a little help, could use a little counseling or something. And so things just worked out right. Then I asked the man, I said, "Will you not close the outer door?" I told him, "My air vents don't work. At least just leave the outer door open." I told him, "I won't scream at nobody or nothing. Just give me a break and leave the door open for a little bit. I can't go anywhere, you know. My inner door is closed. The iron door is closed. At least I could peep out of the crack and feel the air coming in." He said, "Well, don't worry about it." He says, "I think they're going to take you out of here today." I said, "What?" He said, "Yeah, we're going to feed you lunch now. You go ahead and eat and the sergeant's going to be down to talk to you and I don't think you're going to be in here too long."

Oh boy! Those were good words to me. Sure enough, about an hour later the sergeant came down with another cop and they opened my door, said, "Come on out." And I says, "Damn, you letting me out early?" They says, "Yeah." He says, "You got a break this time." He says, "We're going to try something different with you. We're going to give you up. We're going to send you over to the self-recovery tier, mental health tier, and see what they can do with you." I said, "That sounds good to me. Let me go. Shit, I fit right in with those nuts." So I stayed real serious until I got over there, then I cut loose. Boy, I was so happy to be out of that fucking hole. Whew! I didn't care where they put me, just so it wasn't in a goddam cell like that.

I said I was going to tell you about the mental health unit. They had this tier over there called self-recovery. It holds about twenty people, single cells. They used to take the least violent of the nuts, the ones that were able to at least feed themselves and wander around and not get into too much trouble on the tier—because they didn't let you go out here in the population—and they used to put them on that tier and they called it self-recovery. And the infamous Dr. Bunker, he used to run that program in conjunction with the third-floor program he had going. The third floor would be in the other nuthouse, of course, or main number-one booby hatch. So he had both programs. And we had some psychiatric nurses down there supposedly, and we had some ladies from somebody's auxiliary or something from the town, Christian ladies. They seemed to enjoy coming up once or twice a week and teaching us how to make plastic grapes, plastic apples, plastic bananas, show you how to paint by numbers.

Oh, the little old ladies, I love them! They had more tricks for a fella, I'm telling ya. They were all right, though, Chiquita. They were doing what they could do, you know, but they were kind of funny. They were kind of funny to a lot of us. Here we are, you know, [an] old bunch of rowdy hoodlums and shit like that, and the ladies got us all sitting around a big table finger painting! And [we] got clay in our hair and plastic all over everything. They had us making some of the goddamnedest projects, I swear to God! Aw shit! A little therapy, you know what I mean? At that time I couldn't even paint. I'm a helluva good painter and a drawer, you know, a fair artist [now], but I'll be goddam if I could paint anything then, not even by the numbers. But they worked with us, and [had] group therapy where we all sat in circles. And I wish I had had a tape recorder for some of the conversations. I'm telling you, you get ten–twenty nuts sitting in a circle trying to have a conversation and you really got something out of the ordinary, I'll tell you. And they usually would have some young sweetheart from one of the universities around here kind of stirring the whole thing. Half the people would be in love with her, or whatever, you know.

I'll tell you the big trick they had. They kept everybody on Thorazine, see. They give you Thorazine three, four times a day, and that was guaranteed to keep everybody quiet, in line and just kinda shuffling around like zombies, you know. I took my share of the Thorazine, then after a week or so I started hiding it because I couldn't handle it anymore. When you take Thorazine, well, you can't even think. I had a visit one day and I had just taken my medication. Oh, my God, that was a terrible visit! My mind was just completely blank all day. Every time Linda would ask me a question, I'd have to mull it over a little bit and she'd have to repeat it over two or three times to get through to me, so that was the end of that. I never took any more. So I was on the sneak. I'd hold it in my mouth until I turned around and got out of sight, then I would spit it out. Generally I would give my Thorazine to some guy who I thought really needed it, some guy I thought needed a double dose. I made sure to give him mine to go along with his 'cause we did have some pretty rowdy sonovabitches. That was one way to keep 'em calm. They thought they were getting big dope so they'd take it, you know, and that put 'em out for the count, boy.

I was down there for a couple of months. I mean it wasn't no big thing. I didn't mind it down there. Some of the guys even tried to get down there; it was kind of a neat place to live. Hell, it was one of the few places in this joint where you could have a cell all to yourself, and they used to let me leave there and go up to the Indian club just about anytime I wanted to go up there. And my brother, he'd come. He'd stop down there every day, see what was shaking, and we'd bullshit and he'd bring me some cigarettes. I was doing all right, you know; took advantage of the situation and I finally left. I didn't go home from there, but I stayed there until I kind of got my head straight. I did kind of cure that sniffing down there a little bit. Those chemicals started working out of my system. I wasn't quite as disoriented. I was able to pull all the pieces back together and get back on the old track, you know. I mean, some things are pretty tough on your mind. It's the chemicals that are strong. They will build up and blow you apart like a firecracker. It's nothing permanent. I'm not feeling any ill ef-

fects from it these days. I feel pretty together. But I did do that for years off
and on and off and on.

I'd really like to be a social drinker. I can't say that I've ever really tried,
you know. When I do things, I usually do it with a purpose, so when I'm
out [of prison] I decide, "Well, I'm going to drink," and so I drink—seven
days a week. I'd be able to function. I'd drive around and I'd do this and
do that. I'm not drunk drunk, but I'm always sipping on the old jug of that
old pink Chablis, you know. You'd think I was the biggest wino in town,
but it's not that bad. I kind of use that bottle as a friend. In times like that
and I'm by myself, I'm not too interested in running around with anybody
all day because there's always conflicts about which way to go, which way
to turn the car, how long to stay at a certain place, and drive by the school
and see Joe Blow, and I don't want that. So I just completely eliminated
that problem by going everywhere by myself, and then if I don't feel like
going anywhere in particular, which is the case nine times out of ten, all I
do is fill the old tank up with gas and I'm off to the races. And I'll stop everywhere: different friends' houses, my family, my ex-wife, go see my kid,
maybe eat supper there, maybe spend the evening. I might even babysit so
she can go out, which is all right with me because it gives me time to play
with the kids. There are two kids, only one of which is mine. But I enjoy
both the kids. A little boy named Denny Delorme. He has my name though
he's not truly my boy. I still enjoy him and I don't mind doing that. That's
all I do. I do go around in circles. If people don't see me for a couple of
days, they know something's wrong, because it gets to be a real routine,
stopping everywhere. That's about what I always end up doing, drinking
and driving. It's sick. I'm tired of it. I'm tired of it when I'm doing it!

I don't work very much. The last two times I've been out on parole, I
haven't worked a lick. I just didn't get in anything, you know. Last time
I had a good job, too, damn it, and I never went back to it. Too bad. I
should have and I wouldn't have come back to the joint. I know that's
true. I started running around with some real crazy people. I don't know
why I kept showing up there every day, and pretty soon I was right into
what they were doing, just constantly ripping off people every day, and I
just thought, "Aw, what the hell." Fell on back into that and just did that.

I did go fishing for a while. Made some dough. But that isn't a steady sort of thing. You can make money at it, but it's a hassle, a real hassle. You get a little tired of freezing your ass off in that river, too. It's not like you got some fancy boat and you can sit in it and get warm while the fish are jumping into your net. Most of the Indians in the Tacoma area have to get out in that river and fish. They're in small boats with an outboard motor. It's outboard everything. You let the net out by hand and you pull it in by hand and in this process you freeze your ass off. The fishing season doesn't seem to run in the summer. It has to always run up around November. Sometimes September, November. It's colder than . . . Goddam, it's colder than an Eskimo's butt. Doesn't run all year long, either, so it's not something that you do constantly. You just do it while you can do it, while the fish are running, salmon. You can't really make a living doing that. You make extra money is what you do.

I got out in '68 and I stayed out a couple years. I got married during that time. I drank for a while at first, about the first month I was out. I went on a drinking binge with this girl who I eventually married, little skinny blonde. She was a cutie-pie. And we just didn't make it, you know. Originally when I first met my wife, we just were drinking partners. She was nineteen and in a funny state of mind, I guess, 'cause we were off into the booze. Then I got her off in a dope trip and so we kind of had mutual interests, and it was just that she was there all the time with me, you know, so I married her. But it didn't work out as a marriage because I wasn't prepared to quit drinking. I wasn't prepared to settle down.

I didn't get involved with any dope right away but I did go on a helluva drinking binge. Then I went to work at a work-training project, a studio in Tacoma, photo studio. That's where I learned photography. And I trained for six months down there. And then worked for another six months as a photographer and lab technician. Worked a lot in the dark rooms.

I met a lady there. I ended up living with her, even after I got married. Not generally a faithful old chap, Chiquita, you know what I mean? But that's the way it goes, I guess, when I was a little restless. And I married the girl I had been going with for several months because she got pregnant. That's pretty much why I married her.

But this Linda, she was the older woman that I worked with and she had a few material things and she was pretty smart. She was pretty. She was older than me, several years, but we got along real great. [She] had a hell of an understanding 'cause she accepted me better than anybody ever did, pretty much, for what I was, and I really explained who I was and what I'd been up to and how my life had been. And she expressed an awful lot of faith in me, confidence, wanted to help, you know. I wouldn't call her a do-gooder or anything. First, I think she just felt sorry and then we had a lot of fun together and we enjoyed each other's company a lot. To me, she was pretty, and she had class. She was something that should not have been obtainable for me, but I got her. So it was sort of a weird thing I did. She appealed to me an awful lot sexually, too, awful lot. So we got along good. And she had been kind of lonely, owned her own home, car, and everything, and so it was pretty hard to break us up. That was in '68 and she's still considered, probably, the main woman in my life right now [1978]. When I get out of here, I can't say what it'll be like, but I know it has to change, [become] more platonic than anything else. I think it is that way now. But we'll see, you know what I mean?

Linda is fifty-one years old and her and I been getting it on since 1969. It's been a headache and a blessing at times, but I love women. I've got nothing against women and I'm still kind of a chauvinist, or whatever you want to call it. It doesn't bother me, because women like that in a man. I don't care for them attitudes of so-called modern women. If I had one, I don't know what the hell I'd do with her. Absolutely nothing, I guess. I don't like bossy people. But yeah, I met her in 1969 when I got out of here. She was sort of a sponsor. We did have a sponsor program out here. They call it One-to-One and they usually line you up with a business person. That business person has joined the One-to-One program [and] agrees to sponsor one convict and try to give him a hand out there and try to help him find a job. And Linda, she was married and she had two older boys. Actually, they were younger than me. I'm not that much older than them. She's fifty-one and I'm thirty-eight, pushing thirty-nine, Jack

Benny's age. But age don't bother me, not a bit, really. I'm very well adjusted, you know, very well adjusted. Ha!

When I came out in 1968, I had an interest in photography. At that time I was considered a pretty good artist in here and I was making a little extra money by doing portraits of guys' wives—doing a portrait of them for guys to send to their wives. I did most all of them in charcoal, in black and white. But anyway, during this period when I was doing these pictures, I just got interested in photography because I was doing so many pictures, drawing large pictures from people's photographs they'd give me. In art you start paying attention to the way light falls on things and looking at photographs. I particularly was interested in lighting because the majority of the photographs that I got were just snapshots from home, you know, and generally they were horrible and the shadows fell on them, fell crisscross and made them look like they were vampires beside the coffin, with big black shadows under their eyes and things like that. So I got interested in that.

So what I did with this interest in photography, well, I asked questions. I studied books and I checked out more and more books and I read photography magazines and I thought about it, and so when I was ready for parole in 1968 I decided, "Well, that's for me. Photography or nothing for me. I'm gonna be a photographer." So I got out and went back to Tacoma and I went to the Department of Vocational Rehabilitation, the DVR guy—and they're not here anymore, but they used to be, and they'd help you when you'd get out. You'd go to town and they'd help you find a place to train or they'd get you in school and they'd provide money and clothing, and once you finished, they would buy your tools, you know, to put you on the job.

So anyway, this Mr. Hannery, he was my caseworker with DVR in Tacoma. We talked a lot and I said that what I'd like to do was work at a studio and learn, do on-the-job training, all about photography. So I kicked down a few doors, you know. I went to studios in Tacoma and I laid my proposal out to them. They weren't too interested in it. Then I started discovering that they really don't have the time or the money or the facilities to have a person in there to train anybody, you know. They just don't have the time or the personnel to teach you. They're not equipped to be a teaching facility. And it's true that they really can't afford to hire somebody for that position. So when I run into that, I pretty much gave up that idea and [started] trying to figure out how else I could break into the field. But actually, after one turn through the studios I started drinking. I was ready to give up on it. That was really what I was ready to do. I don't know what I thought. I thought, well, they'll just throw the doors open to me because I wanted to learn, but it didn't happen that way, so I was pretty well discouraged and said, "The hell with it." But in the meantime, I told them at the time that I tried and couldn't make it. So he [Mr. Hannery] did some investigating himself and he did a little door pounding and finally one day he said, "Go down to Mardy Studio."—a portrait studio where they do all the portraits, they do senior pictures, they work under contract with dozens of high schools to do their school pictures. They do the yearbooks. And it's one of the largest studios in Tacoma and they employ maybe ten or eleven people at peak times. And they had two photographers, including Mr. Lytle. He did a lot of in-studio photography and he also ran around drumming up business. So he agreed with Mr. Hannery to take me and they told Mr. Lytle they'd pay him back whatever he paid me for six months and then he could either hire me or give me a recommendation and I could go elsewhere.

So that's where I was. I got into that and I backed off the drinking, and I really hadn't got started much. I headed on down, man, just as happy as a lark. My first real job doing something that I wanted to do.

So then I started off just kind of standing around. You know how you start off. Oh shit, I did a little bit of everything. I cleaned water spots on the floor. I guess mostly I stood around. Oh, I moved boxes around for the girls. I did things like that, and sorted picture frames, glass, different kinds of frames, you know, them expensive picture frames that studios sell. Well, we had all of those and I was always getting that stuff in order and delivering things, processing, and asking questions, and I really got off on the job. I liked that job. It was always something interesting to me, so they pretty much had to make me go home at night. I stayed longer than I should have.

I didn't get to touch a camera for a long time, but he [Mr. Lytle] let me borrow one that the studio owned, a Shika D, which is a professional-type camera, and he let me take that home with me. And I had all the free film I needed, so I snapped, snapped, snapped. Everywhere I went I was taking somebody's picture, figuring I could make my pictures at the studio after hours. So I was having just one helluva good time at learning. Well, I had a knack for that, you know. I had an eye for arty situations and compositions. It was good for me right from the start so far as camera work goes. And I didn't do too bad in the darkroom printing pictures, either, 'cause I had an idea of what I liked, contrast and things like that. I had a beautiful hand for making people look good that may not look too hot.

And Linda had worked there quite a while. Previous to that she had owned a studio of her own in the Lincoln Heights area in Tacoma, and it was a pretty nice place, too. And she was a good photographer and was one of the . . . probably one of the best retouch workers in the Northwest. And I started hanging around her because I was interested in what she was doing. Of course, I wasn't particularly interested in her, because she was older than me and she was completely unapproachable, [or] so I thought. And being several years older than me, not just a couple, I had no idea of doing anything or trying anything because . . . I wasn't thinking about it at the time, but I always was attracted to women like that. I didn't like the younger girls. I never could get along with them. But just the way she dressed, you know, and carried herself, and she has some intelligent conversation. Anyway, I was really, really physically attracted to this woman and I didn't know that the feeling was mutual, of course. I had no idea. But because she was married and everything, and like I said, to me it was just something I just kind of daydreamed about, you know, and imagined different good juicy situations that I would get her in and all that stuff. But I never made a move. I just used to sit there and watch her work on her retouch machine and, of course, I sat a little closer each time as we got more acquainted.

She's a real classy woman, real classy, and pretty shy around me, actually. I mean she was secure in her own right, but even so, she acted real nervous around me, kind of giggly, which surprised me. Some of them other ladies, too, I guess they knew that . . . well, Linda was acting a little giddy for her usual self, I guess. Then one day, I was laughing and joking. I got along great with the women. I didn't get along worth a shit with the guys. That's the way it always is, you know. I was always telling them [the women] they ought to ask for more money and that they deserved more money and that they should get equal pay and all that bullshit. Which is true, you know, and so I actually . . . I got a bad reputation with the guys for talking up for the women all the time and causing friction, as they said. But one day the bookkeeper and Linda was working. Linda was working at her desk and her and the bookkeeper was laughing and joking about some damn thing, and I walked up to them and I kind of winked at her and walked on by for some reason, and she says to the bookkeeper, "Betty, boy, I wish I was fifteen years younger." And I told her, "You don't have to be fifteen years younger." And I guess it kind of lighted the torch or something; I don't know.

After that we got pretty tight. I asked her out to lunch one day. It was embarrassing, but I took her in her big Buick Electra to McDonald's and I got her a hamburger. That was a class act. Jesus Christ, I don't know about that other shit, you know. I didn't have no dough, but that was good because that was the only time I ever had to ask her to lunch, 'cause after that she bought my lunch every day. We had a grand time. Boy, we'd go to fancy restaurants for twenty-dollar, thirty-dollar lunches, for chrissake. We'd take an hour. Pretty soon we'd start taking two hours. Goddam! And the boss, he got mad about it, but when he threatened me, boy, she'd be there in a minute, man, right by my side defending me, and sometimes embarrassing me, and, you know, threatened to quit herself if he fired me and all that bullshit and . . . but even then there was no . . . there was nothing physical between us. I mean we hadn't done anything. I guess probably we both thought about it and both the same way, too, because I don't think she . . . she didn't have the nerve to do that sort of thing, especially with some fella that was younger, and it just was completely out of character for her. But she was enjoying it and she was starting to smile more.

And we went to museums together and we went for walks and she showed me so many things and told me so much stuff that I didn't know,

and gave me so goddam much encouragement, and I finally told my story
one day to her 'cause none of the women knew. As far as I know, they
didn't know who I was really, or what I was about or where I was from.
But Linda, it didn't bother her. I did seem different to her, I guess, than
most people. She was curious about where I come from or where I did get
such attitudes that I had about things. She couldn't understand some of
the attitudes that I had and some of the things I did and said. And even my
slowness, I guess, in the romance department. I was pretty unsure of myself. And she's got a lot of insight and she picked up on this stuff until I felt
backed in a corner in trying to talk, have a serious talk with her. And I really trusted her and I just kind of came out one day and I told her about my
background and laid it out on the table for however she wanted to take it,
take it and do what she wanted to do with it. 'Course, she chose to stick by
me all the more, which surprised me, too, you know. People always sur-
prise me. I expected her to not really care to associate with me, and instead
it just turned out the opposite.

And so anyway, we had real good times and of course she was having a
terrible time at home with her husband, who was a real asshole. In my
talks with her, my advice to her was that she . . . with my irresponsible attitude and my outlook on life I told her that I couldn't see why she would
put up with it, because she didn't have to put up with it. The kids were old
enough now; they're pretty much on their own. "You don't have to be sad
all the time. You don't have to put up with that shit all the time, you know.
You're a good woman. You haven't got any of that bullshit coming that he
gives you." And I just kind of encouraged her to file for divorce and move
out, which, surprisingly, she did. My God, I couldn't believe it, but she
did. And I guess that I indicated that, or hinted that, her and I would see
more of each other in a different way if she was living by herself and didn't
have to answer to anybody or sneak home or sneak out to visit me or see
me or whatever, which she was beginning to do. And it went from there,
you see.

She got an apartment. I helped her find a nice apartment. Of course,
she moved from the west side of Tacoma over to my side of town, you
know, lower east side and all that bullshit, and got a nice apartment. And

so we did it, you know. We just kind of sealed the match right there. And we got along so good.

I put her through so much, so much bullshit. God almighty, it's been . . . like I said, she's still hanging in there and it's been since 1969. She's seen me steadily go downhill and she loved me, you know, she loved me so much, and I caused her an awful lot of grief, awful lot of grief. Damn it! But that's just the way it was.

I talked to you about Linda and completely forgot about Marie. She was in there, too, and my baby, because they [Linda and Marie] ran at the same time, if you can figure that one out. They were both aware of each other even though I was with Linda and we was pretty involved both emotionally and sexually in 1969. I got married in '69. I married Marie. I had been going with her when I met Linda. Marie was nineteen when I met her. During that time a baby daughter was born. Her name is Gina. I wanted to call her Adrianne, but my mother-in-law and my wife got together and named the baby and kind of shut me out. But they did call her Gina Marie. So they ended up naming her after me and my wife.

It was a pretty involved situation there because Marie was aware of Linda and the strength that Linda had as far as a hold on me. And Marie was a cute little blonde and she was pretty insecure, awful dependent on me to guide her life, I suppose, to just take care of her. And I was willing to do that and she needed me. I needed Linda. So you see what we had there, and I wasn't willing to let either go. And so I worked it out so I didn't have to let either go. And I moved back and forth during all this time. And I didn't play one against the other or anything like that. I just tried to make them understand that I did love them both somehow. They accepted it at that time and probably just waited for me to make a decision or something, because they didn't dislike each other simply because I wouldn't put up with any backstabbing on either side of the fence there. So I didn't like to hear anything about the other, because I thought they were both good women and they both had that respect coming and there was no reason to fight or anything else. And if they're . . . well . . . that's hard to explain, because you don't plan those things. I hope you understand that.

I don't plan these things. Just so happens that you may be in love with one person and it's not impossible to meet and fall in love with another person. The normal, responsible thing to do—I never was a normal, responsible person, you understand—so the normal thing to do is to ignore these feelings or never let them get started in the first place. When you are responsible for one person, you devote yourself and declare your love for that one woman; then it is my duty to not allow myself to become involved somewhere else. But I haven't been able to do that. And I still do that, and goddam it, I just can't help it, you know. I just think I've got enough love to go around because I can't help it. If you meet another person and the right person, and you spend a lot of time getting to know them, and then it's possible, for chrissake, and there's no reason . . . oh, I suppose there is a reason. There's social reasons and shit.

The only thing I really like about the good old days is that Indians had more than one wife and I like that idea, you know. I love that idea, but it just doesn't . . . nobody agrees with me, goddam it! Nobody agrees with me. I'd like them to all live together and be happy, but for some reason they just won't do it. Pisses me off! Yeah, because you're forced to . . . you hate to have to make decisions and you know I got business I have to take care of at Linda's and there are things that I have to do, then I have to be home. Then I have to go back with Marie and look after things and check on her and stay home for a couple days, and then I'd leave again and I'd go back to Linda's. And she's sad and I stay there a couple days and we do some work or whatever and make up for lost time, and then I go home and . . . see what I mean? It went on for months and months and finally Marie and I separated. And, of course, it was over Linda, and oddly enough, now they're both getting along great, and why the hell they couldn't do that when I was out [of prison], I don't know.

Anyway, I left the studio after I worked there a year. He let me go. He told me, of course, it was because it was slow. I was aware that it was and that he couldn't use three photographers, but by then I was demanding a job as photographer because I was starting to do the actual camera work, so I wanted a little bit more than he was paying me, which was a buck and a quarter an hour. That's all he was paying me, and the other guys was getting six, seven hundred dollars a month. And I noticed I was doing a hell of a lot more work than they were doing, you know. And I guess there's people that just naturally take advantage of that type of situation, and they knew that I didn't really have any other choice. And so I started asking him for a couple dollars an hour instead. And he decided that he couldn't use me any longer. I was doing almost all the film processing also at the same time, so I mean I was doing a lot of the work, you know what I mean? I was more than worth my money. And by then, of course, the women there knew me and were encouraging me to quit and go some- place better because I was worth more money and this and that, and that he'd never give me any money. And it all turned out to be true. So he let me go. And I was creating dissension among the married women, he said, which was a lie. There was only one that I created any trouble with. Of course, them guys kind of had an eye on her, too, but they never scored. They didn't have charm, you understand, and the rugged good looks of this Indian boy.

But so we're still together and her and I went into business together all of '71 and '72. Her and I went into business as a man and woman photog- raphy team. Commercials, weddings, schools, whatever, and we adver- tised and had business cards. I still got a couple old cards laying around the house some damn where. She, of course, had a lot of contacts, so I mean, I had an in right there and . . . oh, I forgot to tell you, too, Chi- quita: In 1970 I won two photo contests [in] what is called national news- paper awards. I won two awards from them in 1970 for black and white photos and I kind of used that, too, to build myself up a little bit. And it built me up, too, because it was my first attempt at competition with peo- ple, and out of eight photographs that I submitted, two of them won prizes, second and third prize. I didn't get a first prize but I got second and third. And a color portrait I took of Linda could have won, but I didn't send it in because I didn't want any color pictures. But it was a beautiful picture that I took out at the park, a natural outdoor setting.

So anyway, I was good with a camera. I'd still be good with a camera, but I've been out of it for quite a while. Of course, when I get out I intend to get a camera. I've had some beautiful ones and blew them. Traded them for dope, and you know, it's depressing for me to even think about some of the things I did to get dope.

I got sent back to the joint for a short period in '72, during that time when me and my wife were separated. When I got out of Shelton, where I was for thirty days, I went back to her. We didn't stay together too long, about three months, I guess, and I split. Said, "The hell with it," and I packed up and I left. Well, actually, she had caught me with Linda, so I couldn't explain it. She knew what was going on, because she was always aware of Linda, even before we were married. She had decided that she couldn't compete and said I should come back when I got ready to settle down. No telling when that would have been, and I agreed to it. When I got out of Shelton I went back to my old lady, and then we had that hassle with Linda and I got caught, not in the act, but I got caught in the act of getting into her car, when I was using my typical excuse to get out of the house. I'd say I was going into town to see my parole officer, while Linda was the one I was going to see. Half the time I'd spend the night with her, or I'd spend a couple days with her, and I'd come home and not give any excuses or anything. Aw, to hell with it, so I just moved, you know; I went with Linda. Me and my wife separated on kind of a sour note then, but it didn't last. I mean I loved her. I wasn't mad at her. I was just hoping she wouldn't hate me and she never did. I did everything I could to stay real good friends with my wife. I took care of her as best I could, even from a distance, even though we separated. I checked on her and I didn't interfere with her life if she wanted to start something new. Of course, I felt guilty, obligated to do what I could do. So that's how that went. That was in '72.

I had a lot of trouble with a parole officer out there, the guy that originally sent me back to the joint. He hated my guts. He was doing things to try to get me in trouble constantly, which he finally did, but he got faked out: they let me go, decided I wasn't guilty. He charged me with eight different violations, and I paid $150 and took a polygraph test the time they violated me and tried to send me back to the joint here. They found me not guilty on seven of 'em [violations]. I pleaded guilty to one count, so I faked him out and I got out of Shelton.

I was back on the road in nothing flat, but I was going downhill then. I was getting off in the dope bag then. When I got out of Shelton that last time I just kind of went whole hog, and so it wasn't just a matter of a couple of months, a few months, and I was a full-blown addict again. So all I did was hustle for a fix every day, man. Take care of biz. I did get half the money [for the fix] from Linda every day. She was working and I was just kind of kicking around all the time, here and there, looking for something, a score, and I picked a couple partners I had run around with. We was steady scoring, you know, burglaries and small-time shit here 'n there, boosting [shoplifting] and whatever. Take off a drugstore once in a while. Everything was just geared to score dope. That was a nonstop job every day. Cost us at least $100, $150 every day of the week. I often wish that I could get that kind of motivation going to do something legal, because if I could find something else to motivate me just staying free to work that hard, well, Jesus Christ, man, the sky's the limit! It just doesn't seem to work that way, though. There's nothing, *nothing,* motivates you more than needing a shot of dope. And you go to any lengths, really. You crash through windows, just take outrageous goddam chances to grab something. And when you get desperate and the end of the day is coming and you see you've got to hit, then if you haven't got enough during the day to cop, you know, to get the stuff, that's when you start doing dumb things. You get a little desperate.

The years I was involved with drugs, God, I hate it so much! Jesus, when I think about it I start hating myself and that's the feelings that I don't like, and I think you understand that, don't you, Chiquita? Those years that I hustled and scuffled to get that heroin and blow that shit off in my arm and just stay in the state of . . . I don't know what you call it, but the pain I caused people around me and times that I was near death, and trips to the hospital in an ambulance from OD's and, God, I hate it! It's terrible, just terrible! But that's the way I think. I don't like to think about things like that. There is nothing good about it that I can ever think of. Yet I hear guys like Duane and them talking about the good times! I was doing it, but I never really wanted to do it. That's the difference between us: I never really wanted to do it! I just . . . I shot that dope out of this frustration because I just couldn't seem to hold the line or have enough self-discipline. I didn't have any self-confidence. I just really didn't feel that I could get up the next day and do a job. I felt lacking in so goddamn many departments, especially education and self-confidence and just social competence. I didn't have any of that. And I still don't have that, you know.

I've got a lot more self-confidence, yeah, but it hasn't been tested, see. This is going to be tough for me. It's not going to be easy because . . . [it's] like building something and you know you never get a chance to test it. You just keep building it and working on it until you think you've got it perfected and then you take it out on the street or the field and start 'er up and see how it works, and it might go crazy and it might work. That's the way I really feel about myself now and I don't know what could be done about that. I believe in God and I have to try to have faith and ask for strength and I ask for wisdom to accomplish these things, the strength to keep going and the wisdom to learn about myself and learn why, some of the whys for these things.

Anyway, I moved into some armed robbery. Originally the first armed robbery I ever pulled was on a drugstore in Tacoma on Christmas Eve. I think it was '72, yeah, about seven o'clock. I don't know what the hell the joint was open for, but they were. But I walked in and took 'em off. Then they closed up after that. I closed them for Christmas, anyway. I got eight hundred dollars [and] about half a box of class A dope, you know. Go in and tell the guy, "Just give me all your class A dope." That's morphine and Demerol and opium, liquid opium, things like that. That doesn't include speed pills and downers. Shit, that's class B junk. Take that once in a while, too, but not in no robbery. Most [of] them druggists keep their class A shit hid, anyway. They stash it nowadays. They've been ripped off so many times they take it and stuff it away somewhere. This dummy had his shit hid somewhere in a box. I sent him crawling around on his hands and knees, old guy about seventy years old. I really enjoyed it, scaring the shit out of the bastard, because I didn't like him, anyway. He'd shot a partner of mine a couple years before. That was in a robbery, so I wasn't about to have any mercy on the dog. I didn't care about him one way or another. But there's people like that. The sonovabitch would have blowed me away, too, if he'd had a chance. I watch for that and that's the most shaky part of a robbery, somebody walking in trying to stop it, or a goddam store owner or somebody plugging you, man, so you got to watch them like a hawk.

I went through a couple of months playing with a gun. Did a little shooting for a while there, but I didn't like it. I didn't really like to threaten the people, taking that much of a chance on killing somebody. You're always on the verge, you know; it could happen by accident. And a lot of times it does happen by accident.

What finally made me retire, hang up the old shooting iron, was an incident in Seattle at a drugstore. I went in and I put one of those silencers on it and drew down on this girl in Seattle. And I had a .44 Magnum, which is a real heavy pistol, and it had a nine-inch barrel on it. It was real awkward, a clumsy gun for a pistol. And I'm whipping that damned thing around, and anyway, there was no neat thrill at all in taking them off. She was trying to help the best she could and I had the pistol cocked, which I don't normally, but when I jerked it out of the damned bag I cocked the damned thing and was holding it level with her stomach. It was wavering back and forth. But there was a customer in the store that I didn't see, down behind the counters. Well, it was a young girl. She was a teenager. She came whipping around one of those aisles and I turned real fast, you know. It made me jump; [I was] nervous as hell any goddam way, and I was kind of dingy from needing some dope. Goddam, then I pulled the trigger and, sonovabitch, I blew cigarette packs all over the damned place, candy and shit. But, man, that girl was so lucky! I was so goddam lucky because the gun wavered from pointing at her and shot beside her. But Jesus Christ, the thing would have tore her in half. So I says, "Well, that's it for me." I got what I was after. I got the dope and stuff, but when I got home, that was the end of that game. I said, "No more. Never." I broke that gun in a million pieces, for chrissake, spread it all over the county. Never picked up another one.

I was in several robberies. We hit a cocktail lounge and we hit a big restaurant in Seattle. These were worse because I did it by myself, with my partner waiting out in the car. And, man, he managed to drive off and leave me alone when the heat came a couple times. And I got away both times. I've never been caught for an armed robbery. I've always been caught for burglaries and things. That was a pretty terrible experience, pretty clumsy, somewhat funny.

This one big restaurant in Seattle, I don't remember the name of the damned place, but there was supposed to be a big doings there. See, my partner set it up. He said, "Man, there's seventeen thousand, eighteen thousand dollars in there in the safe. But you got to take the manager, and he has a coffee break at a certain time," and all this bullshit. So here I goes in here, man. It's the supper hour, too. The dining room's full of people and I'm not a coward, so I slithered up beside a guy who's supposed to be the manager. He's sitting there drinking coffee and eating a piece of pie, having a break. So I got an old navy watch cap on, kind of pulled down, not over my face, though, just kind of down low. And I had the pistol in a newspaper and I had it sitting on my lap. I ordered coffee and I just sat there. I was kind of breaking in the weather. I don't know what the hell I'm waiting for. I sit there and figure out which way to go, kind of look around, see what doors go where, and then when I make my move, I'm just going to stick the pistol in the guy's side and say, "Let's go," and get him to go open the safe.

While I'm checking the joint out, I can see the goddam safe is right out in the open where every customer in the damned restaurant can see the damned thing. So this ain't going to be all that cool, but I'm going to do it anyway. The place had a cocktail lounge, too, and while I'm sitting there having coffee, making my plan, the goddam front door bursts open and these two bulls come running in. Jesus Christ! I jumped up; the gun fell down and hit the floor. They ran right past me. They went into the cocktail lounge. There was a fight going on in the cocktail lounge. Then everybody is moving away from me out there. The cops were moving so fast they didn't even see the pistol. And it shocked the people around me because they were looking at the cops. But after the cops went by, they seen me grabbing around, trying to pick the goddam pistol up. And I went out the front door; I took off.

My goddam partner left me when he seen the cop car drive up. He just

split, so I'm hoofing on down the goddam sidewalk and I cross the street
and I seen him about three or four blocks down, parked in a gas station,
for chrissake! Finally I was able to wave him down and he gave me a ride. I
had a notion to shoot that sonovabitch, he made me so goddam mad.
That was the second time that he had done that to me. In that drugstore
robbery, he drove off and left me and I had to chase him across a mile-long
Safeway parking lot to get in the goddam car so I could get away. Nice
partner. I don't know why I kept going with him but I did. But that kind
of ended it, cut it short. I didn't like the sound of a twenty-year sentence,
anyway, for robberies, and then even worse if you ended up shooting
somebody for it.

When in the hell did I end up getting busted again? I ended up coming
to the joint in '72. Yeah, they did finally get me. I went to this house; I got
a call on the phone that was really weird. I had a lot of dope and I'd been
dealing a little dope around town, on my side of town mostly, and I'd been
trucking quite a bit back and forth to Seattle and making some trades because I had . . . aw, man, thousands and thousands of speed tabs. And I
was trying to trade them for some heavy shit. And so, anyway, you know
how the word gets around when you've got that much dope, and I don't
like speed, so I was trying to trade this stuff. It was all drugstore speed that
I'd taken out of a hospital and drugstore. And so anyway, all of a sudden
I'm dealing in speed.

So I was going across town and I was going up to my wife's apartment
to leave some for her to sell. Just drop a few bags of drugs, Dexedrine, and
let her peddle it and give her half cut on it so she can make a few bucks,
too. And I stopped at this tavern downtown that I always went in and I
dumped a little bit down there. Lots of people I knew there. It was kind of
an Indian tavern. So I sold some down there. Not too much, man; it was
kind of hot down there to do shit like that. So I gets a phone call while I'm
there, and I don't know how my old lady tracked me, but she tracked me
there. She says, "Somebody called and they want you to call 'em. They said
it's real important." So she gives me this phone number. I said, "Okay,
cool," you know, so I hangs up and I called this number that she gave me.
And it turned out to be this little junkie broad that lives in this housing

project where we'd been wheeling and dealing around her house for days. We'd been partying and we'd been shooting dope with her, and all this, buying dope from her and selling her dope. So anyway, I calls her up.

Her name was Cookie, old three-fingered Cookie, man. She called herself Three Fingers because she only had a couple fingers on her left hand because she's been shooting Demerol, and she was one of them dingbats that all her veins were gone, so she was shooting it right in her hands, and shit, and Demerol is kind of dangerous to be shooting in small veins because it doesn't dissolve real good. It dissolves enough to shoot in a big vein, but even then, it'll chunk up on ya so that if you haven't crushed it good enough and you shoot it in the hands and it goes the wrong way and it clogs up your blood veins, then you get gangrene and they have to cut your fingers off, you know. That's what happened to this dingbat.

Anyway, she says, "I got a couple guys that want to buy some speed." I says, "Well, how much you want, for chrissake?" I says, "I'm downtown. I'm ready to cross town. I'll catch you later." She says, "No, they ain't got very long. They have to leave." I says, "Well, how much they want? I'm not going to run up there for a lousy five bucks." Then I heard her say, "Just a minute," and she turned around and started talking to somebody. I really couldn't make out what they said. She comes back and she says, "Well, they want a lot." So anyway I says, "Okay, I'll be up there. I'll come right up." So I left and I turned around and I went up there. I stopped again for some reason on the way to McKinley Avenue. I made another stop. I called her again and I says, "Is everything cool?" and she says, "Yeah, come on over. Where you at now?" I says, "Well, I'm almost up there." I left off about half the dope I had at my sister's house. I used to do that when I went around her just in case. I don't want to get robbed or get ripped off. If I didn't have it all with me, then I'd only get ripped off for a little bit, you know. But anyway, I leave off about half the fucking dope and I had a bunch in the trunk yet, but I emptied out what I had in the car. So I took a couple hundred Dexties with me and I had a bottle of class A dope in my pocket [that] I'd forgot about. The same stuff they use now at these programs.

So I goes up to this house and it's all dark, you know, and the shades are all down and shit. I go up to the chick's house, man. And I had my old lady with me, too, and I drove by the first time. I checked the place out and it just didn't really look like hardly anybody was there. I didn't see any cars. I didn't see hardly any lights. The shades were down and there was a light on in the living room. So we came around the second time. I told my old lady, I says, "Well, okay, just let me out, man. Go slow, and I should be out by the time you come back around." I says, "If I'm not out by the time you come back around, just keep driving. Then come back and check me out again."

So I got out and she split and I walked up to this door and I knocked, man, and the door opened, man, and these goons jumped out and grabbed me, jerked my ass in the goddam house. And these two goddam narcs—this lousy bitch had set me up—so these two bulls grabbed me in and then they arrested me for being on the premises of a doper's home. Then they shook me down, found the dope on me, and they charged me with that. But they originally arrested me right there on the spot. They had traffic warrants on me dating back a couple years. But they had made her call me, all this bullshit. So they put the handcuffs on me and threw me in the back bedroom. I'm fumbling around in the goddam dark in the bedroom and, Jesus Christ, there's four or five of my buddies in there with handcuffs on! The sonovabitches were using the place for a police station! Christ almighty! They're calling every dealer in town up there to sell them some dope and all those turkeys are showing up.

So before the night was over, Christ, they nailed about seven of us, including her. They hauled her ass to jail. They tried to catch my old lady when she came by the second time and she just swerved around them and took off. But they did catch her. They radioed ahead and did all this funny shit and got her way down the street and shook her down and got her with the dope. So when I seen that they got her cold with the dope, I had to cop that it was my dope, you know, to get her out of jail 'cause she's a square john. She'd never been to jail or anything like that. Didn't have a reputation, never been in jail her entire life before she ever met me. Now she's got a suspicion-of-narcotics rap sheet.

I went back to the joint for that, you know. Eventually the charge finally came down to possession of narcotics and I went back to the joint. No, I didn't go back to the joint right off the bat. I went to a drug program, which I blew sixty days later; I blew the drug program and took off. I was back on dope again. Then I kept trying to work a program where I could get some help; instead the judge says I should go back to the penitentiary, and I went to a hearing and I went back. I got a year, which is a pretty short sentence. I only did about six months of that year here and got out again in '73. Went back to Tacoma. Went back to Linda again, went back with my old lady, and I was ready to start again to try to stay off the dope the best I can, try to go to work.

I went to work in Lacey, Washington, as a photographer and I worked out there at a studio. Then I got involved with an old prostitute friend of mine. She kept calling around town until she finally hooked up with me and from there I went over to see her. She was working at this sauna. We sat there and shot dope and shit and she had good dope, you know, and she was all happy to see me and all that bullshit. She was an old dope-shooting partner of mine, so I came out to see her a few times at the sauna. I didn't have to go to work until about ten or eleven in the morning, so I'd go out there early. I'd stay a couple hours. We worked out a little deal there where I was making better money just hanging around the sauna than I was as a photographer. See, it was a whorehouse, too, you know, and about the only thing they didn't do at that sauna there was to sell dope. That's ridiculous to say, because we'd sold dope there, too, because when I had dope, guys were coming out there to cop. After a while I was also supplying the girls that worked there. There was about six girls altogether that worked there, but they worked in different shifts. Eventually I ended up just working for them.

There had been a lot of robberies going on in Tacoma. Some girls got beat up and raped. It scared them. They didn't mind the rape part of it, but they don't like getting their teeth knocked out and all that bullshit; they could pass on that physical violence trip. Then these same guys that had been doing this at the saunas also killed another girl, so all the girls were scared. But they needed to work, so that was one time I did pick up the old gun again. A friend of mine just happened to have a nice little shotgun, sawed-off shotgun, which I had, but I had a pistol, too. I ended up just coming in every day, just sitting around. So all the girls chipped in twenty dollars apiece out of their day's pay—twenty dollars wasn't nothing out of what they were making—and they paid me. And it was a pretty good gig there I had going, you know. Pretty soon they wouldn't open the joint unless I showed up. Eventually they caught the guys that were doing that. They never did hit our place and I just kind of wandered off and got into different trips.

I got tired of the working bag in '73. The only trouble that I had when I was on parole that time was in the first few days. I had a traffic beef on me, a reckless-driving charge. That was all they had for several months there. Eventually I did get in trouble.

I lived with Linda. We had an apartment and I was acting crazy again. I got involved in the dope again, pretty heavy, heavier and heavier. My brother was out [of prison], so me and him was doing it steady. We started hitting the old dope, robbing and stealing all the time. Same old trip. You think you'd get tired of that but . . . I was tired of it, man, I was tired of it. I had my fill right up to my neck with that bullshit, but I just couldn't break it. I just didn't seem to be able to get into anything else. I just kept doing it.

My brother and I got busted for burglary. What the hell did we burglarize? I know, we burglarized a goddam church! We was out running around one night and we're outside in the cold and, geez, we were drunker than shit. We're having a ball. We're driving around, so this stupid goddam car he's got breaks down. I should've had my car but I didn't. The old lady had it. So we ended up walking down the road. I says, "It's colder than shit." It's March and so the only place we come up on is a big old church. Pretty nice looking place, pretty new, kinda fancy looking. I says, "Hey, man, let's get in that place. At least I can use the phone. I'll call Linda and have her come and get us." So we went up to the old church. We peeked through windows and found the office. So I used my old trick: I got a pipe wrench to open a door with and we cracked right on into that goddam place. So we're in there rooting around in this church. I'm on the phone. I called up two, three friends of mine. Them sonovabitches wouldn't get up off their ass long enough to come and get me. And then, I don't know why, me and Donny was just kind of sitting in the office in there getting warm, here come the cops. The old cops drove up, got us cold. Oh yeah, we got busted for this stupid goddam church burglary. Any other time, a guy could have got out of that bullshit. It was such a goddam dumb burglary that even the parole officer believed my story about just going in for a phone call. Nothing had been stolen.

So we went to court on that. My brother got fifteen years suspended and I bailed out of jail. I bailed out and went to the alcoholic treatment center. We figured that was a good scam, especially when my brother got a suspended sentence and they told him to go down to California and stay there or something. But he didn't stay too long. I went through an alcohol program. It was supposed to be automatic that I'd get out with my parole officer. She assured me of it and all that bullshit, but things didn't work out that way. I got a different judge than Donny. The judge I got said, "That's it." He wouldn't even consider it, so he gave me fifteen [years].

So I went back to the joint again in '73 on the burglary conviction and went to Shelton. From there I went to camp to do my three and a half. On the fifteen they give you three and a half [years]. Went to camp, which was a break, a break in the weather. A little side trip is all you can call it because I ended up back here [Walla Walla] anyway.

I went to the forestry camp for a while. Forestry camp at Larchmont. It worked out okay. I got a job there I liked. I was heavy-equipment maintenance man. I fixed trucks, did a lot of welding, and did a lot of operating around camp and things. From there I went to a work release. Shortly after, I got caught. My wife got busted on a forgery charge in Seattle. In fact, it was just two days after I got busted, my wife got busted and ended up in Purdy [women's prison]; the first time in her life, ended up doing time. Then I established contact with her from camp and I used to be able to call her every couple weeks and talk to her at Purdy. She was having a rough go adjusting, but she finally snapped out of it. She didn't do too much time, about thirteen, fourteen months altogether, I think. So we got pretty close to the same time.

After about a year I went to work release in Tacoma. Western State Hospital. And I stayed at Western State there for five months on work release. During that time I kind of forgot I was in the joint and I started boozing it up every time I went to work. I was working with a construction crew. My father-in-law and I did cement work, building foundations for homes. All the guys I worked with were boozers, you know. Everybody hits the tavern. Shit, we hit the tavern for months. We hit the tavern before we went to work in the morning, then we took beer with us when we went to work. I always took a jug of wine or some goddam thing in my thermos bottle instead of coffee. I think we partied more during the day than we worked, for chrissake. But we were making money. So as long as we were making money for him, he didn't mind too much anyway, because he was a drunk himself. We all got along great. They covered for me a lot.

They [prison officials] knew I was drinking a lot at work release, but they were waiting for me to get involved with narcotics again. They were ready to come down on me heavy then. But I didn't. I stayed away from them and I started getting off into the booze trip instead. The thought of just being straight and not doing either [drugs or alcohol] didn't cross my mind. I thought of it, but I didn't think I was ready for that trip yet. I eventually got too much heat on me over the drinking there at work release and they sent me back finally for a drunken binge one night and driving [back] in with the wrong car. I came driving without my sponsor with me, and all kinds of bullshit, so they had a hearing on me and sent me back to the penitentiary.

I had only had three or four months left to do, so when I came back over here to Walla Walla in '75, I did my remaining few months and got out. Worked out to be about five months that I was back here. I got out in '76 and I went home and I wouldn't do nothing. I didn't have any plans. I was going to go to work but I didn't get started. I just kept laying back and I kept drinking and drinking and, sure enough, I got back in the booze again. And I got back into the dope again. And so I went at dope a pretty good lick again with my cousin.

We started burglarizing and we must have pulled a hundred goddam burglaries in the short time I was out. I was only out one month and I already had heat on me, the cops already looking for me. The odd part of that was my car was used in a burglary that I wasn't even involved in. That's the way I got the heat, but I was doing shit on my own. At the time the places were ripped off in my car, I was in jail in a little town over here for a concealed-weapons charge and a credit card possession, attempted use of a credit card. July '76, I stayed on the run in Tacoma. I never even left town, for chrissake, and they had every cop in town trying to find me. I just kind of run around like I knew what I was doing. Had my car repainted and fixed it up, had phony plates on it all the time because I couldn't function without a car. The worst part about that was I had to leave my lady and I couldn't go home. I snuck in for some nighttime visits once in a while. Even then, I didn't stay all night. I'd just stay for a couple hours and I'd hit the road.

So things went pretty bad there, pretty tough situation for a while, and I just ran a while until they caught me finally. They caught me on Thanksgiving Day. Thanksgiving morning, '76. They finally tracked me down, surrounded this goddam house I was in and come in like a bunch of storm troopers. Nailed my ass right there. I woke up with a cop sitting on my back holding my arms behind me, putting the cuffs on me. And this friend of mine that I'd been running around with [who] got arrested a day or two before had made a deal to let them know where I was in turn for letting him go on a car theft charge. So that's how I got caught in '76. He looked all over town. He knew where I was hiding out, because just prior to that he'd made all the rounds with me. He led the cops to me. When he found me, he called them up and told them where I was. They came in and got me, so that's what I'm in here for now.

I got sentenced for first-degree burglary on that one, with a weapon. They used the pipe wrench that I used for a burglar tool, for going through doors. They put that down for a weapon. It was first-degree burglary this time because when I was coming out of the people's apartment, they'd come home. I just opened the door and there they were standing, some guy and his old lady and this friend of theirs. I knew it wasn't the cops, just them, so I just attacked their asses. I went crazy on them. I thought they was all going to jump me, so I took a swing at the guy, and his old lady went screaming across the goddam lawn trying to get a neighbor. And I chased them in both directions then. Mainly I still had my senses, but I was just trying to chase them far enough so I could get to my car. Then I got to my car and took off.

They got my number just as I was going away, so two, three months later when I did get caught, that's the one they charged me with, because that's the one they figured they could hit me with for doing the most time. But when I first went to jail they charged me with thirteen counts of forgery, four counts of credit card possession and theft, two other burglaries, and a first-degree burglary, plus the added threat of the habitual-criminal charge after handwriting analysis, which they [say] can't be beat. But I beat it. The charges were reduced to two possible forgeries. So they didn't press that because they didn't figure they could push that one. But the witnesses came down. They made a positive I.D. on me even though I got a haircut and a shave, the dirty sonovabitches. I must have scared them enough so they remembered my goddam face. Anyway, if I had slicked by that one, I'd been okay. The guy wasn't sure, but the woman was positive and she wouldn't change her mind. And leave it to a woman to remember your damned face! So they had me on that one.

Finally I wheeled and dealed and plea-bargained with them and I agreed to cop to the first-degree burglary and they dropped the habitual-criminal charge and the two forgery charges, which I wasn't worried about any goddam way. And so I went to court in '76 on first-degree burglary and possession of a credit card, and I got twenty for the burglary and I got five for the credit card, and then eventually the parole board, when I got back to Shelton, gave me [an added] three years for parole violation because I was on parole for that sixteen-year burglary charge I had got in '73. So that's what I'm doing now.

When I was out and working, everything I was doing on my job and different things, I'd be always thinking ahead to the fucking time when I'd be back in the joint again, so I defeated myself every time I'd get out. I never did consider being free forever. I always paroled with self-defeating thoughts of returning. Even the things I'd be doing while I was out, I'd be thinking of all the stories I could tell when I got back [to prison]. "Hey, shit, man, this would be fun to talk about next year," or whatever. It was like "Donny's still in the joint. Wait until I tell him about this!" But I didn't plan on telling him like he was going to get out; I planned on telling him in here [when I got back]. It was like I went out and reconnoitered the fucking area and I just come back in. And I'd come back in mostly. Definitely nothing affirmative, nothing I do.

I'm just going to go back a step in time here before [I met] Linda. Okay, when I was thirteen years old I lived in that housing project in Tacoma. I was just thirteen and at that time I was sneaking over and having a terrible love affair with an eighteen-, nineteen-year-old married woman that lived across the street. Scared the shit out of me when I first started it, 'cause, you know, because, goddam, I was a stone virgin. We had just moved from Aberdeen, so I didn't have any girlfriends or anything, so I mean it wasn't too real a situation then. But I mean it was the fact that it was an older woman I was in love with, and that hurt, because she was a real floozie, apparently. Of course, she was an angel in my eyes, you know. And Jesus Christ, she was a cold floozie! Well, it lasted a while and then her husband got transferred to California. He packed her up lock, stock, and barrel and took her out of there. I think he asked for a transfer because while he was working at Fort Lewis, every time he'd be working, all his buddies would come over and all of them would be in there fucking her, for chrissake. And he kicked me out of the house, you know what I mean? So I run on home. Shit, I didn't know what the hell was going on . . . with three or four guys there.

Then one night three or four guys came over and he wasn't home and I was there. Me and her was playing around on the couch and anyways these guys came and they brought a case of beer. Like I say, I was only thirteen, but they didn't run me out. They didn't suspect me and her was up to anything, you know. But they started drinking beer and . . . God, I'm a stupid sonovabitch! I was a naive bastard. I mean they didn't even wait until they got done! I mean, they just took turns. One at a time, they'd go in the bedroom. She didn't even bother getting off the bed. The one would come out and send the next in, you know, so if I wasn't such a fucking dummy, I would of got in line, for chrissake! And I guess she was probably selling it, you know, come to think of it. I never thought about it much; but anyway, I had some idea that they probably weren't in there going to confession and I got a little jealous. And it hurt my feelings that she was ignoring me so long and could have at least called me in to watch, you know what I mean? I could've went for that, too. Maybe I'd have learned a few things. In fact, I know I'd learned a whole lot of shit, wouldn't I?

But anyway I went on home and it wasn't long after that and she tried to get me to run away with her. She was gonna pack her shit and head for California but never did it. And she said, "I'm going to take you and go to California and would you go with me?" Hey, not me! Jesus Christ, I'm not even out of grade school yet, you know, and my mom, she never thought to step in on that, either. I don't know what the hell my mom thought we was up to. I wonder if she'd objected if I'd brought some fruiter home, huh? Maybe she'd put her foot down then. I don't know. Probably not. Not my mom: "Aw, that's sweet. He's such a nice guy." Oh, for chrissake! I wonder what she'd think of these goddam romances and crazy affairs of mine sometimes. She has spent so goddam much time lying for me, one girl after another when they calls up or comes down looking for me, when I might be in the bedroom or in my room with some girl, and my mom would just lie with a perfectly serene and straight face and say, "Oh, my God. I'm sorry, he just left." Or, "Honey, he's gone someplace." Jesus, it just got to be a habit with her, you know, natural. Always protecting.

And she's a beautiful woman, like you said, Chiquita. You got it right. My mom is sixty-four now and she still works her ass off, I'm telling you. She's got one of the hardest goddam jobs. She works at a restaurant and she has the night shift and works from . . . she usually . . . I think she starts about six-thirty or seven and she finishes about two o'clock in the morning. It's one or two before she gets home, and of course, no matter where she works, she's always one of the most valuable employees, if not the most valuable, because she is hardworking and responsible and she'd have to be damn near on her deathbed to miss a day's work. Believe me, that's the kind of people I would hire, and God, if I had a company and I hired a person like her and I hired a person like Linda, I could just pack my shit and go to Hawaii, you know what I mean? There wouldn't be nothing to worry about, because they're such good workers and responsible. I mean they . . . you would never have to worry about the damn business, not with those kind of people working for you, because they will not miss and they will do everything good, the best they can, and they won't steal from you. So you know how people like that are; they always end up doing all the work.

Well, my mom, she is always beat and she gets sick, and goddam, she goes to work anyway. It pisses me off and I try to encourage her on the phone to take a day off or something. I call her up every Sunday at twelve-thirty and I talk to her, and she's usually just waking up and she looks forward to my call at twelve-thirty and I catch her sleepy-eyed all the time. And we talk and she lets me know what's happening with the family, because my mom is also, of course, she's the mother hen of the family. She keeps close track of everybody. She spends many, many hours on her off-time taking care of my aunt, who has got sicker over the years. And this year she's been just plagued with one infection after another, or something's wrong with her stomach.

My mom has always been law-abiding, unless the cops are over asking about me or Donny, then she'd shut up and get smart-assed with them or something, get beat up, get thrown around trying to protect me. I remember one time we was all downtown one night going dancing in Tacoma. Ruby, Mom, and me, us three went. Okay, so we went downtown to the old Milwaukee Tavern, I think it was, where most of the Indians hang out. Mom loved to dance and Ruby loved to dance, and I'd dance and guys would dance with them. And Mom and Ruby and I'd sit alone and buy a pitcher of beer. I wasn't old enough to go in a tavern, but I'd go anyway. Anyway, some guy started giving Ruby a hard time one night, tried to steal her purse. So I jumped up and nailed him, punched him, and the door got slammed somehow and the glass broke out of it, so I fell out onto the sidewalk and the other guy fell in the other direction. Anyway, I still had Ruby's purse in my hand. And the cops came driving up. So they were going to take me away, and my mom reached out and grabbed the cop by the arm, said, "You aren't taking my son away. He didn't do anything wrong." The cop finally jerked his arm away, pushed her down on the street, handcuffed her, and took her to jail, too. I was fifteen when that happened.

My aunt right now is just to a point where she can't walk on her own and she can't see and she can't hear, and it just probably just scares the shit out of her, and you know, it's terrible, terrible. I'd like to write about blind people, you know, because I understand blind people. I've done crazy things, but in the last few years especially, I've tried to understand some things and, God, there's so much that I didn't do. I mean that I could [have done] . . . I love a blind person and I don't know . . . it's just . . . I don't look at them and feel that they're missing anything; they're not missing what we're missing. Sometimes the world is awful ugly. It's like with a blind person, you know, the beautiful snow that we're having right now is ugly and harsh and cold to a blind person. They can't see the snow glisten and can't see the whiteness. All snow is to them is something that is cold and is miserable, you know, so in that respect, there's things they don't see, but they're lucky in that there are some things they cannot see and we have to look at. But they're in touch, you know; they're in touch more than we are in touch. That's the thing, and people have never given a blind person the respect and the credit and the dignity they deserve. That person is more in touch with life than I'll ever be. And I think there is so much, man, that needs to be done. People should understand them more, goddamit, and give them a chance to do things.

I'd like to write my Aunt Ruby's story. Ruby has got a helluva story. I mean her and my mom together. I guess they would set an awful strong example for people on how to get through tough situations and raise a bunch of little goddam Indian brats and bring 'em up in a rotten world, and bring 'em up clean. Okay, we're not clean; we've been in prison, but don't ever say that to my mother or my aunt, you know, because they don't believe it. They blame the world and they blame everybody else. And we couldn't be better to them and my mom has stood by us. And the one and only thing I can think of as soon as I get in jail is my mom.

When I was a juvenile, the one person I thought of immediately and looked for and expected and *knew* she was going to be out there knocking on the door to find out "What happened to Gene, my boy?" was my mom.

My mom would be there immediately, you know. Nobody else but my mother would be there. And she'd always be that way. She's seen me in jails, peeked through little keyholes, heavy wire screens of the cell doors, and had to stand there on her tippy toes to try to talk to me, and her first words were always "You can take it." That's always my mom's first words, "You can handle it. Goddam it and to hell with these people, and you just hang in there and we'll get you out. We'll get you out." She always says that, you know, and "I'll go get a lawyer. I'll get the best lawyer in town." Of course, you know we can't have the best lawyer. God, we can't even have an old average lawyer, for chrissake.

I ain't never had a lawyer that I had to pay for, because we don't have any money. But most of the time, you know, when I'm in jail I tell my mom, "Don't you worry about it now." What I always tell her, "You know me, Mom. I can handle it." And, of course, I've got to handle it, you know, because I don't want her to spend no money, [not] one penny, on no attorney for me, because it's just a waste of money anyway. If I can't talk, cry, and beg my way out of it—which you can do a lot when you're younger—then the hell with it. I'll just ride it out and then my mom hasn't worked her ass off and put every penny in savings [on me] and blown it, see. If it's gonna affect anything, it'll just be her feelings. It won't be her pocketbook and everything else. But she's always there and she's ready and she always makes sure that we got candy and cigarettes, you know what I mean, and five dollars on the books, or whatever. My mom's always there. She's always at court.

Recently I haven't asked her to come to these courts, and the last court, when I went to trial on this one, I didn't even tell my family when I was going to court. I didn't want anybody there because I knew that it wasn't gonna sound good when the judge started handing me those years, because I got twenty-five years and I knew that was a little heavy for even my mom to handle. So I went by myself this time. Then when I seen my mom, I just told her, "Yeah, it ain't shit. I'll head on back and do the best I can. You know me."

You see, my mom was in a mission school when she was younger. To her it was like a reform school and she remembers it, and so she always deals with it that way. It has caused her to be pretty resentful, and I can't say that she doesn't respect authority or laws, you know. She especially respects the law, but she's bitter. Like you say that I'm lucky that I'm not bitter. But I think that the life that Donny and I have led and the things that we fell into and the troubles we've had have caused my mom to turn pretty bitter inside, you know, but she doesn't know who to direct it at. She's bitter toward society in general.

She has her little world of her house, her husband, a drive straight up the hill from my aunt's and then down a street of three or four more blocks to my sister's house, where the gang of kids are, and zoom back down to her house. You see, that's my mom's world and she hates to go out of it. She's got a nice car now, but believe me, she hates to go to doctors and she hates to go downtown and she hates to do any of that shit, you know, and only if she'll have to, she'll go with my sister. Or her and Jay go for their rides in the country when they both have their day off.

My people struggle through every day of their lives just to lay some beans and bread on the table for supper. It isn't something from the old days; it is a fact of life for thousands of Indian families just like mine. And in the toughest of times they remain proud. My mother is a very strong and proud woman. I have only seen her cry once in my life and it wasn't because of me, although I suspect that she has shed buckets of tears in the safety and darkness of her bedroom. She is bitter and angry and resentful at a society that has never let up on its efforts to destroy her family. But my mother is strong. I am sure that you can identify with these feelings, and I see that same strength and determination in you, Chiquita, to overcome all the injustices of the world or die trying.

That is the reason I have never understood how people, men, can call women weak. I have lived under the protection of that strength all my life. It has forced me to hold my head up and stem the flood of tears from the fear I felt each time I was taken away from my family. I was thrown into adult cells even before I knew what a jail was all about. I was beaten and cursed for being different; I was hated because I wouldn't cry. I was slapped by teachers and avoided by classmates because I was quiet and kept to myself. Through all the worst of it, I had my brother with me always. That was my strength. I was one year older. Always, every minute, I was the oldest and so I assumed the responsibility of caring for his feelings and was able to ignore my own. But always, we looked to our mother for strength and she would give us enough love and encouragement to carry us through.

She always held us and said, "Be strong, my boys," and that seemed to be so very important to both of us, to be strong and never show our hurt, our loneliness, to the people that held us prisoners, and especially to our mother. It was known that she loved us and missed us and would do anything to help us. But even at such an early age it was important for us not to make her feel worse by seeing us cry or making it harder for her to leave us after a short visit.

I'm probably making you sad, Chiquita, ain't I? I'm sort of stirring some strong feelings up in myself, so I better change the subject. I'm getting weak these days. I guess my tapes [what is being revealed on the tapes] are affected a lot by my hedging and ducking feelings like this. My [feelings] seem to be closer to the surface then they have ever been in my life. Times like this I want to call my mom and just tell her I love her. She wouldn't know what the hell was the matter with me. It would scare the shit out of her.

There was never much talk of love in my house. The same thing is conveyed with a touch, a look, clean clothes, food on the table, or a ride in the old clunker with all us kids yelling, fighting, throwing the poor little ragged Indian dog of ours out the window about every other block, making him tough, too; my blind aunt in the front seat, laughing and having fun while we competed on who would give her a running commentary on all the wonderful and exciting things we were seeing. I remember my mom saying, "Oh, Ruby, you should see this house," and we would park our Indian car in front of a beautiful home with six heads gawking at all the fancy-smancy lawn and the fancy little white kids on their new bikes. Even the dogs were different. But we liked our mutt okay; he was a Delorme dog. I think I enjoyed those rides more than anything in my life. We were so close and happy and it felt so goddam safe.

This past week I witnessed a killing right outside my wing. Made me mad, sick, depressed—you name it. This was the second one in less than a year for me. I wish the tower guard would have killed all three of the guys who did it.

I was coming back from supper and I was walking toward the wing when I saw a group struggling up ahead. They were stabbing the guy in the front and back. Someone also cut his throat during the scuffle. I hung back until they let him go. They turned and ran into the lifers' park but they weren't lifers. The guy that they stabbed staggered into the wing door and tried to get in but the guard wouldn't open the door—scared. The blood was squirting all over the place.

I just stood and watched. I didn't feel anything for him at the time and that's what really bothers me now. There isn't anything to be done. He was dead on his feet. I knew he was dead. I'm sure he knew he was a dead man. The guard knew he was dead. All that was left was for him to lay down and die, which he did. There was so much blood that it seemed like someone slaughtered a cow instead of a man. I looked at his eyes. They were glassy and he quit moving pretty quick. It was still a while before the stretcher came to pick up the carcass—that's what you're called when your game is up—just another carcass to haul away.

The convict code stinks. It's so wrong I can't tell you. I hate it and it makes me feel subhuman. I don't agree with it in any way, but still I've changed. I can remember when I thought it was right. But I know now it's not right. I have investigated it. I have watched it and seen it work and it's the horriblest goddam thing I have ever seen. It makes you feel like an animal. It makes you feel subhuman. It drains you.

I never had a part in a killing, but I still feel guilty. These killings make me feel rotten. I want to stop it somehow and I feel like somehow I have participated in it. I know that I haven't, you know, but just being here and being a good convict, I guess it makes me partially to blame. These things happen. I do what I can to change things in here to stop it, but it is just a losing battle. This system works hard to turn us all into monsters. This prison is a jungle and makes good men turn back into savages just to survive. Society, free society, sets controls and a man works to become civilized because he has to be civilized to keep from becoming an outcast. In a place like this it works just the opposite. I fight it constantly. I always have.

There have been times in here when my own thoughts have turned to murder as the only way to deal with someone who I didn't like or who I thought did me wrong. Those times were hard for me. I fought with everything I had to understand and cool my temper. It scared me because my rage would be so hot and when I aimed it all at one person it became almost uncontrollable.

The wrongs done me never amounted to much—it would be something like a watch I bought once and it didn't keep the right time. It became super important to keep the guy who sold it to me from thinking he put one over on me. I made some pretty gory plans for him. I had a knife, but I also had my brother to stop me when things became serious. I sat and brooded over that watch for a couple weeks until I thought everyone was laughing, then I felt I had to do it or everyone would think I was a punk. Needless to say, I also didn't want to do it either. I realized at the time that it was this place working to turn me into a monster like some of the others in here. I always call these people monsters, the people I know who have killed another inside or outside the prison. I tried to explain the evil in here to close friends, but it seems like I'm alone most of the time or others don't really care.

Speaking about culture, I often picture us like in scenes in movies I've seen that show groups of people roaming around a bombed-out city after a nuclear war, taking food from other groups, no laws, every man for himself, killing people who have something you want. That's my picture of this place. I don't know about other prisons but I believe that most American prisons are run the same: the strongest survive, prey on the weak.

Sometimes I despise the weak ones and other times I wish I had the power to sort them out and take care of them. I think mostly I walk around and try not to see them, but I'm fascinated by the way they accept their condition and move out of people's way or duck and dodge and run, which saves them from a beating most of the time, because it's funny to see a grown man scamper off yelling for help—there isn't any help—so tempers cool fast. I wonder if they know this or if they are acting on impulse.

It's hard to explain why there is such little regard for human life in here. I can see that it isn't any different on the streets and that's the way it is in here. I'm talking about the criminal element and drug culture. They are always at each other's throats on the streets. This attitude is brought inside. It's a sign of the times—every man for himself. Do your thing and fuck anyone who gets in the way. If a guy burns you for some dope once, dust him so he can't beat you twice.

In a closed culture like the joint every move you make is like being on a stage: all eyes are on you so that even if you don't want to hurt someone over a petty debt, the pressure is on to deal strongly with the problem or your ass will be fair game for everyone else. You'll lose all respect if you let anyone slide. It is easier if the guy is smaller, but you can't take any chances on not kicking some ass, because the prison culture is a deadly culture— we want revenge for insults and a life for an ass-kicking. The attitude says no one has to take any shit from anyone in prison. No man is bad enough to withstand a knife in the heart.

All men want to have respect in prison. Respect does not come easy and it never comes from letting people fuck you over. Nice guys can't win, although in extreme cases you can be both tough and nice and charm the skin off the snake so he can't slip no more.

I was talking to you about the great escape and why we do that in here. What are we escaping from? you might ask. Well, we're escaping from murder, assault, rape, hustling, homosexuality, insanity, phony friendships, empty conversations, boredom, and I guess mostly the coldness, the real coldness of it all. That is the prison. You try not to see or hear, or you ignore these things.

It is possible to give your eye, mind, and body a break from the ugliness, stress, and tension that we're with seven days a week, fifty-two weeks a year, year after year after year. So I think I've said it before, too. I don't want to see this stuff. I don't want to hear it. I don't want to know about these things. The best way to do that is to make yourself scarce. Get up out of it. Slip and slide around it. Duck and dodge it all day. The old saying, which changed in here with just one addition that fits here or any prison is

"See no evil, hear no evil, speak no evil, and evil will not touch you, hopefully." Doesn't always work. You try.

One good reason why you want to escape is you want a place to go. You want a place to be away from the evil, bloodshed, violence, murder. Like hearing a man beg and cry, scream while he's being stabbed sixty-five times. Seeing a man have his throat cut while two others stab him in the back. This guy doesn't scream. This guy makes a wheezing, bubbling sound because his throat's cut. He gasps. It's a terrible sound. The blood foams up and comes out in a fountain. He's wide-eyed. The eyes are glazed. He's terrified because he knows he's dead. Looks around for help and you back away just like everybody else. This is what you're escaping from. This is the thing that you're taking yourself away from. You don't forget these things. You never will. You never forget these things when you've seen them, when you've heard the sounds and you've watched the man die and you haven't done anything about it. You don't forget. You can't forget you didn't help . . . aw, the hell with it!

And when you're in your cell at nighttime sometimes . . . it doesn't happen all the time . . . when it happens—rape—it's generally a real pitiful whimpering, begging sound. Some young guy being gang-raped and beaten, probably spit on, probably being kicked around, cries for help. You can hear his scream to be all of a sudden muffled because someone is holding his hand over his mouth. Other guys in the cell keep watch up and down the tier with a mirror, probably a shaving mirror, and they use it like a rear view mirror, stick it out the bars and watch, tell the other guys to hurry up so they can have their turn. So this happens at night and you can't get away from that.

But there's a strange thing I've noticed about a man that's murdered. Very often the man that's being murdered will tell his attackers, "You're killing me!" My [Indian] brother, Broncho—that's what somebody that was witness said Broncho hollered at the guys that were stabbing him: "You're killing me!" A young guy, twenty-two years old, that was killed on the tier below me once, they stabbed him sixty-five times! And he cried and screamed every time they stabbed him, and that's what he kept saying, "You're murdering me! You're murdering me!" And he prayed and screamed for his mother, screamed for the cops, begged them not to kill him, but they killed him. In a frenzy they killed him. Went completely insane. They were covered with blood from head to foot when they came out of that cell. Three of them. They weren't charged, they weren't convicted. They were caught, but they put them in segregation for a while, then let all three of them go, and they killed somebody else again.

But if you're in your club or if you're having your visit, or if you're over making a phone call, or you're over playing music in the club, or you're out playing baseball, you won't be in your cell and you won't hear those cries and screams. You won't have nightmares. You'll hear it secondhand. You won't hear it at night. You won't think about it five years after it happened. I still hear that guy crying. That's what you escape from. And it does something to you. That's the terrible thing. If you witness it or if you're close to it, it does something to you inside that you have to fight. I don't know how many years you have to fight it. I don't know! I can't describe this, to let a man die. Somehow you've got to convince yourself there's nothing you can do. That's not your nature, you know, to let things like that go on.

I think you can understand the reasons for escape. I wonder if you can see what I'm trying to tell you here, Chiquita. It's important to find a way to avoid these things. And you remember this now and maybe work on it in your mind and maybe expand on it yourself, because that's the same way it affected me, which is very deeply. It's important that you use the different forms of escapism, not so much because you're afraid of it happening to you, but it's important that you don't have to touch it mentally, because that damages. It hurts. It isn't so much that you're afraid that somebody is going to come and jump on you. In some cases you know pretty damn sure nobody is going to come jump on you, but I don't give a goddam how big we are, how strong we think we are; when it happens and when you see it, you're not ready for it. It happens suddenly. Sometimes you're walking around like a goddam dummy and you haven't got everything buttoned up. I'm talking about your emotions and your feelings. So it [what you saw] goes in deep. Then you have another psychological problem that you have to work out, as if you didn't have enough already.

So that's a pretty important aspect of escaping. That's protecting yourself, protecting your mental health. That's just as important as protecting your physical self. You could go on if you see this. If you're healthy it shouldn't affect your life. Only it'll affect you inside your mind personally. It affects you in those quiet moments, you see, until you've accepted and explained, rationalized everything to yourself.

I expect it's the same thing with the veterans from the different wars. They've seen a lot. The only Vietnam veterans in here that you hear really telling stories or talking about it are full of bullshit most of the time. But you got normal, healthy young men that went. They actually experienced, they killed, they saw death; they were close to death; it touched them. It was all around them. These guys don't talk about it. They don't want to think about it. They don't want these images coming back into their mind. It's only the bullshitters who were over there and didn't do anything. Then you get stories from them all day long. And the guys who really experienced death in war, just as it bothers them, they become quieter. It changes them. Their personality becomes introspective. It's not that they're thinking about these things. I don't know what they're thinking about. Maybe the quietness indicates that there is a battle for control going on inside. Maybe it takes a little bit more than subconscious effort to hold these things down, hold these pictures away from them, these memories, so that a little bit more of energy and a little bit more of extra effort is necessary. It takes a little bit more of concentration, so it pulls you away from your outward approach to people and makes you a little more reflective. It just seems that way, anyway. You pull kind of within yourself and that can handicap you. It's a real danger. I think I can handle it. I'm sure I can handle it.

I'm glad I called you today, Chiquita. I really enjoyed talking with you. You have your little dog, Sweet Pea, and I have my tape recorder. I have thought about coming to see you someday. Flying makes me feel that I am going to fall out of the window, even if I stand back about ten feet. I have had dreams that I have gotten on an airplane [where] the Lord reached down right out of the heavens and held me back and I couldn't get on board with everybody else and they left; a giant hand came right out, and I was excited, too. . . . Nothing is going to make me get in some damn airplane. I'll take the train. I got to be able to hit the skids, boy, to hit the ground if I have to. Furtherest I'm gonna fall is a couple feet out the window. They just don't have bad train wrecks anymore.

I'll tell you what happened one time . . . a new high school that they were building in Tacoma and there was a bunch of aerial photos needed, so I agreed to go up and shoot a couple of rolls. Of course I was loaded when I said yes and completely out of my mind. I should have connected aerial with airplane. I guess I thought I was going to climb a tree or some damned thing. I don't know what I was thinking at the time.

Anyway, I agreed to do this and then I was sitting down at home and a flash of light came to me a couple of days before the deadline on a picture that I hadn't shot, either. I thought about it, and the time was coming. Linda reminded me, of course. My conscience, Linda. She reminded me, "You had better get to thinking about how you are going to do those pictures. You have got to have them in a couple of days." And she always explains to me that if you don't do the job then they can sue you and all that bullshit. But I said, "Yeah. Call them up and tell them that I can't do it. You know I can't go up in no airplane." She told me to call them myself. "You can't back out now." You know the old story, "You have responsibilities." And I said, "Responsibility, bullshit. My responsibility is to stay alive; that's the only responsibility I got, you know. Them sonovabitches ain't gonna take me up there and crash me into the goddam field." At that time, of course, I wasn't fit for battle. Like I wouldn't have had no luck at all, as the old saying goes. I mean, the minute that I stepped in that goddam plane, those sons of bitches would get off the ground far enough to crash me and that would be it.

We fought around the house about it and I stuck to my irresponsibility and she was throwing this responsibility shit on me and so, somehow, I went completely crazy and I agreed to do it. In spite of it, my fear, I was young enough then that when I agreed to it that was worse for me, [because] once I finally agreed, then I am bound in my own mind to tough it out somehow. And so I said, "Okay. What the hell am I going to do? Somehow I got to do it. Somehow I got to go up and get some practice so I can relax during the actual picture-taking thing. Let's go down and I'll pay for a ride in the helicopter. Just take me up off the ground and I can take the pictures and we can come straight down. That's not too bad there, you know." I finally decided that that's the way I'd do it.

What I decided on was a practice flight. They got this little airport in South Tacoma. They'd been advertising in the newspaper and on the radio lately. They always get this special little thing going on out there where they have special days when they ride around the city—the scenic flight routine. They only charge you a penny a pound of weight as the price, which is reasonable, you know. For her [Linda] it was reasonable; it still cost me a couple of bucks. So we shot out to the airport. We thought it would be quiet.

A junky little fucker. Planes in all kinds of stages of repair sitting around the apron. None of them looked like the sonovabitches could hold water, let alone get off the ground. So we went in and we signed up for the old scenic flight, see, a ten-minute flight around the city and come back. I am getting a chill thinking about it right now. I waited in the car. I went in and I had to sign and we went back out and the same guy that signed us in said he would take us for the ride. I knew that he was a pilot right away because he had his dark glasses on, slick-looking appearance, you know, jacket and the whole bit, you know what I mean? Just out of World War II, for chrissake! He looked like I could trust him pilot-wise. I figured he could handle it but I didn't trust the crate he was going to fly in, so I went to the car. I figured I needed a little fortification. Just so happened I brought two jugs, so I told Linda that I had to go to the car, I was going to load the camera, "I will be right with you." I put film in the camera and another roll in my pocket.

I couldn't bring myself to get out of the car. She was already standing on the wing, and the sonovabitch, all it needed was some wires coming out the wings and it could have been a model airplane. So Buck Rogers, he's already in the sonovabitch, and I thought he was going to stand outside but he didn't, and she's on the wing, waving, trying to get me out of the car. I locked the car door and said, "This is it." I cracked that bottle of wine and I killed the whole sonovabitch right there and I sat back.

She damn near fell off the wing waving at me and he, he's got the engine idling and blowing her off the wings damn near, and I think I felt sorry for her more than anything else, because I had her so convinced that I was going to go and she was proud of my courage and all that bullshit, so I said, "Oh, Christ!" My jug of wine was working on my courage, anyway; it filled my reservoir pretty good, you know, and I got out of the car and I went waddling across the runway and, goddam it, almost walked right into the prop. The pilot was waving at me and I waved back at him, then I realized that the goddam thing [propeller] was going around. I took a few steps back toward the car. By God, I finally got around and I stepped on the wing. I was under one of those little canopies on top . . . it's open; I don't know what you call 'em, the side windows, you know. A bubble canopy, they called it. I climbed in the back seat there and she was sitting beside me. She had a dress on. Nine years, for chrissake, I still look up her dress! But we got in the plane and I was bumbling around trying to figure out how to strap myself in. Completely ridiculous to me in the first goddam place. The last thing I wanted to do was be strapped in an airplane. I figured it was good for a crash on the runway, but let it all hang out once you are off the ground.

We're ready to go, man, and this fighter pilot up there turns around and he gives us the old high sign or whatever you call the goddam thing . . . thumbs-up shit. He goes bouncing on down the runway. So he makes a couple of turns and, shit, we start picking up speed. If it wouldn't have been for embarrassing her, I would have screamed; it wouldn't have embarrassed me a goddam bit. So we crashed on down the runway. I didn't know if we was ever going to get up and pretty soon we were up, just like an old seagull. I was wishing I was a seagull about that time.

Up we go and I swear, all the trips I been to jail and the things I have done, I can't remember a worse feeling of fear . . . stark terror that went over me then. I just shriveled up like a goddam . . . I melted down into that seat until my eyes were below the level of the canopy, and from that minute on until we set back down, I never looked out that stinking window. She kept nudging me, "Oh, look at that." And I said, "Fuck you. Shut up. Leave me alone." He said, "You folks want to go over the Narrows [water]?" It is real terrible. I did feel a little better when I saw the water. I was hoping he would burn us for our fucking money and take us back. So we zoomed on down and she's talking about "There's your mom's house." She said, "Aren't you going to take any pictures? You know you're supposed to be practicing. You better take pictures."

I reached up and held the camera against the canopy and I started snapping. I didn't know what the hell I was looking at. He was choking that plane and the sonovabitch was bouncing along and I was snapping the camera and . . . I shot a role, thirty-six shots! I don't know what the hell I shot, but I figured anything down there is going to be in the picture. I was lucky. I didn't get a miss. It looked like I was going to die, anyway, so might as well have a picture of it. And then, of course, the ride was over and I had the best feeling of my life when that stupid little nuts-and-bolts thing hit the ground and stopped. I came out of my shell then, puffed my chest out and started talking plenty of shit. Pretty brave fellow.

I came out of that plane sober as a judge. I found out the alcohol don't work up in the air at all. Not on me, anyway. That goddam stupid-looking pilot and his airplane did more for me than any Alcoholics Anonymous could ever do. He sobered my ass up for a goddam month. I never got those pictures of that school. That [experience] never helped me a damn bit. It made me even more afraid to fly than I had been before I went up! I guess it's so goddam bad that I don't even like to watch a plane going over. Now I am scared that the plane is going to fall on me. So if I ever said I was gonna come down to see you, Chiquita, you have to give me about eight days on a highway [at] fifty-five miles an hour. I'll be there by and by.

Some things people have [like a] home, family . . . God, you don't know how much I have always wanted that. Seems so goddam hard. I just push that away as an impossible dream. I pretty much accepted my conditions, my situation in life. I know how hard people work for the things they have, and it's only been the last few years, too, that I started feeling guilty about the things that I have stolen from people. And I don't like to have my things taken. I don't have much anyway, but not everybody can say that.

I had to steal. I usually had to steal at first to get by, because they only give you one hundred dollars when you get out of the joint and that doesn't go far. I didn't want nothing. Then [when living with Linda] my stealing was even worse because I didn't have to [steal]. So I just started doing it out of boredom. I think I did it just to bug her [Linda] and to prove to myself that I could do something good. I really did try to prove to myself that I could burglarize good. I took a certain amount of pride in my ability to open a door, a locked door, and be in and out in a matter of a few seconds, take what I wanted and hit the road and be off. I took a certain amount of pride in that. I did it at night. I did it in broad day, in huge, big apartment complexes. I walked into homes and bang, bang, bang, I'd open the door and close it when I went out with a TV, a color TV.

It started to bother me and I tried not to think about it. I really did. I'd say things to myself like "So you got by with their credit card. It didn't really cost them anything, you know." That's such illogical thinking [to me] now. It's a product of growing up in a place where you don't even learn the value of money. Money was not real, other than to have something to play with or buy some cigarettes. I never had enough money to buy a house or make big payments. I knew about buying it on time but I didn't make the payments. Once I got the article [I stole] I always considered it to be mine. I couldn't see any sense in sending them money. They wasn't going to take it from me and I wasn't going to give it to anybody, so . . . I always have had a problem with money—property, too, for that matter—realizing the value of things. Even things I owned, you know.

It created a lot of problems with me and my wife. It's created a lot of problems with Linda, also. I haven't changed; that was being too generous. They used to say, "Hold on to your things." You know, hold on to things that were mine. I was always giving my stuff away to somebody that wanted it, always lending my car out to people. Of course, I am paying for that right now because . . . what got all the heat on me in the first place this time was [because] I loaned my car out to a couple of thieves!

Incidentally, they both were women. They were women burglars. Both of these girls were professional dope addicts. They also didn't need anybody to help them break into a house and carry out other people's color TV's. It is something they did every night of the week.

It just so happened that I let these girls take my car shortly after I was out of the joint and shortly after I got it, because Linda had a car, too, you know. But anyway, I let the girls take my car and they had it for two days, and I thought it was a little strange that they didn't look me up when they brought it back. They didn't bring it back to my house; they took it down to my mother's house and parked it there. I came down and there was my car. I thought maybe the girls were there for some reason. I didn't know why they would be; my mom doesn't know 'em.

My mom said that the car was there when she came out to go to work. The keys were in it and it was out of gas, of course, [or] almost. So, anyway, a couple of weeks later the police came down to my mother's house knocking on her door and they asked her what kind of car I drove and all that. Of course, the car that they described [to her] really was my car. They said they wanted to talk to me because the car involved was spotted leaving the scene of a burglary at a house or a trailer or some damned thing. And, of course, I wasn't seen, because I wasn't there. Of course, the cops did ask my mother if she knew any girls I might have lent my car to and she didn't. So [when] I came down, my mom said the detectives were there and they wanted to talk to me, and I said, "Well, to hell with it. I guess it's all over now," since my car was in a burglary and I'm a burglar . . . I put it all together and felt that I didn't have a chance. I decided to hell with it. I might as well do whatever I have to do now because I wasn't going to give up the girls. I didn't want to give them up, snitching 'em off, you know, by giving them up. And I was pretty goddam pissed off. I was going to find them and beat the shit out of both of them.

As soon as I found out the cops were there and the story, I knew I was on my way back to the joint, so I figured that as soon as I went down to the police station and I refused to cooperate, it would be automatic for me; they'd put me in a cell and run me back to [the joint] for being involved as an accomplice. If not that, then accusing me of being there, too. So that's pretty automatic, really.

I still wonder what would have happened if I had done things differently. I don't think I would have come out any better, but what I did do was I just dropped my parole. I dropped everything. Like I said, I went undercover; I went underground and stayed on the run for several months and I was finally busted.

And in the meantime, during those several months, I had got drunk with a cousin of mine and we went out to see a friend of his, a doper. We drove out there. My cousin was going to buy a quarter-spoon of heroin. That's all he was going to do, you know. He gets out there to this place and his partner wasn't home. And . . . I don't know . . . the next thing I know was he had the goddam door open to this apartment and came running out with a portable stereo. I went in with him and I was standing around. Then he came back out again and he told me to get the TV, and I thought, Why not? I wasn't afraid of nothing; just being my old drunk self going along with anything. Open house. I figured, Why the hell not? The guy's a goddam dope addict, anyway. Everything he owns he probably stole, anyhow, so why not just take it? If he had come over to my house and I wasn't home, he would have done exactly the same thing: he would have broken into my goddam place and he would have beat me, stole from me. I know the reasoning; that kind of reasoning is a little sick, but I wasn't alone in that kind of reasoning and that's why we was in that place in the first place. If a doper friend comes over to my house and I am not home, I'm in trouble. He can get in and steal my TV or something.

So while my cousin was out to the car, apparently he had hollered at me that a car was coming. I didn't hear him, though. So the people, they came home. I was walking out the door. I wasn't carrying anything. I didn't know they were coming. When I walked out the door, they seen me and I pushed the guy out of my way and took off for my car. He was hollering and screaming at me. I got in my car and I split. He took my license number. I didn't change license plates because I didn't go out there planning to be in any goddam crime. He took my license number down and he called the police. When I got caught I got charged with burglary, and because the people were there, they changed it to first-degree burglary and they gave me twenty years for that. I had a credit card that was hot in my possession. I had been packing it around with me for months. I don't know where the hell I got the damn thing. I used to use credit cards a lot, so guys would give me credit cards that they had ripped off. Somewhere along the line I took a Shell credit card and I used it. I'd just go gas up with it. I didn't have any money for gas, anyway, so I just took the chance. That's what I am here for now.

You know, it's hard when I get out, man, and not even know what it's going to be like, but I feel it's going to be better. I've got so much better a chance this time and if things go wrong I don't think I'll . . . I won't turn to dope. I can promise you that. I won't turn to dope. I might drink a little bit, but believe me, there won't be any dope. I'll find another way, you know. It's good friends and people helping me and having confidence in me and giving me this advice and, you know, this wisdom that I get from you, Chiquita. This is all going to help so much.

I had confidence for a while and when Linda and I started this photography business together doing these weddings, we started making real good money. I had more jobs than I could handle. I had to turn down stuff. I had everybody screaming to come over to their house to do portraits for their families and things like that. And somewhere along the line, most of my old friends, the worst ones, my old friends who looked me up again, including Duane, they looked me up and just . . . well, they just kind of drug me back into it. I was trying to make a go of it and so you would hope those people would kind of take it as a hint and just go away. I mean, why can't he just fuck his own life up and leave me alone? But ex-convicts can't do that. They can't fall by themselves. They have to have somebody with them. And if a guy's doing good and you can bring him down, so much the goddamn better. That's the way it looks to me.

But I went down and I started shooting heroin. And I got more into it, more into it, until the little bit of confidence I had gained . . . and believe me, for Linda it was just a constant chore to try to build me up and try to get me back in shape and to help me do these things, and do most of the work for me half the time and try to keep reassuring me, which she still does, reassuring me that I can do it, I can do this and I can do that, you know, and "just try and things will be better for you." I've heard all this, you know, because this woman has done that for me for years and . . . but heroin is too strong. It's just like you've been ducking along and it's this giant, giant demon and once it gets you, it's got you. You're not going to get away, you know. If you get away with your life, you can consider yourself mighty lucky. Well, I got away with my life, but during that period it was my downfall.

It was obvious to everybody that I was going to go back to the joint. It was just a matter of weeks and months before I went. And I went. I went again and I went again and so here I am. But I've never been able to get back up since that time. I mean it just took all the wind out of my sails when I did fall out. That was the longest I was ever out of the joint and was slow when I did go back. I came back in 1972 for about six months. Then I got out and I got busted in '73. I got out in '75, like I said, and I'm back in [now], so I ain't ever been able to get off the ground again since that one good shot I took in 1968. And I had set my mind on other things other than being in prison, you know, in spite of the help and the love I've got from these people. And I blame that strictly on dope. I blame it on dope. I blame myself, of course. I blame myself. I understand. I see the weaknesses that develops in a person and I really despise it, but you never know when it's gone or how it goes or if it stays. All you can do is to try to recognize it while I'm doing this time here. And I ask myself, Am I ready? When will I be ready? How will I know? You know these things aren't going to be answered, because I can walk around here in the daytime and just feel ready to meet the world. You know what I mean? But deep inside it's shaky, you know. Can you understand that, Chiquita? Sure, you can. I feel great, but deep inside . . .

I can't take any bad-mouthing and shit from people [in the free world]. You know how quick people are running jaws out there. In here, it's different. You don't do it, man. It ain't done. It's just like shouting and screaming at somebody and giving them orders and getting smart-assed with 'em, and they don't expect to get slapped in the fucking face over that shit in the fucking streets. Physical violence never enters their fucking minds when they're running their jaws out there, you know, and it's hard to get used to that shit. My first impulse is to fire 'em up, man. I don't scream and holler at people and I don't expect them to get bossy with me, especially some baldheaded sucker. Cop an attitude toward me, man. You know, they all do it, even the cab driver. I'm shaking in the cab because if he says one of them smart-aleck words to me, like they say in the movies, I'm tending to violence any fucking moment, man. I'm always waiting for it. I'm waiting for him to say something smart to me if I ask questions. Like I see in the movies. Because I wouldn't take that shit from no motherfucker. You know how them New York cab drivers are so smart-ass in the movies when you ask a question? Pow! You know, every fucking answer, "You punk, get off!" Luckily, out here, though, they're different. Most of them are fairly courteous. If they had a rough day they might not talk too much. But I ain't no talker any goddam way, you know what I mean?

I expect a little courtesy from one of the store guys, store people, or whatever, but they pick their shots, I guess. But I've had some of the strangest fucking monkeys get in my face over something. It just stopped me cold in my tracks, man. I just turn fucking cold inside and I'm ready to kill. I try to understand the sonovabitch, you know. What could he possibly be thinking? I'm holding back by a fucking thread, man, and some little sawed-off bastard is telling me to get out of the way, or move my car. "Your goddam car's in my way. Who do you think you are?" Jesus! I'd be turning red, you know. Sonovabitch, wreck his car and my car and I'll come back to the joint, leave that sonovabitch to wonder what happened to him.

That's one of the things *you* don't have to deal with, Chiquita, that you don't think about that much, but I think about it more and more now. I try to bring those things out so I can try to deal with it. What brings it out in me is TV. Like that guy that was talking in the cab, that kind of shit. I can't deal with that. There was a guy like that, too, in the movie tonight. There was this guy's boss. He was a park ranger, but his boss was yelling and screaming at him and smart-mouthing and there was no cops around to hold him back. He didn't have to stand and take that shit. He could have whipped the fucking guy ten times over. He probably was boiling inside, but he was able to hold it. He walked out. I had a boss like that, too, you know. One thing about it, he avoided me like the plague, though. The Walla Walla thing hit him. He knew who he was hiring and why he was hiring me, so we never did have any run-ins, really. I could tell even at times when he was mad about something he never talked with me directly.

Being my old self, Chiquita, I have managed since I've been here to reach out and get myself in trouble all over again. God, why did I do it? I just . . . I mean, I'm here, you know. I have a lot of girls come into the clubs here for our meetings and things and I met that girl that I'm stand-ing with in the picture I sent you, the Indian girl with the long, black hair. And Linda's the older lady that I'm with in the other picture. And Marie is blonde. And I don't think I sent you a picture of her. Marie is an older im-age of my daughter, put it that way. They look like the Gold Dust Twins when I look at them in a picture. And I write to all of them right now and we're all great friends. And who knows, I might end up with Marie again one of these days and take my family back.

But the situation I'm in right now . . . I'm being pressured hard by Co-rinne to marry her. She asked me several times and made a special trip down here from California over the Christmas holidays to visit me. And she wanted to talk seriously about that because, of course, we met and we got along. She is kind of pushy and, of course, she's pretty. I liked her when I first met her. I had no intention of really pushing the matter other than trying to be friends. Maybe that's the trouble. Some girls can't un-derstand being friends, you know, without being lovers. That's tough. Some of the more intelligent women can understand that and appreciate it and feel secure in that kind of relationship, you know, and maybe be lovers once in a while, too, which is nothing to get excited about, to get married over, but Corinne doesn't seem to be that way. She declares herself to be an old-fashioned Indian girl. And I've already broached the subject of multiple wives. I did that over Christmas vacation and I told her, I says, "Listen, you're always telling me that you know I'm not Indian enough and I value material things too much and that's the white way and all that bullshit." And she's bound and determined that she's going to change me and she's gonna do this and she's gonna do that and, of course, I resist and

I've given her fair warning that this is not, it's not something that's done with me that easy. People have tried all their lives to run my life, you know, and all they've managed to do is to lock me behind bars, and I'm afraid that's the way it's going to continue to be.

But this last visit . . . her and I are pretty thick and she visited me a lot and I fell for the girl and I'm wondering now . . . I mean I could stand to lose her without a helluva lot of heartache, you know what I mean, so I'm lying to myself in that respect. But it's pretty complicated. My thinking is kind of cold-blooded, I guess, and I'd better take a good hard, long look at how I'm beginning to make some decisions, because when this started out I was thinking exactly that in building a new life I also needed new people, you see. Now listen to me, Chiquita, for a minute and if it doesn't make any sense I really want you to tell me, because you know that I know myself that there's something wrong in wanting to do that. But there's more to it than it sounds and I'll try to explain the reasoning for looking for new people, not only new friends.

I don't plan to run around with Duane or these other guys, right? Okay, and at the same time I should wait and let love go where it's going to go and meet the girl of my dreams when I'm out there and can kind of sort through to get at what I want. Well, it just so happens that this girl, Corinne, is pretty much the image of what I want. She has three children, and that's not a deterrent to me at all because her children are beautiful and she's got a great little family and the kids are well behaved and intelligent and the son's getting ready to go to college in a year, and she's thirty-five years old, she's beautiful, as you can see. She's in college at Davis, California. The reason she packed up her family and went down there is because her plans are the same as mine. She wants to help her people and she wants some education and she's working on her B.A. now, and, of course, we've talked and our interests are the same.

Well, not always the same. I mean, you know yourself if you're thinking about it what my interests are. She's thinking Indian now, let's put it that way, and although she has spent her life out of it, I mean never really thinking Indian, and her kids and her, they don't have that accent. There is an Indian accent and I think that you might know that yourself. But she's always lived in the city the same as me. Now she declares that my lifestyle is what got me in trouble. And I argued that point because it isn't the society I live in, that isn't what put me in the joint, you know, although it is true, the way I lived my life put me in the joint. So she's bound and determined to change that and take me to the reservation and do this and that, and you know that's not me, so that's a big problem between the two of us. But I did agree to marry her. Boom! Whoosh! And I did do that and I wish I hadn't, but I did. But I was thinking ahead, you know, and I thought, Well, Linda and I, although we still say, "I love you," and this and that and "Miss you," and she comes down to see me a couple times a year and brings my daughter down, I really think that we have to go our own way.

Linda has a son in Tacoma and, believe me, I don't fit. I mean her family is . . . they're family and well-off. They're middle-class people, and my God, how's she gonna look if she ever tries to drag me in there, you know what I mean? And her sons have kind of shied around because of me and I think they've been embarrassed because of me for several years now, and they're pretty happy, really, when I'm in the joint. I think they're relieved when I'm gone, so Lord knows what I'm going to have their mother doing when I'm out. And so they hesitate to bring their wives and families over to visit their mom. And I think they would come over a lot more if, you know . . . when I'm not out they'll come over, but I think it's a little embarrassing to them to bring their wives over and see their mother is with a guy who is almost as young as they are, you know, regardless of how well her and I are getting along. That's it. She was sexy to me, and I'm telling you, it's no mother thing, although you can imagine I've had in Linda . . . I've found an awful lot of protection and security, you know, and actually it's been bad for me because . . . even Marie knew that.

And Marie told Linda that: "Please don't give Gene any more money. He won't do anything. He won't work and he won't learn anything and all you're doing is hurting him." But that is one of the ways she held on to me. But I can't see us getting along that good now. I mean . . . aw . . . I don't know. You know what I mean? Christ, she's . . . you know, she's . . . she just wants what all . . . she likes her family and she enjoys the comfort of her home. She prepares things for herself and gets to do things the way she wants to do them and I just won't fit back into that. I can't picture it. Expecially if I've progressed and I've moved along in life. And I don't know how to talk about it with her. I really hope that maybe she's thinking the same, you know. I've often wondered if she's just worrying about that time when I don't need her in that way anymore, and maybe she can have a break, and do her thing, which is her drafting and art and architecture and her family, her grandchildren now, and not have to worry about me, explaining me, especially having to worry about me being in jail. I'm just wondering if she's thinking about those things, if she's thinking about the future. I hope so, because Lord knows I just don't know how to do it. But you see, that's what I thought about. If I'm going to have to build a new life, then I guess I should, but marriage is no way to start off a new life, either.

So, you know, I really fucked up in that respect and I'm stuck with it right now and I'm really counting on the time I have to work this out. I'm actually hoping that just because of the amount of time that I have that the relationship between Corinne and I will cool itself off, you know what I mean? Yes, you do, and that's kind of shirking the issue a little, but I don't have to rush things, because I ain't out of here so I can't . . . I can't get out of here and hurt anybody, so then I'm just kind of hiding out now in a way. I'm just kind of thankful that I'm in here because of that. And there's been a lot of times when I've been on the streets, as far back as I can remember, when I've put myself in the same situation between the women [in my life] that I look toward the jail to get myself out of it, you know what I mean? I actually felt relief, for chrissake, once I was in the goddam hoosegow! I'd say, "Whew! I got all that pressure off my ass, man, but sonovabitch, I don't want to go back to the joint!"

But I mean it's a relief not to have the hassle and shit like that. Oh, it's a hell of a way to think, I know, I agree, and I'd appreciate a few words of wisdom from you and I know you've got something for me there, Chiquita. You can bawl me out too, you know what I mean? You and I are pretty thick now, so if you feel like kicking me verbally, you just go right ahead, and believe me, I'll listen, because I know I'm wrong. I know I really got to pull myself in and I slipped up and I fucked up and I shouldn't have done it. But I did, goddam it! I'm suffering nightmares over it and I want to get out of it.

Like I said, I came back this time with twenty-five years and the parole board gave me a minimum of twelve years, which means you have to do eight on twelve. It's a lot of time; it's really blown my mind. It's a time in my life when it's really too much time for me. It's weighing heavy on me. I'll make it, but it really drives me up the wall being away from my daughter. I spend so much time with her when I am out. I get to keep her with me and things. She's growing in leaps and bounds and it does something to me. She's really growing away from me now. She has reached an age . . . I don't know . . . so, anyway . . .

I told you why I was here. I never told you that I was here for being a fool, did I? A cold fool; two women, that time. I was a pushover. I was a pushover for anybody. Hopefully, I will make some changes in that department. Hang on to my money, hang on to my car, and get rid of those things . . . friends. I have already gotten rid of them. They are not the kind of friends you have for years. They are the kind of friends you have for a month or two months, whatever it takes for you to get thrown in jail. They can kick back and have a good laugh about you going to prison and them being out. I was the fool. Yep, that has happened to me quite a few times. But it won't again; of that I'm sure. It won't again. And it's the same weakness that got me in trouble in the joint time and time again. Doing crazy things in prison, you know—getting loaded, sniffing, and things like that, hanging with that crowd, you know. Consequently, one more time in the hole and segregation and then out in population. But that has changed. I have been able to control myself now. For the last two years I have had that completely under control. I thank God for that, too.

My prayers are all for strength and for wisdom to carry me past all these things and be on the right road, to guide me. I ask, continually, I ask for guidance just to do the right things, you know; to accomplish some good things. I really feel strong and I really feel like I am getting that guidance that I want and I ask for. It has always been there waiting for me. I am happy when I am secure in that belief. I have pretty strong faith. I have faith in the power of prayer. The Grandfathers are all around me; I feel them, their strength, the Great Spirit, to control life and give us life. If we turn away from him and we don't stay with him, then our life is bad. Our life is bad; I know that.

There's always been that emptiness in me that scared me and made me restless and made me unhappy, always, you know, never feeling at home and never feeling right about anything out there. And it just caused me to run like one of those little animals in a cage, around and around in circles. And that's gone out of me. It's truly gone out of me, because the other times that I've been in here I've had that feeling, that emptiness, that restlessness. And really, I disliked myself so damn much . . . I guess I tried to run away from my own feelings and my life and my situation and . . . I don't know, it's kind of hard to describe, but I was always running. As soon as I woke up in the morning I had to get going. But I never had a destination. I just never knew where I was going to go. I just had to go, just keep moving and drink and do things that would take my mind off my own problems and my own hurt, because I did hurt. I hurt all the time inside. I was always so damn disgusted with myself and the things I was doing and the things I had done with my life. I was so goddam sad and disgusted and, "Poor me," you know. "Look what's happened to me; I'll never be anything and fuck everybody," and that attitude, you know.

And I used to write that on all the walls all over Tacoma: "Fuck the world." There's still evidence all over town that I'd been there. In different sections in Tacoma you will find in spray paint "Fuck the world." But I had a symbol that I used rather than write the words, because I didn't want 'em to erase the words, so I put an F and a T and a W and they're all joined together and they make one symbol. And I think I drew that for you once when you were here. I used to wear that symbol. I had it made by a jeweler on a silver chain and the symbol was cut out of stainless steel and polished, and I used to wear it and I used to wear a ring that had a little silver FTW on it. I used to have all that stuff. Some people wear swastikas; I used to wear that, and even my dog . . . I painted a FTW with red fingernail polish on his forehead. And my little daughter, whenever she'd go home [after being with me], her mother always had to wash tattoos off her, 'cause I used to sit and draw FTW on her little shoulder.

Oh, my God, that is terrible! But what the hell; I guess it just shows by itself [what I felt]. I know now some of the psychology of things like that, and that knowing it, of course, didn't have anything to do with those feelings going away. But over the course of the last three years that feeling has gone. And I've always had it in prison, too, you know. Even in prison I've been restless and I've felt lousy because I always was dissatisfied with myself and I didn't like myself. And I guess maybe that might be one of the most important things: I didn't like myself and I knew if I accepted punishment as . . . I felt I had it coming for being such a rotten kid and being such a rotten adult, and maybe I asked for more [punishment]. Maybe I went out and deliberately did things so that I got my just deserts, you know what I mean? I think I did. I believe that.

I have a feeling that . . . well, it's obvious, too, from the record, that nobody's done anything to me that I haven't gone clean out of my way to ask for. And I've never complained about being picked on, really. I've never had complaints about parole officers or police. I never have felt that, because I've always known that each time that I got here I worked hard to get here. I truly worked harder than other people to get myself put in this goddam place, you see, and I think the way that I did my time also indicated my willingness to accept the punishment as my lot . . . and I was happy to do it, you know what I mean? I mean more than happy to do this.

And what do you say? It's horrible, goddam it! It's terrible [the feeling that I need punishment] and it has to end somewhere. And it's ended, I truly believe, and I know that because that feeling is gone and, oh, my God, I wish that I could really tell you about it, Chiquita, but . . . I don't know . . . it's like having a wart and the wart's gone. That's ridiculous to try to simplify that, because that emptiness and that pain that I had in me was the cause of everything I did. It was the cause of when I used dope to try to get rid of it [the pain] for a few hours. It was the cause of my drinking. It caused the way I drove, reckless and fast, a hundred miles an hour, never really caring. I'd drive a hundred miles an hour on the streets and roads and backroads, and I'd drive one-handed and relaxed, you know, which shows I really didn't give a shit. I didn't care if I went off the road. And the things I faced and the things I did and faced death, and OD'd on dope again and again and . . . oh man, it's so sickening!

Somewhere, somehow . . . I don't know how it's possible and I don't know if it happened to other people, but there's always been a part of me that said and cried, "I don't deserve this. I'm a better person than this, and this isn't me." And that part of me has always been afraid and looked to God to help and save my life and change things somehow, sometime, somewhere. Maybe it would be with age, and it was a . . . I begged inwardly to be allowed or be shown somehow to, you know, to grow up. I've asked this of myself and I wanted, you know . . . I know, I always knew that I was stuck somewhere, and then I was in my thirties and I was still an adolescent and an asshole. And so I've always been afraid and I actually thought for a while that maybe I was retarded. I did. "Why?" I said. "I just don't act adult and I don't think adult. How am I going to get [hold of] this thing? Where am I going? When am I going to become responsible and [do] all the things that a responsible person does? When am I going to have some confidence?" And I have so little self-confidence that I really couldn't even grasp a concept. I thought I was stupid. What the hell, it was only by looking at other people and I didn't recognize those type of people, your type of people, Chiquita. [He's talking about the middle class, about being middle-class himself. He never thought he could join that world, the world of the law-abiding, hardworking, achievement-oriented. He sees himself as unworthy and unacceptable since he is a lawbreaker, a person who belongs to the criminal subculture or underworld. People in the square world won't accept him because he's a felon, and also he doesn't trust the middle-class world. It has been his enemy in his eyes. His "people" are underworld people, lawbreakers who refuse to join the system, who live by exploiting it.] I didn't look at you. I'm going to use you as a model for while I'm talking here, and I think you'll know what I mean.

I didn't recognize you as people, that I could possibly be like you, see. I've always seen [people like you], but it didn't mean anything to me. It was like another type of human being, and I was this type of human being and you were another type of human being. And there was doers and I was a nondoer. There were haves and I was the have-not, and somehow I was delegated to this position in life and I was born to it and my . . . you know . . . I accepted it with my can of spray paint and I said, "Okay, I'll take this. And here, fuck the world. This is all I can have and this is all I can do." Outwardly, that's what I did, the way I acted. But I did want it [to be middle-class], you know, although I had so goddam many fears that you could never put 'em in a book. And inferiority! I felt inferior! I lived inferior! And I acted inferior to everybody around me, even including some convicts, for chrissake!

There's a funny thing about the convict code. Although a person like myself can't seem to do anything right in your normal society and neighborhood communities, I guess growing up in prison . . . I never felt normal and I never felt on an even level with people unless it seems like I was in prison. I never knew why, you know, and I never really questioned it until the last two or three years, and I think that you had a big influence in that part of my life, too, ever since you and I have started working together. I have to say that although I didn't believe so much in the convict code, I never questioned it and I never really looked at it for what it was.

And the thing about it is, there is a certain amount of dignity that a person can gain in the penitentiary. There's our form of social controls in here and in most penitentiaries. The ability to take it, you know, and endure mentally what you can't avoid. That's kind of the big thing. So you can [endure] if you're abiding by the convict code. Then . . . let's see, well, dignity. And you need composure. Oh, lots of composure. You need courage; you need to at least show courage outwardly. You might be scared shitless inside, which is the case most of the time. And more than anything, you have to be able to take it, and you have to be able to hand it out when it's necessary. These are the traits that really are affirmed by the convict code. Actually, they're also the traits that are most commonly defined, I guess, as masculine. Right?

Well, by the whole population, that's what they look for in each other. We're always judging people by that in here, and, well, I guess from what we lose on the street, being so goddam inadequate out there in everything we try to do, we sort of lose our masculinity [in the free world]. In this case, when you get back in prison you can recapture that part of you in a different form. You can recapture what is normal for the male role in here. And it doesn't have to do with any sexual aspect, you know. It's just in terms of your behavior around here. Like I said, the ability to hand it out and take it and keep your composure under every situation that comes up and to not show weakness and to have our former dignity and hold your head up, and no matter if somebody's trying to chop it off. So if you live in[side] these walls and you're living as a good convict and you're living by the convict code to the letter, you see, you gain back all that you've lost out in normal society, because the only way we can have those things out there is, in my opinion, through education, through living a meaningful life.

And the word *meaningful* to me means a lot. I'm not going to explain what it means to me, but it means a lot. And I'm clear in my mind what it means, and it's accepting that responsibility of caring for your family and yourself and if you're doing a good job and your children are in school and they're well fed and they have fairly good clothes and your wife is relatively happy taking care of the house and you're not beating her up and you're not separating all the time and you're not a drunk, then you've got dignity coming, you see. You're doing a hell of a job. You may not be middle-class. You may be goddam near poverty-stricken, but if you're holding your own, you've got dignity, and that takes strength, you know; you got respect coming and you're a man. You are what a man is supposed to be and [doing what a man is] supposed to do.

But if you're out there, and I think [when] we get out of these places, we're just like goddam mutts that run up and down the alley, you know what I mean? The local neighborhood goddam dogs. We assume that position and we run—in my case, I drive—and you move and you run and you take a bone here and you take a bone there and you bury a bone here, you know, and you stop by and get a few strokes from this person and that person and they don't have anything to stroke you for, because you don't do a goddam thing. And if that's all that you know, life is tough. That boat the guy's got down the street, the nice house Joe Blow's got, that just isn't us, you know. And the reason it isn't us is because there's no way that we can do [what they do]. You don't know anything, you're unskilled, you haven't even begun high school, and if you did get a job, then the job that you get is going to be the lowest thing on the scale. It's gonna be unskilled and so your pay is going to be the lowest the law allows and how are you going to buy that car? That house? That boat? Take care of those kids and have your kids look as nice as the rest of the people's kids if you ever could get that way? How are you gonna do it? So if, even if you have serious moments and you sit down and you consider what you've got to do to put it together, and if you marshall all your strengths and you've got all your shit together and you went after it and you took what you've got and put it on the job market and set a goal, chances are you're not gonna reach any goal to take you above the economic level that you're at.

So, of course, there's other ways. That's to drop everything you're doing and pretend, maybe, that you haven't got all these bad habits, to somehow get motivated enough to get up out of this rut you've been in for the major portion of your life, ignore all the psychological chains, the barriers, just somehow bounce up out of this and change your mode of living, change your education, acquire all this education, ignoring the fact that you're too damn old to go to high school and you think you're a dummy any goddam way. I mean, that goes without saying, so that even a GED test, the thought of a GED test is tough. It defeats you. You don't think you can pass . . .

Sounds a little discouraging. I'm not gonna discourage myself, though, because I'm through the tough part, goddamit! I'm not no dummy. The thought of college and the thought of a GED scared the shit out of me. I swear I just didn't think I had it in me, you know, but that's the way my life's been. I didn't think I had anything in me other than a lot of goddam dreams and, oh shit, just so damn, damn many of us live like that and we believe [we can't do it] and we've accepted that and even if you somehow get the courage up to even take the GED test, that doesn't say that you can do college-level work, you know. It doesn't help. It doesn't give you any self-confidence. So you got through the GED test. Even if your grades are high, that doesn't do a damn thing. It doesn't mean you can do high school work, as far as I'm concerned and as far as anybody else is concerned. It just means that you've lived and you've done a few things and maybe you've read some books, you know, and you got through the goddam test so somewhere along the line . . . Say that you really want to do this—I mean you have to really want to change your life—you've got to seriously believe that education can be the answer.

So it takes something else to take that first step. It takes some good counseling by people. It takes real concern from teachers, the staff, because you're certainly not going to get it from friends; you're not going to get encouragement in here from friends. You're constantly laughed at when you start, really. They actually try to encourage you to drop out of everything, get back in the old swing of things and miss classes, do nothing, to drink, to smoke dope. That's all you get from your friends. So people constantly . . . aw, it pisses me off. They keep saying, "Aw, you're too old. You're too old to do that. You'll never change. You'll never . . ." Oh, God, I hate that! Geez, I hate that when people talk, when people tell me that because I've gone . . . I've grown up believing and doing and acting the way adults told me my life was gonna end up, when I was younger, you know, all those negative things that grown-ups told me when I was younger and getting in trouble and having problems. People didn't encourage me even at the tender age of ten, eleven, twelve, and that is still an impressionable age. All I ever heard from people was "You're no good. You're gonna end up in a penitentiary. You're gonna do this, blah-blah-blah," you know.

So now when I hear that from people, you only hear it from your friends. Even officers will encourage you, you know. When you're trying, they'll say, "I hope you make it," and "I think you'll make it." "I think you're gonna be all right." That's what you need. You have to have that, you know. I look for that, and goddam it, the people can really make my blood boil when they belittle my effort. Somehow it's affecting them, I guess. They try to tell me, "Oh, you'll never change, blah, blah," and "Look at this guy and look at that guy. They've been here all their lives." Aw geez. Well, you understand what I mean.

I wanna come back here one of these days so goddam bad and say, "Look, you sonovabitches, you can make it. All you assholes out there that stop these guys from trying to change, from trying to learn something, from trying to do something for themselves, and hold 'em back and believe that this is what it's all about, baloney!" I want to be able to stand there and I want to be able to talk, to drive this point home and show these people that it can be done by doing it. And I'll do that one of these days, mark my word. I will do that. I will come back, and when I come back I'll be driving a nice car and I'll be dressed better and I'll have a family and I'll have some things, and more than anything else, I won't have any more arrests. I won't be on parole. I'll be in that other world. I'll be part of the system. I'll be working to change the system in any way that I can. I'll be working to stop people from coming to prison.

It all sounds so good, doesn't it? But it's also possible for me. It's all open to me and I know I'm good at it, so I have confidence. I know that's where my ability is. I know I have talent for that. I have a talent to influence people. I am a leader. People will listen to me and, number one, I have quite a reputation in the Washington State Penitentiary and other institutions [in the state], and I'm not a snitch. I never have been. I've never been a weakling. I've never been a punk. I've never used punks. So nobody can put me down. Nobody can turn on me in that audience of convicts which I want to face alone. And I'll tell them, "You ain't turning to your partner next door and saying, 'Aw, he's full of shit. He wasn't nothing. He didn't do anything.'" There's nobody will ever do that with me. I know for a fact that I'm gonna finish school. I'm gonna go as far as I can. I'm not gonna starve out there, so the pressure isn't gonna be on me. There's not going to be that much pressure that I can't go to school, that I have to work constantly, because I'll make room for it. That's a priority with me and will remain a priority until I get all that I can get. I'm not worried about that at all.

So I'm luckier than a lot of people in here in that respect that I will have the time, the opportunities to take advantage of what's offered, and I'm not ignoring the fact that I'm a minority and I can take advantage of plenty of programs to take care of the financial end. I'm aware of that. And I'll be more aware of that when I start investigating the sources. So there's so many beautiful things that's gonna be. Nothing's gonna be easy. God, don't ever get the idea that I'm thinking that, because it hasn't been easy and it's not going to be easy at all in the future, I know. *This* is easy. This is so easy right here. I just have to . . . I've got my little old house here, regardless whether I like it or not. I've got my place to study. I don't have a lot of pretty little girls running around to distract me. I haven't got any reason to be late in the morning because I'm not going anywhere. I don't have to worry about gas; I just walk over to the school. This is easy, you see.

And people like myself, we don't have a hard time in prison, you know. It's fat city. I mean it's a piece of cake. Some people have a hard time, as you know. I don't have a hard time and people like me don't. We can get by and our friends will help us get by. So I mean it's a tight society in that respect. You do look out for each other. We are concerned for each other and there is a certain amount of love, you know. The closer you are, like our cell partners here, I worry about these guys constantly and I look out for them and I expect them to look out for me. And when I'm sick, I expect them to be a little concerned and watch, and my partner over there in the next bunk, if he's got a real bad cold or if he's got the flu, I worry with him because I know about pneumonia and things like that. So I'll even find myself at night when he's . . . if he's . . . I'll lay here a long time and I'll watch his breathing, you know, and make sure he's breathing good and everything, and I don't relax until he gets well, you see, and that's something. Maybe that's just me, but they do [the same for me].

When I was real terribly sick a month or so ago, my brothers here they felt with me. They were concerned, you know. They did little things that they could do to make me more comfortable. They stole food from the dining hall because they knew I was too sick to walk over there, and I didn't ask for these things, you know. They took a chance on getting tagged and they stole some biscuits, doughnuts, and brought me these little things while I was sick. So, you know, I get mad and I get sad and I get disgusted with the guys in here, but they're not a race of animals, maniacs. And I can't help but love them and be concerned about them.

Of course, you're in a culture that doesn't have feelings. There's no value in emotions. *Emotions* is a dirty word in here; to be compassionate or tender, those things are useless in here. But they're a part of being a human being, the part that you have to hide. You have to consciously cover up that you feel bad because this guy got killed. You can't express that, man. You gotta hide it. That's gotta make some scars, man. That's hard on your psyche, man, to do that.

It ain't easy for people, believe me. You get to the point where things get so bad that you learn how to control your own emotions, wrap 'em up and put 'em in mothballs. You can't play with 'em like that, man. It's a risk. But if you try, you can lay back in your bunk and cry. If you try hard enough you can reach down just like sorting through a box. I can, man, I really can. I picture it in my mind, a bunch of spools of thread, you know what I mean? And I got 'em and I know what they are and I can pick that one. That's my daughter, and if I sit here by myself and nobody's in the house I can start toying with that. That thread is my daughter. It's the binding thing between us. I can start pulling that out in my mind's eye, pulling it out, pulling it out, thinking about her, and I start to get a lump in my chest. My feelings start a lump in my chest, man. A couple times a year I get to see her and I start thinking about my feelings for her and my being gone so much. What does she feel? And what have I done to her? And this and that and build it up and wham! Unless I consciously reach down and touch them feelings, they'll never pop up with me and then they don't bother me.

Had a visit yesterday. My daughter was over. A friend of mine brought my daughter. It was a good day, a good day. She's growing fast, as all kids do. I guess when they get nine years old, they start really sprouting. She's nine now, a little blonde. She's getting clothes-conscious, getting music collections of records. You know, all the kids do. All the girls, of course, start that a little earlier. Their interests are quite a bit different. It's tough on me because I don't keep up. I kind of fall behind on those things. I tend to keep thinking back a few years and keep . . . in my eyes she's still a baby, of course, so I think our conversation probably isn't what it should be, the father-daughter conversation. That worries me a little bit but it'll come along. It'll work itself out.

I ask her . . . I expect her to . . . if she has anything to talk about, serious questions, you know. I just ask her if she's got anything she wants to tell me and she says no. And we get back to nothing. Anyway, it's been kind of a real strong relationship between me and that kid. Being back in here so many times, I miss her for a while and she's . . . what, a couple months old? And I leave. When I come back, she's two years old. I leave her for a few months and I come back, I leave and I come back and she's four years old. And I'm with her for a little while and we have fun, we get super tight and I get busted and I come back here. And I get out and she's six years old, seven years old. Oh, God, it's . . . you know, it's just kind of impossible to keep up with the growing pains or whatever you want to call them, stages in her life. Even though we've all been through it, I still fall behind in that area because I don't understand the stages that a kid goes through that good. Only that I sit back when I'm thinking about her . . . I sit back and I . . . my thoughts are . . . things I wonder about . . . I mean I wonder what she's thinking about, things like that, what's important to her.

I know probably what's real important to her. I especially worry about what she thinks of me, and I don't suppose that she could ever understand the whys and the wheres of my situation, why I'm always gone. And that's what I've been waiting to try to answer when she asks, but she didn't ask. She accepts these visits as "That's our day." And I see her twice a year and that's our day and that's it. She doesn't seem sad. She's a little shy when we get started off. She's a little shy, but thank the Lord for even two visits a year. Could be worse. Could be like some people [in here] and be on the outs with my ex-wife or something like that, and then it would be a problem to ever see her. But in my case my ex-wife cooperates every way she can and agrees that it's best for now that we should see more of each other, so she encourages my daughter to write, sends me her grades, and makes it convenient for Linda to pick her up and bring her over here. And I really appreciate that fact. It means a lot to me now.

You know, in prison every man's nightmare is a death in the family. A death in a family is a tragedy on the streets also; however, this kind of grief is multiplied for both the prisoner and family because of restrictions imposed by this particular prison. I recently experienced the pain and anger connected with the death of my father. I was pretty fucking mad because of all the changes they put me through when I asked to attend the funeral.

Anyway, when my dad passed away I went straight to my caseworker and asked if I could go. Several months before, my brother and I had made a trip to see him in the hospital in Tacoma. So believe me, it was really a fight to get someone to approve this second trip. It was approved and I was due to leave at five in the morning. I felt pretty bad, but from the time I got the news of my father's death I never had a minute alone. I had to choke it all down and never shed a tear. I cried inside and that hurts even more.

When I got up the next morning, I packed up my medicine bag and eagle feather. I also had a nice Indian prayer to say at the church. They cracked my door and I headed for Control. That's an all-night pig station; it is always open for business. I'm getting mad just talking about this. I was escorted to the visiting room to wait for the two guards assigned to be escorts. After a few minutes they came into the visiting room with their arms full of chains. "What the hell are these for?" I asked. They had cuffs, a waist chain, and leg shackles. "You'll have to wear these while you're away from the Joint." I said, "You mean every minute? You going to leave them on in church in front of my family and friends?" "Every minute," he says. I had to make a hard decision. I could see my mother and family, especially my little daughter, watching these two sloppily dressed goons lead me into the church and graveyard. You can't even get in and out of the car with all that shit wrapped around you, not without help anyway. It really wasn't hard to decide what to do. I said, "Take me back to my cell and cram those chains in your ass." It took a long, long time to cool down, *months*. My attitude was bad. Anytime I had to talk to a guard or the administration, I would freeze up thinking they each had a part in it. I built the whole trip around the chains into a conspiracy against me.

I know that you worry about me, Chiquita. You're right when you say that the world's a prison, too, and it's pretty cold-blooded out there. I know that, too. And it's cold in here and it's cold out there, but it is what we make it. I really don't look for the bad things. The joint's bad. Right. Sure, there's bad things about it, but there's good things about it, because

I've come back here but my whole life has changed. I met you and that's an A-number-one nice thing and it's good and I've benefited from it, and I've learned from you and I've learned what real friendship is and I've really learned to admire somebody else and see the beauty of a person. And if I hadn't come back, I'd never went to college. I'd fumbled my way through life with a seventh-grade education. There is so much good that I've got. And I've avoided the bad things, you know. The bad feelings are here [in the prison], but since I'm not involved I really don't actually have my hand in. I don't hurt anybody and I don't even wish anybody to be hurt. I get awful mad, but it's more sad than mad, you know. I don't hate the people that killed my [Indian] brother here . . .

You have to pray. You have to ask God to help you get rid of those feelings, because you can't let them take root. I can't live anymore with hate and resentment and bitterness toward anybody. I know how that must sound to you. It must sound ridiculous coming from me, but you just can't. And it's not a matter of just sitting and accepting anything that happens, see. I'm not that way, but, goddam, I guess I've grown up enough to know what I can do and I know what I can't do as far as being in prison, and it's not a matter of fighting back, because it's just a matter of knowing, accepting reality. I can't throw a rock and hit a cop in the head and change a goddam thing. All I can do is hurt myself and hurt the others around me. So I'm just lucky that I see that. And so I know how the outcome's gonna be and I know there's no satisfaction, there's no such thing as revenge in here. I know about revenge and I don't believe in it and I never have, because I don't like that feeling and I don't like living with feelings I don't like.

4

The Old Rebel
in the Free World

[The material for this chapter was collected in June 1992 in Tacoma, Washington, and was a response to my specific questions, unlike the previous chapters, which were tape-recorded ten years earlier in prison, where he was free to tell his story without direction from me.]

Yeah, I was devastated, as you say, when my brother died. What happened to him? He was drunk, already passed out drunk, and I went home to babysit him as I was doing every night, but I had to be back at the treatment center by ten o'clock. So when I decided I had to go back, he was already passed out on the bed. So I said, "Don't nobody give him any dope." I said, "He's already passed out." I figured it was safe to go, so I went back and went to sleep, and I got a call about six in the morning from Harry, the guy that was staying with us. He said, "Hope you're sitting down." That's all he had to say. He said, "Donny's gone. I'm sure of it." Said, "He OD'd last night. He got up long enough to shoot some heroin and he passed out on the floor. Everybody took off running every which way."

Nobody stayed there to help him, so I felt pretty guilty about that. I could have saved him if I'd been there, because I've saved him more than once. When he drug-overdosed I used C P R on him and brought him back two or three times. Only this time, that was it.

I got the phone call and I just said, "Okay," then I hung the phone up and I went back and laid down and covered up my head and passed out. They woke me up about ten o'clock saying, "Don't you know your brother died?" And I said, "Yeah, I know he died." I said, "Why should I hurry now? There's nothing I can do now." They said, "Well, hurry up. We'll give you a ride home."

And I was just dreading everything, having to tell the family, you know. So I had a guy give me a ride home. And when I went home, nobody was there. It was empty and I went next door to Mrs. Korlevas' house and used her phone and called up Mary Jan. Mom answered and I told Mom on the phone, I said, "Donny's dead." She screamed and hollered and dropped the phone and pretty soon Mary Jan got on the phone and I told her and she freaked out. And it went from there.

Everybody kind of gathered at the house. There was still a few dope addicts hanging around. [They] didn't know which way to go, so by the time Mary Jan got there, she started kicking everybody out except the family and, of course, started blaming me again, as if I had anything to do with it, which ain't unusual. She blamed me when my younger brother died, too, and I'd only been home from prison a couple days. It was pretty awful.

It didn't sink into me, hadn't sunk into me. Months later I was still in the angry stage. I started having dreams about beating him up with sticks and everything, you know, and that was pretty obvious. I was in this angry stage of him leaving me; as far as I was concerned, he just left me. We had a lot of plans together, a lot of laughs together. We thought alike, we talked alike, and our lives were going on the same path, of being drunk or being good, and I just never felt so totally alone in all my life. When I try to even think about it, my insides just turn to jelly. I was just paralyzed. I didn't know what to do, where to go, how to think, how to laugh. Couldn't cry. I just wanted to go with him. That's when I started getting self-destructive. I thought it would be better to be dead than go on alone. Seems like we'd . . . over the years we pretty much planned our lives together, even though we may have separate families. We were still together, same neighborhood, so that we can do things together, fish together, fix yards together, just anything, and . . . I don't know, seemed like my life just went out from under me. I had no plans on being alone. I didn't make any. I had no options. I couldn't imagine . . . just like a drunk who can't imagine living with alcohol and can't imagine living without it. And it's pretty much been that way ever since.

I haven't calmed down that much. I still can't talk much about him or think about him. I get choked up so I just try and wander around aimlessly, no direction. No direction, no escape, no hopes, no plans, no interest in anything anymore, no joy in life, no escape, no kind of peace. That's what it's come to as far as concerning Donny. I can't bring myself to go to the graveyard, and then when I went to the funeral, I got as loaded as I could on heroin and they almost had to carry me in there. And I couldn't . . . couldn't look at his body or anything. Just like looking at a mirror image to me. I think that's why I even shaved my mustache . . . by looking at some pictures of us together, him without a mustache and me with one.

Sometimes he'd be around and I'd hear him say, "I'm here." It come out of my own voice: "I'm here." I started hearing voices at the house at night, a man and a woman talking, so it wasn't . . . it wasn't Donny. A man and woman would be talking real low and muttering. I'd turn the stereo on. I'd turn the TV on and try to drown them out, and you still couldn't drown them out because they weren't even talking loud. They were probably in my head. That's when I started getting real disoriented; I *thought* that was happening.

So it hasn't left me with much. I haven't been able to come up with anything constructive. [Can't] even think constructive. Now when I get by myself, nothing happens. I'm just like a rabbit sitting behind the bush and just looking. It's a real helpless feeling. I feel helpless, hopeless. That's just the way it really is, helpless and hopeless. I'm really depressed, very severely, very severely. I don't know how I can overcome it. I want to be on lithium but the doctor wants to wait until I get more stabilized. What he means by that, I'm not sure. Does he mean stable in the sense that I don't know where I'm at now all the time? Or does he mean stable in the sense that my moods are at a point that are acceptable, livable? They have to do blood tests all the time [when you're on] lithium and I'm very hard to get blood out of because my veins are all shot up and gone from shooting dope. That was my hope. I had a lot of hope [about lithium] because I've studied lithium carbonate a lot. I went to libraries and got books on it, did research on it. One of the things that particularly interested me was that a lot of people that had alcohol problems, once they started on lithium, it did something to alleviate the craving for alcohol. So the [doctors] got two positive results out of it, and that's what I was hoping for. I was hoping Dr. Long would hurry up and do something. I'd like you to meet him. He's at Puget Sound [hospital] and he tries hard to help me a lot.

I got depressed a lot even when I was little. Yeah, I got very depressed. I had, according to the records . . . I had seen some of my records—you know the state really digs [into your life]. My file, they weigh my file. They don't count pages anymore. I seen reports in my case records from Olympia at Walla Walla [penitentiary] that said that one of the nuns in the third grade said I had a major inferiority complex. In the third grade, for chrissake! Where the hell did they get this stuff? My God, they got my life from day one, you know. I guess I did [have an inferiority complex]. I was always bummed out. The only way I could get out of it was for me and Donny to go out and do something exciting. Exciting was climbing those fences and breaking into cars.

See, my bipolar goes back to my teenage years. I've been manic-depressive since I was a teenager and now my depressive stages are lasting a lot longer. Instead of just lasting for a week or a month or two, they're lasting for months at a time. I don't hardly have a manic stage anymore. I can't remember the last time I had a manic stage. I just keep sinking further and further into the mud. I was always depressed when I was young. I recognized that, especially because it seemed that I was picked on. It seemed I was picked on by white society and it seemed that I was picked on by Indian people because I was a half-breed. And what was happening in my family bothered me. It's always bothered me. I was real quiet, a very, very, very quiet child. I didn't trust adults. I didn't trust women, period. I didn't trust anybody bigger than me. Of course, I trusted my mom and my Aunt Ruby.

I went in taverns since the time I was fifteen years old. I was drinking a lot of beer. Started when I was twelve. Never did think about my father's drinking problems. No, never did. I didn't even think like that. I'd say, "Hey, this is me." Maybe he could drink for twenty years and get in trouble and maybe I could drink forty years and not get in no trouble. I still feel that way, but I know it's wrong. I feel cheated. I feel downright cheated these days that alcohol affects me so bad, because I would like to drink another twenty years. I know guys in their seventies that have been drunk for forty years. I'd like to do that. I mean, if I wanted to.

I feel like a goddam weakling not being able to drink. I don't even like to admit to anybody that it makes me sick. I'll go ahead and take a drink and get sick. Yeah, it's sick, isn't it? But that's the Indian culture, too. All Indians drink. Well maybe not before the white man came, but they all drink now. What do you think they got "Thunderbird" on that bottle for? Because Indians believe the thunderbird is a powerful bird and they'll buy more of that wine. So they put an Indian thunderbird on the bottle and the Indians drink it [the wine].

I was expecting to be at the joint for another four years, but they decided to let me go. I was doing a good job [compared] to my record before. I had so much trouble with the prison authorities. I was always getting tagged. I had infractions for drinking, sniffing, any possible way I could get loaded. But I changed because I was getting too goddam old to do that much time. That twenty-five years made me think a little bit. I figured the least I could get, the least they could give me to do, was eighteen years, the minimum, so when you're in your thirties, thirty-four, thirty-five, that's a long time.

Working on that book with you made a difference, too. I was doing okay just before then, but helping you gave me a little more freedom inside the walls to go to the library when I wanted to. The majority of the staff there cooperated and let me get around there to do things for our book. I remember when I first met you. I think it was 1977 or '78. I can't remember for sure, but it was so strange that you should appear just at the time I was searching for someone to help me write about the prison. Here you come from Ohio State University, all charming and full of personality, and the convicts trusted you and so did I. I was lucky. They told us you were a folklorist and I thought, "What the hell is a folklorist?" I couldn't figure out why you wanted to study the prison lingo. I thought that was weird. But anyway, I remember a bunch of us met with you and I ended up working with you. I never for a second thought that your project would combine with my objectives, but the result was pretty damn good.

I've always been proud of the book we produced, because it was a study of *real* prison life as seen from the inside and it covered every step, through the court system right on into the prisons as seen and told by the men who were under sentences ranging from a year to double life for murder. I used to look forward to your visits to the joint when you and I would get together and talk about prison life. Because the convicts trusted you it made my job of interviewing them easier. Unlike rag-mag interviews or publications about the joint which only covered a brief period of unreal prison life, our book was a true picture of life in the joint. Like I said, all the cons trusted you and I'd spent so much time in the prison system that I no longer needed to worry about being trusted as a good convict; I am and was a good convict and my people [fellow prisoners] spoke truthful and most were sincerely interested in the creation of a truthful account. In fact, I believe you could find no better realistic book for the study of the legal system and institutions than our book. And I learned so much from you, Chiquita. You were the one person in my life that was able to inspire and encourage me to continue my education. I will always love and respect you for your dedication and helpfulness throughout all these years. I truly found a friend for life in you, and although we are separated by thousands of miles, you're still there for me. I know you have a lot of hopes and dreams for me and are disappointed when things don't turn out right. I wish I could make you happy and not disappoint you. I try to do the best I can. It's depressing when you're mad at me, Chiquita. Smile.

Anyway, I transferred out of Walla Walla [in] late 1981 after I got into the work-release program out in the minimum-security building. I stayed there for three months, which was plenty of time to get me registered [at the University of Washington in Seattle], get me the grants I needed, and then they transferred me and let me go.

It took about six months for my brain to catch up with me. While I was in the University of Washington I was a student, but I was still a convict. I was afraid to leave the campus. It was like a giant invisible wall. I just walked the edges of the campus and just looked out at the activities across the street. But I was paranoid, too self-conscious to go into a tavern or go where any groups of people were, because, of course, I felt older, out of place and stupid because I just came out of prison. Seemed like everyone could tell just by one look at me that I was an ex-convict, thief, a dope addict. So I really stayed by myself in a forty-thousand-student university. I was always by myself. It's pretty hard to find a seat in the dining room by yourself, I'll tell you that. So I used to eat on the steps a lot, or out on the grass.

But I was lonesome. I was lonesome for my old convict buddies because I didn't have any street buddies. I was lonesome for Donny and those guys back in the prison, kind of wishing I was back there. And it took a lot to get over that. It took a lot to be comfortable at the university. A long while. I had to go in to counseling there. Guy said, "What's the matter with you?" I told him, "I'm lonesome. For one thing, I feel out of place. I'm from the prison, man. I don't know anybody. Everybody's young, riding bikes around, playing games here and there. I don't know what the hell to do. I can't find anybody to talk to." He says, "Well, you probably don't talk to anybody anyway." I said, "That's true." He says, "You know what I am?" He was a psychology major. He says he was an ex-convict out of California, and that was cool. We hit it off pretty good. He says, "Fuck them people. You don't have to talk to them. If they want to be cliques and clans, let them be cliques and clans. Go on your own and do what you want to do. Eventually you're gonna meet up with somebody. There are a lot of Indians on campus that think they're alone. They just haven't found each other yet. Find the Indian clubs where they congregate. You'll find new friends."

That's exactly what I did and that's exactly what happened. Found a couple of new girlfriends real fast, a couple of my buddies, and started getting friends with other people and getting involved in Indian things and politics on campus. Events mostly. For the most part, Indians stayed out of politics. They stuck with their own. They ran for elections or something like that. Then it was just a popularity contest. It ain't who's smartest; it's just who's got the most friends. And it took a couple years. It got better, it got better and my grades went up.

I had a lot more time to study because I didn't party all the time. Then once I did get out of the university and started coming home, I had to learn all over again how to be a neighbor to a white person or a regular person. How to say hello, good morning, good-bye, and good night, and not just stare at them out the window like I used to do. I had a cop living next to me, of all goddam things. Right next door! So I thought he was after me all the time, watching me all the time. But he wasn't; he just lived there. I was real suspicious, real paranoid, a real loner, just like I am now.

But anyway, when I first started at the University of Washington I tried to compare it to a positive institution rather than negative. It didn't work. There is no comparison. I loved being there, yet was scared shitless. I never cared for crowds, and that was crowds. It was so strange and different from what I was used to in life: picking classes, getting registered, getting signed for the loans and grants was a major step, a major change. Just doing things on my own was different as hell. I was proud as hell for even getting enrolled without help. Well, maybe just a tiny bit [of help].

I pretty much walked around like a sleepwalker for the first week I was there, following the other students. Talk about culture shock! I was like a farm boy come to the big city. I lived on campus in a dorm or "cluster" reserved for guys from the joint. I would say there were thirty of us at any given time. I really hated school when I was young, but the university gave me a better perspective. I was treated as a man rather than a child. My classes were for the most part in social work. Of course, I had a lot of Indian studies (Northwest Coast). I studied the language and culture of the tribes here in the Northwest where I grew up.

Classes were not really hard as long as I studied, but I did need to learn new tricks, or old, about studying. I went to private counseling on campus because I wanted to learn not to isolate so much. It didn't help. Anyway, I enjoyed each day and built my self-esteem up. I met good people, took part in events, held [lectured to] a couple classes on my own for fifty bucks an hour twice a week. Picture that! I was teaching about institutions and the court system from step one. I was invited to a couple sorority houses to talk about prisons.

Although it took a couple years, I did come out of my shell. Once the campus newspaper did a front-page picture and article about me, it was impossible not to be noticed. It was really exciting picking up a copy of the daily and seeing my picture on the front page. Another high point was a scholarship I was awarded for being an outstanding minority, one of two thousand entrants. I was awarded three hundred bucks and was invited to speak. Gina, my daughter, was very proud. I'm still thrilled or awed about seeing the Queen [of England] close up [She visited Seattle and the university while he was there.]. I could have almost grabbed her hat. Special invite: I was the only minority selected to attend a reception for her. There were about two hundred people there. It was cool. And none of my pictures that I took [of her] turned out!

The University of Washington is a beautiful place to be. Students are proud and work hard. I think our professor once said that maybe ten out of a thousand students are accepted and half of those fail. I was a society and justice major, then changed to social work, so one B.A. is in society and justice, and the other is in general studies, which I enjoyed more.

The university allows the Indian students to sponsor powwows yearly. It turns out to be a big event for all tribes in and around Washington state. I met relatives all the way from the Dakotas there. We had a fine Indian club on the campus where we could sit for coffee, talking, or just reading. I enjoyed the Indian arts classes and learned a special type of art form. I also learned wood carving. For the most part, I was happy.

I graduated in 1984. The university honored me for grades and achievement, you know, nonacademic things, counseling, helping out, volunteering, and doing good in classes. And my professors had a vote in that, and a lot of them said I was valuable in their classes once I got the nerve to admit that I'd been in prison. But I kept that quiet for two years, not wanting the students to know, not wanting anyone to know. But when they published my picture in the daily, every student on the campus knew who I was then, so I couldn't keep it quiet any longer. Then I started getting invitations from a lot of the college professors to come and talk to their classes . . . talk about prison, talk about the prison system, talk about plea bargaining, talk about jails, talk about homosexuality in prisons, things like that that their classes needed to know. But they didn't have any books on it. I think our book that we did is the only real good book on corrections. While I was a society and justice major, we never had a good book to use. We had to use a book that was published by a convict in California, but it would have been ideal if they'd taken our book and used it because then they would have really learned something.

My first job was . . . before I graduated I went down to the Puyallup Indian Tribe in Tacoma and I talked to the lady that was a director there. I told her I was interested in being a therapist and that I'd been studying it and she said to bring in a résumé. It just so happened they had an opening. Somebody told me about it. I said, "Well, I'm not even out of school yet. I don't know if I should go down and apply." But I did apply. I told them a lot of my history, about being in prison. Told them I was just on the verge of graduating and that my interest was in helping people because then I feel more responsible to stay straight because of that person or persons. And so I got my résumé together. And it was a real good résumé, definitely good. I got excellent recommendations by teachers in the Minority Department, the head of the department, and all that, and they hired me. Yeah. They hired me a month before I graduated.

They hired me as a Counselor II, put me to work the same afternoon [I graduated]. They had a crisis come in and they had nobody to handle it and they sent me in there. This woman was bawling and going on. I didn't have the slightest idea what to do, just sit and listen to her and say, "I'm sorry," and pat her on the back or something. Well, she went out of there feeling good and wanted to be my client. She made a request that she'd get to see me. So a lot of my clients did that. I ended up with seventy. Had the biggest caseload down there. And I took all the guys that were out of prisons [and] all the women that came out of prisons. I got all the nut cases, alcoholic cases. The women counselors, they were afraid of certain guys that had just got out of prison. They were afraid to work with them. And generally the guys didn't want to deal with them either. They were just young girls, you know, and when these ex-cons would find out I was there, they just came in. A lot of guys that had been out of the prison quite a while found out I was working there and they'd come in for counseling.

But I discovered that convicts that have done a lot of time also suffered posttraumatic syndrome like the Vietnam vets suffered. I was comparing my nightmares, my stress, to the experience of some of the guys I was talking to from Vietnam and some of the convicts I knew that had done a lot of time, and I found it was the same. I don't think it applies to just doing a year or so of time; applies to doing a lot of years like I did. And even now, I'm still having those nightmares of people trying to kill me and calling me a snitch and rotten shit that I never been in my life. I used to wake up sweating, guys coming at me with knives, people that I know. And they cut my head off and everything. And I compared my dreams with several other convicts that's been in a lot and they been going through the same thing: waking up with a cold sweat at night back in prison and surrounded by friends that want to kill them and stuff. I had several Vietnam vets as clients and we compared notes. And we sat and talked and we tried to figure out why and what could be done about it, because it was a fairly new symptom among people. We didn't hear anything about that in World War II. And there were things that happened differently in the Vietnam War. Once you were done, all of a sudden you were in the states, immediately, all by yourself on a jet plane. You didn't come back in parades and group ships and all that stuff. And I compared that to being let out of a maximum-security prison without any preparation for the free world.

A lot of times I stayed late at night working. I also visited people's homes. And I worried about them all the goddam weekend, scared they were going to kill themselves or something like that. So by Monday morning I was anxious to get to work just to see who was going to show up alive, you know, because I got mostly all crises cases.

I told you I got drove into the bay by one guy that was going to kill himself. He said he was going to drive in the bay. I said, "Not without me, you ain't." He just hit that gas and away we both went into the water. Colder than a witch's tit, I swear to God. It was wintertime, too. I got so mad I punched him, then drug him out of the car and then back up to the shore.

I'd be with people when you've got to go out on crisis call and they've got guns. That's really scary. Somebody's going to hang themselves, that's all right. I went on almost every crisis call after I did the first couple. I was the only male counselor there. The girls [counselors] were scared to go on crisis calls because they didn't know what to say, so I ended up going. Sometimes they [the clients] wouldn't even let me in the house, so I had to stand on the porch and talk to them for an hour before I could get in the house. I wouldn't call the police. I'd stand there and stand there and try to talk them out of hurting themselves and eventually they would open the door. We'd start talking about booze and that was something I could talk about. And then we'd start talking about stealing and that was something I could talk about. The guy might be mad because he'd been in prison and he's all depressed. We'd talk about that. "It don't have to be over because of that, man. Look at me. I did seventeen years of my life in the joint." Sometimes they'd make me prove I was in the joint by using the language and all the things that you know about Walla Walla that you only know if you did time. Pretty soon the door would fly open and the guy would be shaking my hand and stuff.

But anyway it worked out good and I worked there for three years. We had to write reports on our clients, kept track of their home life, and I opened my home to nine or ten of the girls and I let them use my address to get their welfare checks. I got bawled out for that and getting too involved emotionally, but I did it anyway. I knew that was unprofessional but I couldn't help it. [A] girl's been raped two or three times and she's sitting there crying, I'd just get so goddam mad I'd damn near cry with her. I know she's gonna get it again, because I know what kind of girl she is. I know she's gonna be back in those taverns. That kind of bullshit I can't deal with very well.

But my job, when they started cutting back on the money, they cut back on the job positions and I was the last one hired and the first one fired. They eliminated one job position. They kept two counselors and the director and they turned my job into a case-manager job and they give it to a girl that had been there longer than me. And they promised me that anytime I needed a good reference, they'll give me a good reference. I've never taken advantage of that.

I wasn't taking drugs or drinking during that time, but I did start drinking when I knew I was going to get fired. Then I started drinking heavier. By the time they fired me, I was well into it again. I didn't even come pick up my last paycheck. Jackie went down and did that. I was with her by then. And by then I found out I had diabetes.

I met Jackie when I was in an alcohol treatment program. There's a standing rule that when you're in treatment programs, you're not there for romance; you're there for yourself, to be treated for addiction. But oftentimes people become attracted to each other, not necessarily because they're pretty, but because you kind of have the same problems and you get together and you start talking about things and you do hook up, you get clannish together. And in my case, her and I . . . she was so mixed up in her mind that she clung on to me. She was thirty years old; I was in my forties. She clung on to me and clung on to me and it just happened. She was pretty and I didn't have anybody. I was lonesome, so I fell in love with her. But I also told her to go home; I didn't encourage her to leave her children and her husband. They were already getting brokenhearted, but she wanted drugs so damn bad, she picked drugs over her family.

So when I left the treatment center, they took her aside and preached to her about being with me so much while I was there, and so she got pissed off at them and packed her bags and left. She showed up at my doorstep about ten minutes later. I let her in. She asked if she could spend the night. I said, "Yeah, I'll fix the couch up for you. You can stay the night or whatever. You get scared, just call me." But when she got scared she crawled in my bed with me, snuggled up. From there on she stayed in my bed. And we stayed together and we got married eventually.

But from the day both of us got out of the treatment center we both got back into drugs. She knew I was a heavy drug user and she wanted that. She had never had heavy drugs in her life. She was a drugstore cow-girl; she just did prescription drugs. She had doctors that would write [prescriptions] for her because she was pretty, and she took a lot of Valium and stuff that women like. First time she seen me shoot dope, she said, "I want some." Made her sicker than a dirty dog but she wanted some more after that and I knew that was the end of the game. When somebody gets real deathly sick and they turn right around and do it again, that's it; they're hooked immediately. She puked all over the house and when she was done puking, she come over and asked me for some more. I said, "Aw, Christ, I created a monster now."

And so after that we got married and for the next three years it was a rocket downhill slide for me and her. We worked our dog asses off twelve hours a day and, hell, all the money we'd make . . . sometimes it'd be three or four hundred dollars . . . we'd spend every bit on drugs and not even have money for a pack of cigarettes that night. We just worked selling cardboard. We'd sell cardboard; we'd get fifty-five dollars a ton and we'd take in at least a ton a day. And we'd sell metal, things like that. And we stole cigarettes. We sold them for five bucks a carton. We'd steal fifty cartons of cigarettes in a day. We'd steal from any store that had cigarettes. She had a giant purse. She'd fill it up and I'd . . . she walked through the aisles, then I'd come in five minutes after her, like a different customer. Then we'd meet in certain aisles. I'd just take them from her, shoving them in my belt, my big pants, and then when she walked back up to the counter, I was out the back door or side door and she'd walk up to the counter and she'd have a loaf of bread in her basket and pay for it and leave. And we'd have the cigarettes. And we'd do that everywhere.

Before I lost my job I wasn't stealing. No, hunuh, no. I didn't do that until I just didn't have anything left. I had no money, no savings, so I started stealing again. I didn't want to work anyway because I was sick. I found out I had diabetes. I couldn't work. They told me at that clinic where I worked that I had diabetes. I was feeling rotten all the time, feeling too tired to work through the day, and they gave me a physical, did my blood and determined my blood sugar was way up to five hundred. They said they don't know how long it had been like that but that's why I was feeling so tired. My mood swings were so bad I couldn't hardly work on some days because I'd be more depressed than my clients. As soon as that diabetes hit, my mood swings started going up and down, up and down. One client come in, I was all happy, talking to him; another client come in, I wouldn't even talk to him. I'd say, "Aw, sit down. I got things to do."

And so I started working on this diabetes, but to me it was like a death sentence. I figured . . . the first thing in my mind I pictured was friends of mine that had diabetes. Didn't have any legs, didn't have arms, were blind and all that. Even now when I read a diabetes magazine it's depressing; there's no good news in the thing. They're still cutting people's legs off. My best friend's sister just died of it. She always took care of herself. She wasn't like me. Christ, everybody that's Indian isn't like me. She took good care of herself.

Anyway, after me and Jackie broke up, aw, I just kept drinking. Sent her home. I was alone. Her folks give her one last chance. There were gonna disinherit her and said they wouldn't help her anymore if she stayed with me, and so I tell her, "Well, you better go home. When this van breaks down, we're broke down, because I can't take care of you. I can't take care of myself and I don't want you on coke and all this bullshit, and I don't want to turn you into a prostitute so we can get some dope. If I ever catch you downtown, I'm gonna beat your fucking ass. Might kill you, because I will be downtown, I will be watching." So anyway, she did good. She remarried a young guy, younger than her, and she got what she wanted because his folks had a horse ranch and she loves horses. And she's been over to my place a couple times and I haven't been home. What I was afraid of was [that] the only reason she came back to see me was because she wanted me to buy her some dope. She knew I could get it. I guess it didn't turn out that way. She was okay. I didn't recognize her when I seen her, but she did okay. She went to some treatment programs and come out in good shape. She's got her own little cleaning business now and she cleans offices at night. Looked mighty fine.

I don't care much about being in the free world. Too tough, too tough for me. I'm too institutionalized, been in prison too much, been taken care of too much as a youngster and as an adult by the state and it kind of gets into your system. When I come up against bills that they send me in the mail, I can't even imagine being able to pay a bill. I must have ten different creditors suing me now. They sue all they want; they're not going to get anything because I ain't got it. I owe the hospital pretty damn near eighty thousand dollars but they keep taking me back in anyway. You figure what seven weeks in a private room alone costs, you know, intensive care and all that bullshit. But they keep taking me back. Now I got a letter from St. Jo's that's several thousand dollars.

Since I got out of prison I been in hospitals about twenty times. I got into this pattern of moving in and out of hospitals when I started drinking too much after I had this diabetes. My pancreas would get inflamed and it's a horrible pain. And I'd be in the hospital for a couple weeks for that. Then I'd get out and I'd quit drinking for a couple weeks, then I'd think, "Aw, that's good enough," and I'd try it again and a week later I'd be back in the hospital. Mainly it was my pancreas. And then the last time they told me I had a heart valve that's getting screwed up. Caused from shooting dope, some kind of fungus that will grow like that on a heart valve. My sister was there. She wasn't too happy about it either, because the doctor come right out and told me, "You're not socially acceptable for a replacement, so I'm just telling you now what's going to happen, that you will be at the very bottom of the list if they put you there for an operation." So I said, "Yeah, that figures. What the hell."

All the doctors concurred that I was a drunk and a dope addict ex-convict. She was nice enough to me, but she was frank. She was just telling me that's the way it is. When they do transplants, they have to all vote on it. You have to be worth something in the community, plus you have to have a helluva insurance. So anyway, I have that on my heart, a little irregularity, a fungus. She tried to describe it to me, that it grows right on that valve. It comes from the garbage that's on needles, the garbage that comes from dope, that's mixed with dope. The dope itself doesn't hurt you at all. There's nothing more pure than heroin. It doesn't hurt your body but the cut that they use in it hurts you. They'll mix like powdered sugar with cocaine to make it look like it's more. You can't shoot straight cocaine; it will kill you. You got to have it mixed with something.

As for the prognosis of that heart valve trouble, oh, I don't know, I never talked to them about it again. I almost forgot about it as quick as I could and just went on about my dirty business. That's when I was shooting dope. I said, "So what? I got cirrhosis of the liver, too. So what?" I've known about this heart valve problem for about two years. It develops over a long period of time. It will kill you.

It would be nice [to make it]. It just seems like too much of an impossibility. It's not worth the effort, not really. I never know how things are going to go from day to day. I don't plan and plan ahead, "Maybe I could do this, and maybe I could do that." If it happens, it happens. I know how you feel about it. I know it pisses you off, but I don't really need to hear that, because I say that to myself all the time. I'm my own worst enemy; I'm my own worst critic. I think exactly the same way you're thinking. "Why in the hell do I do this? Why don't I do this? Why don't I do that? How come everybody else has a home?" I could have had a home by now, you know. I could have had this thing and that thing.

It's just that there's a horrible part of me that's always there, you know, that would just as soon destroy me. It's a part of my personality. I have a destructive personality. I don't know why and I wish I did. It pisses me off. It's like fighting another person. It's exactly like a dual complex, a dual personality. I'm constantly fighting with myself. I think I need to be exorcised or executed, one of the two. Yeah, lobotomy. See, I do fine when I'm in institutions like this little place I'm in now. Can't get a better guy. I help cook, I help do this, I help do that, but you let me out on my own, I won't do a goddam thing for myself. Nothing. It just all goes away. I haven't figured that one out either, but I know you and I got the same thoughts, the same angers toward myself. I have the same argument toward myself, but it doesn't seem to change anything.

Maybe if I'm healthy and I stay sober long enough, maybe I'll get the strength back and start doing some things. Right now I've only been sober about two weeks. I feel a lot better until I get depressed, angry, angry as hell. I know people don't like me drunk, so then I will get drunk. I say, "Here, you don't like me drunk, so then I'll get drunk." I say, "Here, you don't like me then, you won't like me now, for goddam sure." I guess I'm a rebel. I don't really want to be, but I am. See, there's a lot of . . . what do I call it . . . conflict inside me that's tearing against each other. I don't want to be like I am, but I am. I am what I am and that's all that I am. Of course, I'm making choices, [but] they're not conscious all the time either. It's my choice to do this but there's a part of me that don't want to do it. Of course, it's not that important, so I can go ahead and do it. There's another part of me that would rather be drinking and being in a fog, not seeing anybody. That one [part of me] doesn't have the strength right now because I'm not depressed, hasn't got the strength to take over and do all this bullshit.

Oh, I don't like success, really. I like success of a different nature. I don't like to be in the spotlight or anything and that drove me out of it in the first place. Being on TV and that kind of shit, that drove me the hell away from it, scared the fuck out of me. I don't want to have anything else to do with it. They wanted me to do another show after our book came out and I got that publicity, but I just never called them back again. Said, "That's it for me because everybody will know who I am, a rotten-assed convict." I probably got plenty enemies that I don't even know about from that newspaper article that time. You know, "Why are they writing about this stinking convict for? Why don't you write about people that do good things, that aren't thieves?" That was one of the most depressing weeks in my life when I seen that in the newspaper. I just wanted to bury my head in a hole and never come out. It scared me to look at a newspaper and see my face looking out on a Sunday edition. I couldn't get home fast enough. I couldn't come out of that apartment for a fucking week. It wasn't like being in a newspaper like that time when me and Donny pulled that caper where the car burned up. That was different because that was more like me. More like us, I mean.

I don't know who in the hell I am anymore. I don't know. I feel sorry for myself, I suppose. Depression is feeling sorry for yourself. Major depression is being sorry about something that you can't even put your finger on. My depression's just got to be chemical; the doctor's already determined that. But like he said, I need to be in control before I could use lithium. It's too dangerous for me, doing lithium and drinking and crazy shit like that. It would kill me. But I want on lithium. I want to get out of this so I can keep my spirits up instead of up and down, up and down all day, exhausting. I try to hold that line so I don't get crabby. Try to hold that fine line so I really don't get too bad, because that's when I start arguing with people that I work with, like at that home where I'm at now. It's sad. I bit my fucking tongue yesterday. They'll throw me out. I come close to being thrown out a couple times. I already almost said some smart-assed things to a couple workers there. Bit my tongue and said shut up to myself, turned around and left. I'm not great with authority yet, or [with] people that think they're an authority.

Then I have that thing about young therapists trying to tell me about life when I know a helluva lot more about life than they do. I have to sit there and listen and nod my head and say, "Oh yeah, gee, that's a good idea." Damn assholes! I don't think I'm better than anybody else; I think I'm worse than most people, [but] I think I understand me a lot better than a lot of people do. But as far as finding the magic trick to change it all, I don't know if I need to meet another person or what the hell. Like you said, I need to feel safe. That's one thing that has to happen before I can get any strength at all.

I haven't been drinking. To me, drinking is drinking every day. Drinking is drinking. When I stop drinking, I'm not drinking. Of course, I might stop for ten years and start up again. You never know. I'm the one that requested Antabuse. Dr. Long gave me my Antabuse. I said, "Start me on it before I leave this hospital or I won't make it home." So he did and I made it home. I been doing fine ever since, except I been out of Antabuse for two days now. I could drink if I wanted to. I thought about that already this morning, but I haven't been drinking. My body's feeling healthier. My color's coming back. I'm not so damn yellow. My blood sugar's been under two hundred the last two days. That's good for me. But I can't do that when I'm alone, damn it. It's so fucking discouraging. You can't go home and feed yourself like the hospitals feed you. They get me all regulated and I get home and I'm wild. I'm out of control with my diabetes in two days. Two days. No food, you know, got no food. Got no money to buy food, so don't eat right. A sandwich a day or something like that, that doesn't do it. You gotta eat this, you gotta eat that for breakfast, dinner, supper. You have to have a meal in between meals and I don't have that kind of shit. Even the CARE packages you sent helped a lot. I won't take a job because I don't trust myself. I might go to work two days and be drunk the third day.

You said I probably would have been a Sioux warrior if I'd lived a long time ago. Yeah, I probably would have. Well, we all try to be warriors in our own way out here. It's pretty sad when Indians try to be warriors now. The young Indians try to be warriors by going to taverns and fighting all night long. That's the reason they go, to fight. They got that in their blood. They got no other way to prove anything except try to be a bad-ass in the neighborhood. There's no other way for them to prove anything. I got caught up in that at a young age. Sure, I wanted to be somebody. I wanted people to respect me for my violence, just my toughness. I didn't care about other things, about being a nice guy or anything like that at that age. I been in gangs ever since I've been thirteen years old. Just wanted to be like that so they'd say, "Aw, don't fuck with that guy, man. He belongs to the Rebels, the Rebels on Portland Avenue." Me and Chuck Conway, another Indian boy, and Jimmy, we ran Portland Avenue. All we did was fight and drink and steal cars, and we had a lot of girls. Those guys changed their lives when they grew up. They all ended up in prison with me during the Monroe years, but most of them never went back again. Two of them are dead now. Drowned right out there, like I said. The third one owns a smoke shop. The fourth one owns another smoke shop, and they fish on the river here.

You ask me where my rebellion comes from. My rebellion comes from trying to fit in somewhere. I didn't fit in the white world. I didn't fit in the Indian world that well, so I had to choose to stay in the Indian world regardless of how it was until they accepted me. And they finally accepted me. I never been accepted in the white world even though I look half white. To them I'm still a damn Indian. So you look half white. It don't work. From the time I was little, I lived in Aberdeen, Washington, and although there was Indians around there, I never seen any Indians, so my brother and I were like niggers to the people that lived in Aberdeen. They treated us like niggers. And so that's the way it went. So we acted that way.

We acted bad, even though we was small. We did as bad things as we could do. But people acted bad toward us even though they didn't know us. Grown-up white people.

We were just young and I realized early I'm not going to get suckered anyplace, so I decided, "We're Indian, we're Indian or we're white." And I couldn't be white because my brother looked Indian. But I was growing up in the white world; I wasn't growing up on a reservation. Donny didn't understand, either, but he got along good with Indians and Mexicans because he looked that way. Me, even when they sent me to Indian school, all the Indians there called me white trash and shit, tried to beat me up, so I fought my way through Indian school. Did just fine. Took a year and a half before they left me alone, but after that it was okay. And Donny always got along good because . . . he got along worse in the white world because he was darker and had dark hair, but it never seemed to really bother him that much. We talked about it jokingly. I used to be called white trash in the Indian school and I'd be called a goddam Indian in the white society. I'm a helluva fucking half-breed. Don't know which way to go, so I decided to go Indian. I forced them to accept me. I did it by just being there all the time.

The Puyallup Tribe accepts me as a Puyallup. I'm not a Puyallup. They give me money, though. They're always ready to help me out. I identify more with them than my own tribe. I'd never go to my own tribe, my reservation. Too ugly, ugly. I never want nothing to do with it. I never want to see it [too much poverty]. I'd like to show you the new Indian housing development up on top of the hill. The Puyallup built them themselves.

Maybe you're right when you say you think a lot of my problem comes from when I was a kid, being called "blanket ass" and "siwash" by people. Maybe so. That's why I say fuck them people. Maybe I have internalized that stuff and let it damage me. But it can't be helped. It can be helped with some really heavy therapy, but I'd need hypnosis or something like that to get all the anger out, because I've got a knot of anger that's as big as a baseball in my chest. It burns like fire. *You* can touch it real easy by saying things to me that hurt. I need to cry but I can't. I got to get it out, spit up a fur ball.

I haven't been able to cry even over Donny. You say I've got to talk about it. I'll try to. It's just a lot of hate and anger. Anger and jealousies all crammed together. I don't feel so much pain over it anymore because I swallowed it down. But I'm sure it caused me to be the way I was, to be a rebel, to do everything I could to get back at them, get back at adults, specifically white adults. You know, they made me feel homeless and out of place no matter where I was. "Get out of our yard!" "Who brought them goddam Indian kids here?" "Get out of here, you little fucking siwashes," and shit like that. "I'll cut off your ears if I ever see you talking to my daughter." That's when we was just little. I used to be scared to death of some of them fathers. They all acted like that. They thought it was funny, of course. They all made jokes about my dad, you know. But I had a lot of anger, I guess. I didn't realize it at the time, but I felt good every time I destroyed something that belonged to them people. I felt good when I destroyed school doorways and windows. Felt good when I stuck my head up underneath a nun's dress. That always felt good. Pretty dark under there; even her panties are black. But I used to have to hide behind them nuns all the time. I think I told you that before. During recess I used to have to spend the whole recess standing by a nun.

That anger didn't go away. I was angry about the way they treated my mother. I was angry about the way they treated my dad. My dad couldn't get a good job because he was Indian, and he drank until he became an object of ridicule. See, even the other winos . . . He was always falling down drunk and his Indian squaw wife would have to come and get him. "Siwash," they called her. I never ever figured the name for "siwash." I thought it meant "half-breed" until you told me it meant "savage." Yeah, whatever . . . and, well, they called us all that, so I did what I did, not growing up Christian-oriented, although we grew up in a Catholic church. I never believed in any of that bullshit. I'd go in that confessional and lie like hell. "Yeah, I did this, I did that." I was mad from the start that I even had to go to the goddam church after a while. They put the fear of God into me, but not good enough. I wasn't that afraid.

I blame myself for my anger, my rebellion, my refusal to conform. Everybody's tried to help me through the years. You and everybody else. I know better. I know what I'm doing. If I want to do it, I do it. I want to go to jail every time. I want to be a nut just to have a place to live. I tried being a chronic mental case; they wouldn't go for it. I wasn't crazy enough or something like that. I know how the nuts act, their symptoms. I can fake them real good. Once you work through that system, you got it made, get checks all the time. That's what I'm doing now.

I'm not nuts. I was afraid of it for a little while because I was having a bad time, hearing voices and stuff. I could overcome it, but the booze made it worse. I was hearing voices because I'd been drinking. You hear voices when you're coming down when you quit drinking, not when you're drinking. I drank because I heard voices. They were there right at my shoulder. I'd see somebody standing right at my shoulder. I'd turn real quick. It still happens to me. Last Saturday it happened to me. Sitting there watching TV and somebody was standing right here and there wasn't nobody there. I was thinking about Donny and all of a sudden he said, "I'm here." Comes out of nowhere. Out of my mouth, said, "I'm here." Thinking about him, and that was last night, too, I heard it. I said, "Well, you're not helping me much, buddy." Maybe he is.

I just ask God to help me stay at this place. If that don't pan out, what am I supposed to be doing? Keep asking for help? Be down at the mission with the rest of them bums? It ain't gonna happen. I guarantee it ain't gonna happen to me. There's one way out, one way or the other: go back to prison; die or go back to prison. Go back to prison, more than likely, and let them take care of me the rest of my life. You know, like the old-timers in the movies? That last big one. Go for the last big one. You either make it or you break it. Win some, lose some. If I win some, then I got enough for rent and everything else. If I lose, I go back to prison. Federal prison this time, because they got more money. Holding up a bank is a federal crime.

But it's better than living on the street. A lot better. What's my world amount to anyway? A little room. Hell, a prison's bigger than that. I don't spread out. My room is a little teeny, little teeny circle, unless I could get a bus pass. Then I could go to all these things by myself. That was what I was going to do, get a bus pass first, and that lasts for a month, then I can ride the bus anytime, like a taxi, go to comprehensive mental-health therapy and stuff. They're all on bus stops downtown. You need a bus pass.

Since I been out, I've had a lot of stress, a lot of weird stuff. [I] feel good about myself, do well for a while, then it starts breaking down again. Start coming up against things I can't cope with and start getting weak. The weakness comes from alcohol; I know where it comes from. Can't do nothing when you're weak. I get real bad physically. I can't even walk. I stagger. I don't have the strength. Alcohol got my strength. Can't eat. I eat Popsicles. That's about it. I buy a giant package of Popsicles. I eat those for three days. That's one of the reasons my blood sugar was so high. It makes you thirsty, terribly. Steve [a friend] kept saying, "Well, can you eat? Can you eat soup? I'll get it." I said, "Popsicles." I've had a very hard time accepting it, dealing with it. I've had a hard time curing it, switching from pills to insulin. It's been a pain in the butt. But I could've took the time and energy to learn about it. Learn how to take care of myself, which I did learn to do, but I didn't do it [take care of myself]. I decided I can't throw away all my food. I'm not going to make all them exchanges. I'm just going to eat what I eat.

Donny's death just ruined my life completely, all the hopes and dreams I had. Just ruined everything. We just always did things together, even if it was just visiting. We had the same sense of humor. I can't talk about this. You say I need to cry, to mourn . . . He's still with me, in my head. Stays there all the time. He's not in the house. Like you say, he's in my heart. Like I lost my other half. I did. We gave each other strength to do a lot of things. Even quit drinking. He was trying to quit, too. He was watching out for me and I was watching out for him. I don't have close friends. He was my close friend. So there isn't much left.

He's probably doing better than I am. It was an accident. He was drunk. A lot of people think he wasn't, but he was. He OD'd. I've done it myself twice since he died. I've OD'd. Ended up in the hospital. Not on purpose. Taking my pills. My pills don't mix with dope at all; they don't mix with alcohol. Knock you cold. That's why I didn't make it home from the hospital last time. I bought a bottle of wine and I had taken my pills and whammo, that was it. Normally I can drink four or five fifths of wine a day. People don't even notice when I've drank two, don't even notice it except they can smell it. This time I just drank one and I was out. Complete blackout. Back to jail. [I] said, "What the fuck did I do now?" Then I remembered I took all those pills in the morning before I left the hospital.

They don't tell you, "Don't drink." They said, "Don't operate heavy machinery," but I hadn't planned on operating a Caterpillar. Just like some cigarettes. I only buy cigarettes that say, "May hurt you if you're pregnant." I buy those; those are safe. No. Some say they cause cancer; you don't buy them kind. I wanted to start a chapter against MADD mothers. Drunk Drivers against MADD Mothers. I'm a helluva drunk driver. I hate people picking on me because I can't drive right, so I'd say on a sign on my bumper sticker: "If you don't like my driving, get off the sidewalk." That comes true every now and then. "Get off the street, for chrissake!" "Oh, okay." "What happened? You better let me drive." "Fuck you. I'm doing great. I can drive better when I'm drunk, anyway."

Donny's been dead more than a year now. He died in December 1990. It's been a year and a half now or something like that. Donny was like a little kid. He functioned as an adult, he worked and everything, but his fears and his hopes were more like a child. He had things that bothered him a lot. He couldn't talk to nobody but me. We did everything together. He was smarter than me in a lot of ways. He didn't care for book reading that much, but he was smart with math and he was a better worker than I was. He worked hard. And it broke him up when his old lady just left. He broke down very bad. He wasn't afraid to cry. I'm not afraid to cry, but I don't want people to think that his being gone bothers me forever.

But I can't move forward. I've never been able to do anything right. I mean dealing with the past. I just say, "Forgive yourself. God forgives you." So how many times do I have to say I forgive myself so my fucking life can go on? I still fall backwards. My wheels are spinning. I can't make any progress. You say that I need to forgive all those white people for what they did to me. Oh, I don't care about them. I don't care what they did. Too many other things in life. I seen that happen to the little colored kids and the Indian kids all the time. They're not all going to grow up to be thieves and shit. I don't know why we grew up that way. I guess my behavior was get-backs. Yeah.

I got a lot of things I need to process through my head but it's not easy to do. Counselors can't really help me. I've been to grief therapy several times over this. Didn't help me. I just sat there cold. I couldn't think about it. I couldn't go back. The therapist tried to make me go back, go back, go back. [I said,] "Forget it. Forget it. I don't want to think about it; I can't. It's bigger than both of us, buddy." He said, "Everybody has somebody die." I said, "Yeah. Easy to say. How about if your wife and kids die when you go home tonight? How are you gonna say, 'Oh, everybody dies sometime'?" Sure. We all die. I'm gonna die, you know. [Crying.] Just a lot of times I'd rather be with him than here just because of the way my life's going. I just see a lot of lonely years ahead of me if I stay alive. Oh shit, it seems too complicated. I can't get my head together to even make these goddam welfare appointments right now. Somebody stole all my stuff, stole my food stamps, stole my welfare papers I had to deliver. Second time that's happened.

I don't know if there's a way to deal with the anger I feel because of what whites said and did to me when I was a child. Well, it was a pretty impressionable age. It's a self-fulfilling prophecy almost when they say to you at that age, when somebody tells you, "You're gonna end up spending your life in prison," that you're gonna hang someday. I had a fear of that for so many years. I can't even button my shirt up to the neck; I start choking. Can't have anything tight around my neck. And it goes back to a grown-up person telling me something like that.

I don't think there's any way of getting rid of those angry feeling I have about people. I'm a therapist, I'm suppose to know, and I don't know how to tell people . . . See, I try to tell people, "You're good people. The hell with what happened in the past." I said, "Forget about it. Cry about it. Do something about it now and it will be gone." But it don't work that way. I guess you're right about there being a connection between forgiving them and forgiving myself. Well, I can do that. Sure, I can. Yeah, I can forgive them. How do I know? Well, you don't know. All you can say is "I forgive them." It's all you can say. Just like I say I ask God to be in my heart, but I don't feel nothing there. My life still stays fucked up. I've spent many a night trying to turn my life over to God. Then I figure even he fucking give up on me. I ask, What the hell did I do so bad in my life that I have to be like this? Damn, what did I deserve this for? I can't figure out nothing. They harmed my whole family. It's not that easy to forgive them. I can say it, see. I can say it quietly. I can say it out loud: "I forgive you, you know, whatever you did. You died anyway, you sonovabitch." Most of them are all dead any goddam way.

My heart, half my life, there's a demon . . . There's no room for anything. Once it comes out, it comes out. At one time in my life . . . you know at one time in my life I had that connection. I was strong. It was like a volcano power that came to me when I worked hard toward studying, trying to believe and asking the Great Spirit, the Lord, whoever you wanted to call it, to take my life. Then I'd say, "I don't mean really take it, but take over my life, take hold of it and show me what the hell to do. Thy will be done." Man, I keep trying to do that, keep trying to do that, but it's just empty. Empty. Nothing there. Why in the hell me? God's supposed to love everybody. How come he ignores me? Just because sometimes I just go ahead? I'm impulsive and I do what I want to do anyway. I'm not a quiet listener at night. I don't hear the Lord talking to me. If I did, I'd probably get scared.

I don't know. I'd like my life to be better. Anybody would. It just seems that I missed so darn much growing up. One thing I missed is the work ethic. That's a handicap now, a real handicap. I don't generally go after something like people do. They work hard. They buy their little toys, their little campers and boats, and it just seems I'll never have it like that. I know it's material things, but it means that person is adult whoever owns it. He's adult and he's worked hard for it. It means more than he just has it. I see the person with things like that and I think, Why can't I be like that? No, it can't be. It's been too long I've been out of it.

It's true what you say; I *am* a rebel: "No, I'm not going to do that because that's what those white people did. I'm not going to be like them. No! I'm going to make them mad at me. I'm going to make them hate me. I'm going to do everything I can to go against them. I hate those bastards.

I'm going to do everything that they don't like. Do [be] like they said I was going to be. They don't like drunk Indians? Tough shit. I'll be a drunken Indian." Yeah. I forgive them. Rotten asses. Do good to those that harm us. Well, as an adult, I don't have enemies. Jesus Christ, everybody's grown up with hurts in their lives. They don't all end up in prison. Hell, I had to live in white society. I still don't fit in. I'm a half-breed. I know I look more like a white man than an Indian. I know. So see, both societies, it's still the same. I'm fifty-one years old and I'm still trying to fit in the Indian society now because I had to make a choice.

Well, I've grown up that way, with get-backs, doing some damn thing [to get back at white society] all through my teenage years and my younger years. I've been on the outside of society, the outside edge looking in, just like they used to treat tribes in the old days and run them to the reservations and push them around like Jews. I identify myself with Jews more than anything else. I read more about the Jewish Holocaust more than anything else. I read more about that than Indian things, although they're both the same thing. They're a holocaust in a different fashion. Persecution, genocide. If you realize you belong to a race of people who they planned to execute, genocide, get rid of off this earth, it makes you feel like a cockroach. Indians are getting washed out, year after year, generation after generation, anyway. They're trying to cling to what they had but they can't. White society keeps moving on; it wants that land and is going to get it some way or another.

My brother hated white people. When he got drunk he'd punch white people in the taverns for no reason. He talked about it a lot more than I did. I used to say, "Cool it, man. That guy ain't saying nothing." "Aw, that white bastard's talking about us. I can tell." I'd say, "He ain't doing nothing. He's just sitting there laughing and joking with his friends." Pretty soon he'd go over there and start a fight with them for no reason. Get us kicked out. "Couple goddam siwash drunk sons-a-bitches." He was fine when he was sober. His friends were white down at work, you know. But when he got drunk in a bar, that shit would come out in him. He's fine when he's sober; when he gets drunk he starts talking that crazy shit about white people. I ain't never done that, even drunk. Just want to be left alone most of the time. I don't mind fighting but there's gotta be a reason for it. I've attacked people for no reason and lived to regret it. Beat up by the cops later. Of course, them drunks could never beat me up.

Hardest thing to get rid of on parole is the convict code, living on the convict code out here in society. Must take a year. Takes a year for your brain to follow you out of the penitentiary. It really does. That's why you go back so damn fast, because when you get out, your mind's in the damn joint. You get busted thirty days later, it doesn't bother you a damn bit to go back. You never left any goddam ways.

I woke up this morning at five. It's the longest I ever slept. I've been up ever since. Day before I was up at three-thirty in the morning, ironing clothes and shit. Just something to do, stay awake. I asked if I could come out and watch TV. They let me sit out there and I sat out there for about a half hour and I went back and started ironing clothes and puttered about my little cell. I put a broom in my door to leave it open a little ways because I can't sleep in the dark. I used to always leave my TV on, turn the sound on and leave it on for the light.

How about healing the goddam disease of alcoholism? That's what's killing me, the disease. You know what AA teaches you? "It's not your fault." And I don't believe in that teaching, either. I don't believe in saying, "I'm alcoholic," but you have to say it. That's what they say, "Oh, gee, it's not your fault. It's a disease. It's the disease. You couldn't say no." It makes me mad when a therapist even tells me that, because I know we have choices to make.

I certainly don't want to go on like I'm doing. I was hoping to hell by now to leave something to my daughter, to help her somehow. But I need her help. And I told you I don't know one day from another. I just take each day, "Well, here I am again. Goddam, there's the sun coming up. I'm here again. Now what? What's today? No plans. What's going to happen today? Am I going to get kicked out of this place? Am I going to just sit and do nothing all goddam day?" What the hell. My biggest thing is to get a bus pass, stay sober, and get my goddam paperwork taken care of.

When my friend, Steve, brought me to his house, he called the doctor and told him, "He's too sick. I can't take care of him. He's got to get help

somehow." So my doctor told him on the phone to take me to St. Joseph
Hospital, direct admit, and he'd take care of it on the phone. But Steve
didn't know what was wrong, just that it didn't look right. My skin pallor
was real strange and I was acting strange. I'd been drinking, but not very
much. My blood sugar was too high. It was diabetes. I hadn't ate for a
week. I hadn't taken any insulin for a week. And so we got up to St. Jo's
and they admitted me and the doctor took a blood sugar test and he sent
the lab guys up to do it again because he couldn't believe how high it was.
It wouldn't even register on the meter. I knew it was high because the meter goes up to five hundred and it was over that; it was up to eight hundred. I should have been in a coma by six hundred, so they moved me
down to intensive care for the night. Insulin. They got it down to three
hundred and something and they sent me back up to the nut ward, said,
"He'll be okay. Just watch his insulin." They increased it from thirty-five
to eighty, which I don't like. I can't take that much insulin at home because I don't eat. Don't have nothing to eat. If I stay where I'm at now, I
can take it because I got food to eat. My doctor put me up there in the nut
ward to start with because he knew if I was doing all that, something bad
was wrong again, that I wasn't taking care of myself. He didn't want me to
go home alone anyway when he released me before. He was sorry, because
he didn't think I was going home. He thought they were going to take
care of me at the hospital.

And my drinking, my alcoholism, well, you see, generally it never gets
better. It always stays the same. I mean it doesn't stay the same: you stop
and you start. Like they say, you start right from where you stopped.
So it's getting worse and worse. And I got cirrhosis of the liver. And I got
problems with women: You don't love me anymore. And I got problems with my pancreas. I drank it up. I burnt it out. They won't give me a
transplant on that either for the same reason; I'm not socially acceptable.
Like I told you, they vote on transplants, the doctors and all those people.
"Why do you want a transplant?" "Oh, so I can go on drinking. Oh, I
wanna be a good citizen." No. There's votes. They have a big election like
the parole board or something. They get together when they do a transplant.

You asked me when I knew I was good at art. Aw, I knew I was good at art in grade school, making pictures and things like that. And as the years went by I kind of stuck with my drawing. I didn't try to learn. I just tried to draw things I seen. For one thing, just to be able to get the angles just right, you know, like that bench over there? That bench, to make the angles look right? The shadows, I got interested in shadows and little things that you have to do. Can't have a tree up here and the sun down here. Just kind of self-interest, you know. And then self-pride of being able to do it [and] getting compliments. Made me want to do it more. Then I decided maybe I'll be a commercial painter someday. But when I seen what commercial art was, I didn't want anything to do with it anymore. No fun in that. All you're doing is advertisements, dumb shit like the newspapers. You know, models and stuff. So I learned myself through the years. I learned to do portraits. Learned to use charcoal by wasting a lot of paper and charcoal, but you gotta waste a lot of things to learn a lot of things.

I finally met a Canadian guy when I was in Walla Walla and he was a professional artist, commercial and professional, and he taught me a lot of things on how to do landscaping for blueprints, or do landscaping for your own paintings, and how to transfer something small to big on paper by using the lines, crisscross, filling in the little lines. That made my portraits a lot easier and a lot more accurate. But a lot of times [in prison] I'd blow the portraits of the guy's wife because I'd make her look better than she was. If she had crooked teeth, I'd straighten her teeth. They'd say, "That ain't my wife." I'd say, "That ought to be your wife. Tell her to do something about her ugly face. I'm not painting ugly women. Fuck it! I fixed her up for you. You ought to be proud of it." "But it don't look like her." "I know. She's got buck teeth, for chrissake! You like buck teeth?" "No, but that's what she looks like." "You like fat women? Look. I slimmed her down for you." So I quit painting for people because they were always critical. I started painting on my own, like Barbra Streisand, people I liked.

After I got out of the joint, I studied art at the University of Washington. Indian art, Northwest Coast Indian art, strictly Northwest Coast Indian art. I didn't want to learn, see. I've always been freehand, do what I want with art. Then once he [the teacher] explained it course-wise, and he explained how hard it was going to be, I decided it would be a challenge and I wanted to do it, because right away out of a class of about sixty, there was only about ten of us stayed after the first week, and from that ten there was only about six of us graduated. It's so structured. Artists like to be able to do what they want to do. They don't want to have to . . . it's almost like blueprinting [creating Northwest Coast Indian art]. I mean, there are certain things that are there or they're not there, or they're not Northwest Coast Indian art because through the centuries the Indians found ways to do their totems the same way they do their drawing, but their drawing came last. The drawings are modern. They're all taken from old totems, carvings, and once I learned that, shit, I could go to town with it, see. I can take one design and make four or five different pictures out of it. Keep turning it around, do this, do that, the ravens, the eagles, and all the little things that go with them that identify them. Those that know the art can identify them; those that don't know the art just look at them blankly, "Oh, that's pretty." I say, "You ought to like it; it's part of your culture, part of your Northwest Coast." "No, I'm Puyallup." "You're Northwest Coast, Puyallup."

When I first got out [of prison], my concerns were about going back to the joint. Concerns about going back and eventually different kinds of concerns about not getting picked up for drunk driving, when I started doing that. And then, waiting for my brain to catch up with me, because my brain was still locked in prison but my body was out. I was acting like a fool by still trying to live by the convict code, which you can't live by out here in free society because all these neighbors are stool pigeons and snitches and call the cops on each other. This don't happen when you're in prison. In prison you gotta look out for yourself. By looking out for yourself, that means you don't tell on your neighbor, because that gets you hurt. These people here are different. They use the police. They call the police all the time. But real convicts that come out of prison, their minds stay in prison; they won't even call the cops if they get beat up. They're so dead set against the police, you know. And I've tried to tell people, like Cindy that got beat up so damn bad, to call the damn police. But she's been against the law for so many years from being a hooker that she wouldn't even call the police to protect herself. I told her, "That's what the damn guys get paid for, for chrissake. They get paid to come and protect you. Call them." "You think so?" "Yeah." "Do you think that would make me a snitch?" I said, "No. That's their job, to protect you. Those guys want to beat you up. Have their asses arrested."

I'm a super loner now that my brother's gone. Now I just don't have anybody. Well, I have you now for a few days, but soon you're gonna go. I had a friend for a few days. Now I'm back to square one. Now I got to figure out where I'm gonna go from here in a couple days. All my shit will be thrown out on the sidewalk here and I'll try to figure out where in the hell I'm going to go to. Oh, I got to get to that welfare [office] and I got to get them papers or else they're not going to do anything for me. It's my job to deliver those papers where they're supposed to go and they haven't been delivered. They're stolen; now I gotta get new ones. They're for doctors. The doctors have to send the forms out and send it back to welfare saying I'm handicapped and this and that. My diabetes doctor has to send the form back in and say, "Yes, it's severe; it's brittle diabetes." Which they haven't really explained to me what a brittle diabetic is compared to a diabetic, but apparently it's not good. They been trying to get my blood sugar under control for about a year now. They can do it sometimes for about a week and a half and then it just goes crazy on me. So along with my depression, anyway, diabetes causes highs and lows, highs and lows.

It drives you insane trying to hold on to that one steady line. My brother used to say, "God, go take a shot! For chrissake, shut up!" because I'd be bitching like an old lady or something. Bitching about this and bitching about that. I didn't realize it. I don't know if I am. It don't seem like it. I try to be real quiet and not do that. I suppose I do. I try my best to hold my temper. Makes me so goddam nervous I'm shaking by the end of the day. Can't sleep nights. My medication is to help me, but I've got a helluva lot more medication than these other guys. It's all supposed to calm my nerves, calm me down. It barely does it. I've taken enough to knock three guys out already this morning. I need coffee. If I don't have coffee, I'll die. I have to control my temper when my blood sugar gets out of whack along with when I get depressed about something. Then I start seeing things and I start really getting nervous. I start walking around and around the block. See people standing beside me. I look over my shoulder and they're not there. In the daylight this morning when I was hoping you'd be here and I was sitting by the phone, this girl in a red T-shirt and red pants sat down beside me and I turned to say something to her and she was gone. That happened three or four times this morning. There wasn't nobody there. I see my brother, but only in my dreams, not real life.

But lately it's been figures coming, walking right up to me and sitting right beside me. I look and they're not there. One yelled at me in the bathroom, something really kind of funny. Made me giggle. Something about "Piss, piss, hit and miss," and their voice is right in there with me. And I started laughing. They give me them Klonopin pills and that doesn't happen; that holds that bullshit down. It stops it, so maybe I am getting a little bit psychotic. The same reaction as when I was sniffing carbon tet except I know what's real and what's not real here. Some of these guys sit there like this and they have to try to sort through the voices. They're so bad you have to try to figure out what that person is really saying. That's getting pretty tough when you can't tell what's real, what isn't real. I still can, but I still jump. I still talk out loud. Nobody's there. "Good-bye. See you tomorrow."

My future's really dim. At this point there is no future because . . . that's just probably because of the way I've been thinking. You go a day at a time, see. You get real depressed, you get suicidal if you can't see ahead. You got to get over that first. I consider myself suicidal. I've already tried twice. I still think about it. I tried to overdose on insulin. First time, I woke up at Tacoma General [hospital]. Second time, I was at home and two people came over and I just barely made it to the phone to tell them I'd already shot it and they came and picked me up and took me to Puget Sound [hospital]. They brought me out of it. I was in restraints for twelve hours. That was about four weeks ago, in April, early April [1992]. I went from there to Western State Psychiatric [hospital]. From Western State, I got out, I went to jail, and went back to Western State.

I'm not real hopeful. I can't see any bright spots. Of course, in a way

I'm hopeful, like I'm waiting for something to drop into my lap. I don't have the energy and drive, so you really can't go after something like you really want, like I used to. Now I just hope for the best. Just hope to live from day to day. Every morning I just thank the Lord I'm still alive. Some mornings I don't [thank the Lord] because I might have to live in a dirty old van or something, or I've gotta sleep out in the cold. Then all I do is cuss the Lord. I cuss everybody. I'm very bitter. You can see what I'm going through, depression. I'm hopeful these chemicals will help. Right now the doctor's giving me too much. He did that before. Feel groggy all the time.

Everybody says, "Oh, you can do this. You can do that." But I haven't got the thing that makes you do it. It's part of your soul, part of the drive that's given to you. I'm just sitting, moping around. Today it's just like the fires went out. Worrying about yesterday. Sad about things that's happened to me, feeling sorry for myself. And I isolate myself more and more and more, so I'm not so able to get help, you know, because when you're totally isolated, you don't have no friends anymore that you'll even see. And they think you don't like them or something. Then I've got a couple [friends] I'll explain things to, why I do what I do. I don't know that I talk to myself [but] they tell me I do. It's embarrassing. It's happened a lot when I sleep. It scares them. So my future . . . I just hope to live for a couple more years. I'm even doubtful about that sometimes. If I could go without drinking, I think I can. I think I can make a comeback even. I want to get my Antabuse so damn bad because now I can drink, see. I been off of it for four days now. I'm not anxious to drink, but that doesn't go on forever. People like me . . . if friends are having a good time, you end up with them. So it looks pretty bleak. But I'm trying to do these things to brighten it up.

If I could get some kind of income coming in and I know I'll have a little place to stay—this has been just a constant drag week after week, trying to do this and it's so slow. They gave me food stamps to live on and then they got stole. But they're so slow with getting your check and stuff like that. And then they try to make me jump through all those hoops that I don't want to [jump through]. I've been through treatment programs. I'll go through another treatment program if they want to pay for it. It doesn't make any difference to me. It's a place to live. They aren't going to teach me anything that I don't know. I could be an alcohol counselor myself; I know all the tricks. I know how to talk that talk and walk that walk, you know. Come out with the best of them. Go down faster than any of them will. That can happen.

I was hoping I could stay at the place I'm in now but they say I'm too highly functional. Yeah, I'm functional all right. I suppose because I can get up in the morning, take a shower, and comb my hair, I'm highly functional. I was asking about congregate care. They say, "I can't do anything for you until you get money." See what I mean?

Psychologically I've just had a horrible time. It just started when I was working. Started getting depressed again. Should have been happy; I was getting good checks. But then I started getting worried about it. People I was seeing [clients] was reminding me of things I was going through. Listening to them, I got depressed an hour afterwards. I was thinking, "Gee, am I going to get that bad? I can't cure them." Pretty soon I was getting so bad [when] they'd come into the office, I'd say, "You got a minute?" I'd sit and talk for an hour and let them listen. But I started experiencing what I call posttraumatic stress.

When I got diagnosed as diabetic, I immediately pulled my horns in. Said, "I'm out of here." I said, "I'm just going to go off in a blaze of smoke." I figured I hadn't long to live after they told me that. I should have studied it to see what it was all about. Instead, I started drinking real heavy.

I met Jackie at the treatment center. We got married. She was a pill freak, too, so we didn't help each other one damn bit. We just tore each other up doing dope and running around and acting crazy. I went from bad to worse, from worse to worst, and neither one of us was happy with the situation. I wasn't happy being with her any more than she was happy with what I was doing. We didn't argue that much . . . well, I guess we did. She's scared of me. When I would get drunk, I'd get violent. She'd be on Valium and she'd be acting like an idiot and, of course, I was, too. After, when I got alone, psychological effects didn't come on until Donny died and I ended up in the hospital myself.

Donny was drunk. He was real drunk, passing-out drunk. He was passed out when I was there and then he got a shot of heroin from the Mexican drug dealers we have here and it killed him. But apparently he woke up and demanded his ish, his daily ish of dope, because they gave it to him without any argument. They were paying him rent with drugs, you know. He was charging them rent for Mexican tar, black, black heroin. Real strong stuff. And I had gone back to the treatment center because I was supposed to be back there at ten o'clock and I thought he was safe. He wasn't safe; he woke up dead.

So from there I really went downhill then. I didn't grieve at all. I just was in total shock, disbelief, and anger. That's where I'm still at. I haven't . . . I haven't gone through the process because I can't get through the denial stage. I still am [in denial]. I've denied it to a lot of people who said it was a suicide, as far as they could see. Like they knew something better than I did. But I hadn't been around for a couple of months. They figured his death was suicidal, though. They figured he just did that on purpose, that he just didn't want to go on any longer. He was in love with his hound dog girlfriend. She was no good. She stole his money and stole his car and went to Canada and he didn't see her anymore. They wouldn't let him in Canada because of his prison record, so he came back home, and when he got home, all he did was pout. He was depressed. Cried a lot, talked about her.

That never changed. He stayed that way even though he went out with several other girls, including my ex-wife, Maria. But Maria couldn't handle it either because he'd still talk about his ex—old lady even when he was with her. No girl wants to hear that bullshit. That's all he seemed to want to do was talk about her. So that's what he kept doing. I tried to talk to him about it [but] he didn't want to hear it. I didn't want to tell him she wasn't no good, but she wasn't no good. He talked to Mom a lot. Mom would comfort him, pat him on the shoulder, give him twenty bucks. He'd go get drunk and stay that way. He was a bad drunk; he wasn't a good drunk.

I think it helped Donny a lot, too, me staying out of prison. It made him proud that I was going to school. He held his head up a little higher when I was doing something. It made him try harder, and he tried and he quit stealing until he got with a couple of drunk women who were boosters and he started stealing meat out of stores, selling the meat. That's when he got back into drugs. But other than that, he wasn't trying to compete with me, but he felt that if I could do it, he could do it. So he did put an effort into it.

I guess my breaking up with Linda had been coming down for some time. She was getting real moody, real pouty. I don't know, something happened. One day I called her from a cocktail lounge in Tacoma. I was really drunk. I called her up and asked her to come and get me. I had my car there. Normally I would go out and drive it, but this time I couldn't get off my stool, so I knew I couldn't drive. So I gave the barmaid my number and she called Linda and Linda came and got me. And then I was flirting with the barmaid and Linda drove up. We was going home and then she started arguing about my drinking, about it getting worse and worse. I was still working then and I [had] started drinking cocktails and rum and coke and that hard stuff and getting blackouts. And then we argued and argued and it got worse and worse and she just . . . just like she had a nervous breakdown . . . she just started screaming and slamming the gas throttle as hard as she could as she was going down the street and I just backhanded her like this. Couldn't get my foot over to put it on the brake or nothing. Looked like she was going to drive us head-on into a pole or car. She screamed and hollered at me. Then after that, we got home.

We never talked to each other for several weeks. We just passed each other in the house. Then I went to work one day and first thing I did was go pick up mail [and] there was a letter from her in there and it said, "Please find a place to move to. I'm too old to take any more physical abuse and I don't want to see your death. I still love you, but you need to move. I'm going to be retiring pretty quick and I've got a lot of trouble with my arthritis and I don't want nobody feeling sorry for me," and this and that, so I did [move]. She rented me a place and after that I took over the rent. I thought she was kidding. I didn't want to leave. I had plans on taking care of her when she got crippled. I knew she was going to get crippled from the rheumatoid, so I was just going to pay her back, stick with her. I had no plans on leaving her like that. I didn't plan on getting drunk like that and getting violent either.

I'll admit I hit her before. I did through the years. Why? There was a certain line you cross, and she crossed it every time. She knew where the line was. If people get in your face you just hit them. I don't believe it's all right, but there's a certain line with anybody. If you cross that line, they should do something about it. She was with me thirteen years. When you're with somebody thirteen years, you know what their temper is. You know when to stop or turn around and walk away. You say there's no excuse for hitting a woman, but I say there's lots of excuses. I know it's against the law, but it's against the law for a woman to hit a man, too. Once she got mad enough to hit me. I started laughing. It didn't hurt. I said, "About time. About time you did something." "Well, you make me so mad." I said, "When I make you that mad, scream. Do something about it. You act like a mouse. I'll treat you like one." I didn't do that to Jackie. Jackie'd stand right up and fight. I taught her how to fight.

However people treat me, I treat them the same. Try to. I had the same argument with Donny about beating his wife all the time. The same thing: telling him it made him look like a coward by beating a woman. But after I got to know her [Donny's wife], I wanted to beat her up, too, the old slut. Even you'd want to beat her up. It's easy enough to talk; not so easy to practice.

On good days, me and him would leave everybody behind and go fish for the day. Get away. Let them [the women] go drink or do whatever the hell they wanted to do. "See you tomorrow. Just do what you want to do. Spend the night at somebody's house if you want to. Get drunk if you want to. You know where to find us. We'll be at the dock." That's the way it went. That's the way it went with Jackie. She always knew where to find me. I'd always tell her where I was going to be and she'd never worry about me looking for another woman, because I loved her and I wouldn't mess around. I might be sitting in a booth drinking with two or three other women, but I wouldn't be having my eyes on nobody. If they decided to have their eyes on me, tough shit; they never got nothing. We never fought about that.

We did [fight] only in that she didn't want me drinking so much. The more it [the fighting] happened, the more I was drinking. But then by that time I couldn't seem to bounce off. [It] got a foothold on me again. Alcohol gets its teeth in you quick. There's plenty of truth in that saying "Don't take that first drink." All the truth in the world. Then it just dulls the hurts, dulls all the fears and the pain. Just puts a damper on them. Makes everybody rowdy. What little control we have consciously, we lose completely when we drink. I have a lot of control when I'm sober, but when I drink I lost that control. That's why the police beat me up a lot. It's not their fault always. Most of the time it's my fault because I start a fight with them, call them names and stuff. I really get myself into real hurt. Get in deep shit, as they call it. The harder they hit me, the more I call them names until they get tired of hitting me, [then] they call on the radio, "Bringing in one fighting male." There's a whole herd of them waiting for me at the elevator by the time they get me down there, which is just part of it, part of the game—win some, lose some. I know you can't never win [with] the police and I don't go around looking for fights anywhere. I don't go to taverns at all [now].

I'm a very lonesome-type person. I can't get in trouble that way. I don't even care to have a woman around me when I'm home drinking, because I don't want to hurt anybody and I don't want to argue with anybody. I don't want to talk to anybody. I don't want to be criticized by anybody. I don't want to be seen by people because I don't shave for days. I don't wash.

My first years out of prison, it wasn't bad because I was still in an institution. I still had rules and regulations to go by at the university. It was easy that way. But when I graduated, it scared the shit out of me. Then I was out here by myself. The first thing I did was try to run to Tacoma. As soon as I get past a certain geographical point coming into Tacoma, I get all the urges coming back for drugs and booze. It all hits me. An environmental trigger, you call it. And I kept coming, kept coming, and I kept getting in more trouble, more trouble, and pretty soon my boss . . . I started just trying to drink on weekends, but it wasn't a month later and I was starting to hide a bottle in my office so I could sneak a swig every now and then between clients. And then my boss finally give me a choice of either going to treatment or just not working anymore. So I went to treatment for twenty-one days. My insurance paid for it and my sick leave covered it. And it didn't do me a lick of good. I was drunk before I got home. Didn't do a lick of good.

Took Jackie home with me from the program. Her and I was good for about four days; that was it. I went downhill from there. From there I went right down to being a regular hobo, except that I owned the van. We spent a lot of time digging in dumps, digging out food, digging out canned goods. We knew all the places to go to get stuff, the warehouses that threw out dented cans and stuff like that. We'd get them. If there was enough, we'd sell them. I wasn't working at all. We called ourselves self-employed. We was doing garbage. I was doing cardboard and we were selling all the canned goods which the groceries would throw out. Sometimes they'd throw cases of food out. We'd get it and go sell it. We'd go to Northwest Fruits and we'd get watermelon, we'd get oranges, we'd get all that good stuff down there, we'd take it up and sell it. Bags of potatoes, we'd sell it. We didn't steal it. They'd give it to us or throw it out. If they found one rotten potato on top of a fifty-pound bag, they'd throw the whole bag out. We'd pick through it and run around and sell it. We'd put ten-pound bags together and sell those. We'd pile our cardboard on top of it. We'd steal transmissions when we'd find them. We'd crawl under fences at night and take aluminum and take different things and we'd sell it in the morning.

We went through a hundred, two hundred dollars a day every day on our drug habit. Heroin. Just heroin. She could get legal codeine from her doctors, so we had that, too. It helped when we didn't have any heroin. We were shooting up heroin three or four times a day. Started the morning off and the evening. I loved the drug. I didn't like all the work that went to get it, but I loved the drug itself.

So I forgot all about all my good resolutions, just like Pinocchio. I never thought of it. Hell, no. The drug takes over. I didn't even think about my wife. The drug was number one with me from then on. She was

second. She could go out the door and never come back as long as someone traded me . . . I'd have traded her for a couple of grams, just traded
her ass. When we got married she sold her wedding ring the next night for
two grams of dope, Black Hills gold with diamonds in it. She thought I'd
be mad. I pretended I was mad. I said, "Aw, go ahead and sell it. I don't
care." This Mexican wanted that ring so bad and he was our dealer, so we
sold it to him. That's how much we thought of wedding rings. I told her
this was going to happen. I said, "We keep doing it, this is what's gonna
happen. I'll be third in your life; you'll be third in my life. You'll always
choose the drugs over me." Drugs are first and she's the third. If I got a
choice between meeting her here and knowing I'll never see her again, or
meeting her and paying for and picking up some dope, I'll pick up the
dope.

My daughter, why haven't I seen her or how did she luck out and raise
up so good? How come I didn't straighten up for her like I promised?
What happened? Well, I didn't keep my promise, obviously. I didn't do it.
Without the drugs I probably would have. Drugs just stop all that kind of
positive thinking. And then your mind is totally devoted to getting those
drugs, then the hell with your loved ones, the hell with people that care,
and that's what happened. And if I didn't have my dope and I didn't have
some booze to replace it . . . I've never figured out why to this day; I keep
thinking about it . . . I feel good now, so how come a person don't wanna
keep feeling good? If I went right now and take that twenty dollars you
give me and buy some booze, I'd feel miserable. I'd be sick and throwing
up and hurt all over. And still, I seem to choose that over feeling good and
healthy. It doesn't make no sense and I haven't been able to . . . psychological addiction, they call it. I ain't got hooked on drugs physically where
it make me kick and scream and have pains. It's just up here in my head.
Whole days are just depressed, horrible, if I can't get some. We'd start
early in the morning. We know we'll get some if we keep driving. We'd
steal a lawn mower off somebody's porch, anything that's not nailed
down. Took picnic tables out of parks and sold them. Anything. We both
called it the most horrible years of our lives, our marriage; we both called
it that.

And my daughter, she got angry at me for marrying Jackie. For one thing because she thought Jackie was darn near her age. They looked alike. And Jackie took her place, because Gina was number one with me, then after I got married and started seeing Jackie, I never seen Gina again. She was horribly jealous and mad that I could do that to her that easy. And I felt bad about it, but I thought she was old enough to understand or something. I don't know why I expected her to understand. I just never seen anybody after me and Jackie started messing around with drugs. You don't wanna see anybody anymore. Nobody counts. And so I didn't see Gina for those years, and now I haven't seen her for over two years because she knows I'm still drinking. When she knows I'm not, she'll come back. I let her know I'm not going to go to her wedding when she gets married. She's probably mad about that.

On June 12, 1992, I flew to Tacoma, Washington, and spent seven days with Gene. The last time I visited him was in 1986, shortly after he had married Jackie. At that time he looked fine, appeared to be his same old self. This time, however, it was very different: he had lost his lower teeth, which not only made his speech difficult to understand but made him look much, much older, sunken-cheeked. Most troubling, he had lost over one hundred pounds. It was painful to see what had become of my friend.

I found him living temporarily in a halfway house. He had just been discharged from Saint Joseph Hospital. His diabetes is complicated by his alcoholism. He was penniless. I spent several days driving around with him in my rented car trying to help him get medical and financial help. We went first to the state patrol to apply for a new I.D., then to the social security office and the state welfare office. While driving we talked about what had happened to him since leaving the Washington State Penitentiary.

Earlier in the year, in April, I had bought him some clothes. I also got him a tape recorder, an art table, and art supplies, hoping to encourage him to work again on his beautiful Northwest Indian paintings and to keep in touch with me as he used to when he was in prison. I sent him packages, hoping to supplement his inadequate and meager diet. At the time, he was living with his niece and her children in his mother's dilapidated old house. Although his niece paid for utilities, he had no income to buy food for himself. Sometimes he would walk to the Puyallup tribal headquarters to join the elders who were served lunch there each day. Efforts to secure him assistance with the complicated process necessary for state assistance failed. When his niece suddenly moved away, his telephone was disconnected. I called the telephone company, offering to pay for his telephone service, but they refused to let me do so because I lived out of state. Finally the electricity was cut off and I lost track of him. I called the Puyallup tribal office, the Tacoma jail, the hospitals, to no avail. Finally, an ex-prisoner friend of his and his wife told me where he was—in a psychiatric hospital. I then decided I needed to go to Tacoma to see what I could do to help him.

Things were in a mess: he looked and felt dreadful and I was upset, worried about him and at the same time angry at him for not having lived up to *my* expectations. Unreasonably, and although I knew better, considering what his life has been, I had wanted him to join *my* world, the square world, but he hadn't, and so during our time together he had the added burden of having to cope with my disappointment.

Shortly after I left Tacoma, he moved into a group home for alcoholics. Some of the other men in treatment there had also been in prison. He seemed in much better spirits and told me that he was comfortable living there. He had been approved for medical and financial assistance because doctors had determined that his health and psychological problems were so severe he was unable to support himself. I began to feel less anxious about his situation, since he now had not only shelter and food but a support system that included care of his severe diabetic condition. But then I learned that he had been evicted from the group home for drinking again.

On December 28, 1992, I received two letters from Gene. The first was dated December 18:

Hi Chiquita. I'm in jail again. The weather is cold. I am O.K. Once my money starts I won't come back here. Make any sense to you?

Can't seem to get your telephone number so I decided to write. No, you can't send stamps. Maybe money for stamps. I'll buy a few next week and borrow one from someone tonight.

Second degree theft, possession of stolen goods, namely a set of car keys that somehow fit a car near by. I'll never understand the way God works or plays tricks on me at times. Well, there must be a reason.

I'm tired. Been here three days and no sleep! It isn't because of the jail. This jail is good compared to most. I'll sit here for a month or two getting well again.

Don't get mad at me again, please. I really didn't do much except obstructing justice. They beat my head in so my debt should be paid now. Actually, I told them to! I said, "Why not just beat my ass then maybe you'll feel better?" I wasn't being too obnoxious, I don't think.

The twenty-third is a pre-trial date. I'll meet my lawyer then also. He will be a dump-truck [public defender], no doubt. I can handle myself in court.

If you could spare some money in the form of a money order addressed to me, $25 or $30 bucks, I could use it just to get soap and other things. We don't smoke here, you'll be glad to hear. Don't worry about the money. I'd appreciate a care package. But do write me when you can. I'll call you when I get your phone number.

I met a few guys I know so they are able to help me with these basics. I'll sort of be sorry to miss Christmas but it is no big deal to me. It's too cold outside and I don't really care one way or the other about leaving. I know I won't go to the Joint, so don't worry about that because I'm not. Besides, I would go Federal, anyway. More money to spend for its prisoners there. Never mind. I'll never go back.

Haven't slept for three days so I'm tired. Hope I'll sleep tonight. I am in a special unit and I will help tutor and write letters for guys. It is much less crowded here. I have a room or cell. There are no bars so they call them rooms. These doors are locked just at night.

I doubt that I'll be out before January or February, so I'll have some money to get a place of my own. I'll look forward to that day.

Please get hold of me. I may call before you even get this letter. I think I'll say good bye and wish you a good Christmas. I know I'll eat good and have a roof over my head, so I am really in no rush to leave, if you can imagine that. I do want to talk to you. Love you. Gene.

The second letter was dated December 24, 1992:

Dear Chiquita,

Greetings, my love. Haven't received your letter yet and am looking forward to it. Mail from a person you love and care about sets the tone for the rest of that day and the next in here.

I am sure acting like a sick person, yet I don't want to be sick. It affects my chances to get a roof over my head.

It is 4:00 A.M. Another restless night. I would give a lot for a long sleep. Six full hours would be plenty. It is quiet because all the other prisoners are sleeping soundly. It will help them to be rowdy all day tomorrow without having to stop for a nap.

I have had you on my mind a lot these last couple weeks. I sometimes think you are the only reason I stay half way sane. It would be so much easier to just let myself sink in the tar pits.

Hey, I am sure I'll find a place to live when I leave here. Mary Jan [his sister] can take care of my rent money so I won't forget. Then all I'll need to do is steal a TV and cooking stuff. I expect I could buy some but it isn't easy to live on so little.

I figure I will be ready for a care package from you every now and then. I'll go to the Goodwill for a lot of things like lamps, pots and pans and all that junk. Even blankets and strong bug spray. I would hate to use blankets that someone used. I'll get new ones. I'll really start from scratch. What I need to do is go to the hospital for a few days, then I would get all my sheets and towels.

I really miss you. Wish you were not so far away. I could visit now and than. I have your phone number memorized now. I think I'll call you today because I'm feeling lonesome.

I'm supposed to be helping the Mexican guys write letters and learn English. What little Spanish slang or street lingo I know is great help because I can't read a thing.

Well, my sweet lady, I keep taking breaks. I just finished breakfast. Check this out: The food was so scarce this morning that I already put a request in for medical [attention] because I *know* that in a couple hours I will start getting sick. I need more food because of the insulin shots. Already my head hurts and my eyesight is worse than two hours ago. Soon my lips will get numb like a dentist shot. I'll start to sweat, then get weak and confused, then if I have ignored all the signals, I will pass out for hours—and everyone will think I'm asleep! How's that scenario? So my beautiful lady, go figure that out, right? Enough already and all that stuff. Now I am afraid to lay down.

It is still very early, like 5:45 A.M. I am now locked in my little house for at least an hour. At 7:30, the doors will magically open and guys will scurry around cleaning their houses for inspection at 8:00 A.M. I think it sucks but I cleaned an hour ago.

You'll never guess what the hell I was doing now. Morning exercise! By myself already. I'll do it every day barring a stroke or something like that. Maybe my poor abused liver will just explode and turn to dust. Enough of this drivel. On to more important subjects. Yeah . . . like I take anything serious these days.

Tell you what. I do seriously try to make changes, to find a niche that will please me and make my days worthwhile. But after a few months of normal existence and tending to my own affairs, I just fucking lose it and go back to things which are dangerous, one step ahead of the long arm of the law.

I'll tell you a fact you can chew on and believe it or not: I am requesting a polygraph test, because I can beat any polygraph machine. That's because I am a pathological liar. I have done the test twice now and both times I lied my ass off but the dumb machine and the fool giving me the test didn't catch a thing. In fact, the first test cost Linda $150 but it was a small price to pay because I was already in Shelton and when the Parole Board heard the test results they let me go home the same day!! Is that cool or what? Is America great or what? Home of the brave, land of the free, stand beside me, *don't* guide me, 'cause I'll do what I want when I want and fuck life.

Sorry about that. I sort of lost control. Yeah, like I have some control to start with. Actually, I feel fairly smug and smart assed even if I am in jail. It doesn't bother me a bit. I'll sit here 'til the cows come home.

I better say good bye for now. I love you very much. Don't forget that. Gene. XXX

August 1993. For the past four months, Gene has been in the psychiatric unit of a state hospital in Washington. It has been very hard to get in touch with him and I have had to rely on just a few telephone conversations when I have been able to reach him. His sister told me he has tried more than once to kill himself. Whether or not he was serious about this, I do not know. He does not want to leave the hospital and has found, I believe, another institution to protect and care for him. He was released for about five days into a structured group-home situation recently but was sent back to the hospital for drinking himself into unconsciousness. In some ways, I believe, he is playing a con game, but I also recognize that he is very ill. Brittle diabetes, cirrhosis of the liver, alcoholism, and drug addiction are a deadly combination and Gene may perhaps be doing the only thing that he can to keep himself alive: he recognizes that in order to survive he must be under lock and key. When I recall that he was first institutionalized when he was ten years old and that he has spent most of his life within the confines of one institution or another, it is small wonder that he is unable to function successfully in the free world.

Inéz Cardozo-Freeman

SELECTED BIBLIOGRAPHY

Abbott, Jack Henry. *In the Belly of the Beast: Letters from Prison.* New York: Random House, 1981.

Allen, John. *Assault with a Deadly Weapon: Autobiography of a Street Criminal.* Edited by Dianne Hall Kelly and Philip Heymann. New York: Pantheon Books, 1977.

Bachman, Ronet, *Death and Violence on the Reservation.* New York: Auburn House, 1992.

Bataille, Gretchen M., and Kathleen Mullen Sands. *American Indian Women: Telling Their Lives.* Lincoln: University of Nebraska Press, 1984.

Bauman, Richard. *Verbal Art as Performance.* Prospect Heights, Ill.: Waveland Press, 1984.

Braroe, Niels Winther. *Indian and White.* Stanford: Stanford University Press, 1975.

Brasfield, Philip. *Deathman Pass Me By.* In collaboration with Jeffrey M. Elliot. San Bernardino: Borgo Press, 1983.

Brumble, H. David III. *American Indian Autobiography.* Berkeley: University of California Press, 1988.

———. *An Annotated Bibliography of American Indian and Eskimo Autobiographies.* Lincoln: University of Nebraska Press, 1981.

Cardozo-Freeman, Inéz. *The Joint: Language and Culture in a Maximum Security Prison.* In collaboration with Eugene P. Delorme. Springfield, Ill.: Charles C Thomas, 1984.

Cloninger, C. Robert, and T. K. Li. *Alcoholism: An Inherited Disease*. Washington, D.C.: U.S. Department of Health and Human Services, Publication no. [ADM], 85–1426, 1985.

Crapanzano, Vincent. *Tuhami: Portrait of a Moroccan*. Chicago: University of Chicago Press, 1980.

Crow Dog, Mary, and Richard Erdoes. *Lakota Woman*. New York: Grove Weidenfeld, 1990.

Cruikshank, Julie. *Life Lived Like a Story: Life Stories of Three Yukon Native Elders*. In collaboration with Angela Sidney, Kitty Smith, and Annie Ned. Lincoln: University of Nebraska Press, 1990.

Dickens, Charles. *Oliver Twist*. Edited by Fred Kaplan. 1st ed. New York: Norton, 1993.

Dorris, Michael. *The Broken Cord*. New York: Harper and Row, 1989.

Dudley, Joseph Iron Eye. *Choteau Creek: A Sioux Reminiscence*. Lincoln: University of Nebraska Press, 1992.

Dyk, Walter, and Ruth Dyk, eds. *Left-Handed: A Navajo Autobiography*. New York: Columbia University Press, 1980.

Eakin, Paul John, ed. *American Autobiography: Retrospect and Prospect*. Madison: University of Wisconsin Press, 1991.

Fire, Archie (Lame Deer), and Richard Erdoes. *Gift of Power: The Life and Teachings of a Lakota Medicine Man*. Santa Fe: Bear and Company, 1992.

Fire, John (Lame Deer), and Richard Erdoes. *Lame Deer, Seeker of Visions*. New York: Simon and Schuster, 1972.

Freeman, James M. *Untouchable: An Indian Life History*. Stanford: Stanford University Press, 1979.

Hale, Janet Campbell. *Bloodlines: Odyssey of a Native Daughter*. New York: Random, 1993.

———. *The Jailing of Cecelia Capture*. Albuquerque: University of New Mexico Press, 1987.

Haley, Alex. *The Autobiography of Malcolm X*. New York: Grove Press, 1965.

Hassrick, Royal B. *The Sioux: Life and Customs of a Warrior Society*. Norman: University of Oklahoma Press, 1964.

Jackson, George. *Soledad Brother: The Prison Letters of George Jackson*. New York: Bantam Books, 1970.

King, Harry, and Bill Chambliss. *Box Man: A Professional Thief's Journey*. New York: Harper and Row, 1972.

Krupat, Arnold. *For Those Who Come After: A Study of Native American Autobiography*. Berkeley and Los Angeles: University of California Press, 1985.

———. "Native American Autobiography and the Synecdochic Self." In *American Autobiography: Retrospect and Prospect*. Edited by Paul John Eakin. Madison: University of Wisconsin Press, 1991. Pp. 171–94.

Langness, L. L. *The Life History in Anthropological Science.* New York: Holt, Rinehart and Winston, 1965.

Lazarillo de Tormes [anonimo]. Adaptación de Elisa Criado y Matilde Taboada. 2a. ed. Madrid: Sociedad General Española de Libreria, 1980.

Lee, Nella. "Native American Crime: The Invisible Tragedy." *Wacazo Sa Review* 9 (1) (1993):38–46.

Lurie, Nancy O. "The World's Oldest Ongoing Protest Demonstration: North American Indian Drinking Patterns." *Pacific Historical Review* 40 (1971): 311–32.

Maracle, Lee. *Bobbi Lee, Indian Rebel.* Toronto: Women's Press, 1990.

Marken, Jack W., and Herbert T. Hoover. *Bibliography of the Sioux.* Metuchen, N.J.: Scarecrow Press, 1980.

Martin, John Bartlow. *My Life in Crime: The Autobiography of a Professional Criminal.* New York: Harper and Brothers, 1952.

Maurer, David W. *The American Confidence Man.* Springfield, Ill.: Charles C Thomas, 1974.

———. *Language of the Underworld.* Collected and edited by Allan W. Futrell and Charles B. Wordell. Lexington: University Press of Kentucky, 1981.

———. *Whiz Mob: A Correlation of the Technical Argot of Pickpockets with Their Behavior Pattern.* New Haven: College and University Press, 1964.

May, P. A. "Contemporary Crime and the American Indian: A Survey and Analysis of the Literature." *Plains Anthropologist* 27(97) (1982): 225–38.

Medicine, Beatrice A. "An Ethnography of Drinking and Sobriety among the Lakota Sioux." Ph.D. dissertation, University of Wisconsin at Madison, 1983.

Meyer, Roy W. *History of the Santee Sioux: United States Indian Policy on Trial.* Lincoln: University of Nebraska Press, 1967.

Moore, Frank (pseud.), and Robert Straus. *Escape from Custody: A Study of Alcoholism and Institutional Dependency as Reflected in the Life Record of a Homeless Man.* New York: Harper and Row, 1974.

Mullen, Patrick B. *Listening to Old Voices: Folklore, Life Stories, and the Elderly.* Urbana: University of Illinois Press, 1991.

Neihardt, John G. *Black Elk Speaks.* New York, 1932; reprint, Lincoln: University of Nebraska Press, 1979.

Paquin, Ron, and Robert Doherty. *Not First in Nobody's Heart: The Life Story of a Contemporary Chippewa.* Ames: Iowa State University Press, 1992.

Reed, B. J., and P. A. May. "Inhalant Abuse and Juvenile Delinquency: A Control Study in Albuquerque, New Mexico." *International Journal of the Addictions* 19 (7) (1984): 789–803.

Shkilnyk, Anastasia V. *A Poison Stronger Than Love.* New Haven: Yale University Press, 1985.

Shoblad, Richard H. *Doing My Own Time*. Garden City, N.Y.: Doubleday, 1972.

Spradley, James P. *Guests Never Leave Hungry: The Autobiography of James Sewid, a Kwakiutl Indian*. Montreal: McGill-Queen's University Press, 1972.

Standing Bear, Luther. *My Indian Boyhood*. Boston: Houghton Mifflin, 1928; reprint, Lincoln: University of Nebraska Press, 1988.

Standing Bear, Luther. *My People, the Sioux*. Edited by E. A. Brininstool. Boston: Houghton Mifflin, 1931; reprint, Lincoln: University of Nebraska Press, 1975.

Stone, Albert E. "Modern American Autobiography: Texts and Transactions." pp. 95–120. In *American Autobiography: Retrospect and Prospect*. Edited by Paul John Eakin. Madison: University of Wisconsin Press, 1991.

Suvak, Daniel. *Memoirs of American Prisons: An Annotated Bibliography*. Metuchen, N.J.: Scarecrow Press, 1979.

Swann, Brian, and Arnold Krupat, eds. *I Tell You Now: Autobiographical Essays by Native American Writers*. Lincoln: University of Nebraska Press, 1987.

Sykes, Gresham M. *A Society of Captives: A Study of a Maximum Security Prison*. Princeton: Princeton University Press, 1958.

Thrasher, Anthony Apakark. *Thrasher: Skid Row Eskimo*. Toronto: Griffin House, 1976.

Unger, Steven, ed. *The Destruction of American Indian Families*. New York: Association of American Indian Affairs, 1977.

Vizenor, Gerald. *Interior Landscapes: Autobiographical Myths and Metaphors*. Minneapolis: University of Minnesota Press, 1990.

Watson, Lawrence C., and Maria-Barbara Watson-Franke. *Interpreting Life Histories*. New Brunswick, N.J.: Rutgers University Press, 1985.